Policy-making in Britain

C000093142

Policy-making in Britain is a broadly based introductory text on the policy legacy of the Thatcher era and the new developments in policy-making in the 1990s.

Examining the policy process within its ideological, political and economic context, the authors show how it is affected by domestic and international considerations, including the influences of both local government and Europe. The book is divided into two sections, the first establishing a broad critical framework for analysis and the second focusing on case studies of particular policy areas. These include public expenditure, the NHS, Next Steps, water privatisation, pensions, training and education, and immigration.

Policy-making in Britain gives a clear sense of the dynamics operating in policy-making. The inclusion of both practice and theory in this text encourages students to think about the likely outcomes of policy change. It also makes plain the connections between British public policy and the environment and conditions under which it is shaped.

The book brings together leading authors on policy, and provides a lively and accessible introduction to the subject for students of public policy, public administration and British politics.

Maurice Mullard is Lecturer in Social Policy at the University of Hull. The contributors are: Tom Burden, Richard Common, John Dickens, John Kingdom, John Konrad, Ian Law, Robert Leach, Kirk Mann, Maurice Mullard and John Williamson.

Policy-making in Britain

An Introduction

Edited by Maurice Mullard

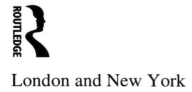

London and New York

First published 1995
by Routledge
11 New Fetter Lane, London EC4P 4EE

Simultaneously published in the USA and Canada
by Routledge
29 West 35th Street, New York, NY 10001

Typeset in Times by LaserScript, Mitcham, Surrey
Printed and bound in Great Britain by
Mackays of Chatham PLC, Chatham, Kent

British Library Cataloguing in Publication Data
A catalogue record for this book is available from the British Library

Library of Congress Cataloguing in Publication Data
Policy-making in Britain: an introduction/edited by Maurice Mullard.
    p. cm.
    Includes bibliographical references and index.
    ISBN 0–415–10849–7 – ISBN 0–415–10850–0 (pbk.)
    1. Great Britain – Politics and government – 1979–
    2. Policy sciences. I. Mullard, Maurice, 1946–
    JN231.P643   1995
      320′.6′0941 – dc20   94-48178
                                                     CIP

    ISBN 0–415–10849–7 (hbk)
    ISBN 0–415–10850–0 (pbk)

Contents

Figures and tables

FIGURES

TABLES

Contributors

Tom Burden works for Leeds Metropolitan University and the Open University. He is co-author of *Business in Society* (1981), *Capitalism and Public Policy in the UK* (1985), *Features of a Viable Socialism* (1990) and *The Operating Environment* (1995).

Richard Common lectures in public policy and management at Leeds Metropolitan University. He was a research officer at the London Business School and at the LSE until 1992, when he began lecturing at the University of Luton. He is currently studying for a PhD at the University of York in the area of government reform.

John Dickens is head of department of Politics and Public Policy at the University of Luton. He has taught politics and public administration at diploma, degree and postgraduate level since 1978, and during that time worked as research consultant and adviser to David Blunkett MP at the House of Commons. He has also been an Open University tutor, examiner and moderator.

John Kingdom is Reader in Politics at Sheffield Hallam University. He is the author of *Government and Politics in Britain* (1991).

John Konrad has worked for over twenty-five years in further and higher education, holding posts in teacher education and information technology. He is currently an Associate Lecturer in Education and Professional Development at Doncaster College and a self-employed training consultant. In the latter capacity he has worked for the European Union and for a number of Training and Enterprise Councils in the UK.

Ian Law is lecturer at the School of Sociology and Social Policy and director of the 'Race' Public Policy Research Unit at the University of Leeds. His publications include *Race and Housing in Liverpool* (1984), and he has co-authored *The Local Politics of Race* (1986), *Local Government and Thatcherism* (1990) and *The Nature of Care in a Multiracial Community* (1994).

Robert Leach is a principal lecturer at Leeds Metropolitan University, where he is currently responsible for running an undergraduate degree in Economics and Public Policy. Among his more recent publications are *Local Government and*

Thatcherism (1990, with Hugh Butcher, Ian Law and Maurice Mullard) and *British Political Ideologies* (1991). He has just completed a study of British politicians who have changed parties (*Turncoats*, forthcoming).

Kirk Mann is senior lecturer in the School of Sociology and Social Policy at the University of Leeds. In 1992 he was Visiting Fellow at Sydney University where he carried out research on the Australian superannuation scheme.

Maurice Mullard is lecturer in Social Policy at the University of Hull and visiting professor at the University of Liberec in the Czech Republic. His major publications include *Understanding Economic Policy* (1992), *The Politics of Public Expenditure* (1993), *Citizenship and Democracy* (1993, with Hugh Butcher) and *Market Liberalism and Leisure Policy* (1994, with Norman Barnett).

John Williamson completed his PhD thesis on 'The Fragmentation of the Welfare State Consensus' in 1992, and since then he has been teaching at Bradford and Ilkley College where he is senior lecturer in Political Economy and Public Policy.

Introduction

Maurice Mullard

The Scott inquiry on the sale of arms to Iraq, the revelations of the subsidies offered to the Malaysian government, the report on Westminster City Council, the criticisms of the Public Accounts Committee on the new public sector financial mismanagement and the expansion of quangos which spend about one-third of the nation's income without any form of public accountability: all these factors seem to point to a malaise in the governance of the United Kingdom. Where previously corruption was used to describe the politics of 'Europe' or 'the Third World', it is now being frequently asked whether it is justified for UK citizens to continue to put so much trust in their public institutions. Where UK institutions were once assumed to be somehow superior, the experiences of the 1980s and 1990s indicate that the behaviour of these institutions is no different to the practice experienced in other countries. There are in the 1990s problems of accountability, problems of too many decisions being made by too few and behind closed doors, and problems of too many political appointments and of increased disillusionment with the political process.

According to Joe Rogaly, the political commentator of the *Financial Times*:

> Local government has been hobbled. The behaviour of parliamentarians has brought political life into disrepute. Ministers spend too much of their time dishing out money and jobs to favoured individuals, companies or organisations. Fifteen years of continuous office has resulted in the creation of a patronage state . . . Britain is replete with opportunities for patronage, secretive deal making and good old fashioned corruption. . . . The Conservatives have torn the heart out of the unwritten British constitution. The democratic checks on executive power have been replaced in the name of consumer choice. What the latter phrase often means is placemen's self preservation.
>
> (*Financial Times*, 27 May 1994)

The 1990s are therefore being associated with new forms of political crisis. It is, however, paradoxical to describe the 1990s as years of political crisis when the incumbent government elected in 1979 was seen as being the solution to the political crisis of the 1970s. Political commentators reflecting on the 1970s had asked whether Britain was governable. They pointed to the failed corporatism of the Heath and Labour governments and argued that clientele politics had undermined the conduct of policy-making and made government by consensus too politically costly for both Conservative and Labour governments.

The trade unions had refused to cooperate with Edward Heath's pay policy, the reform of industrial relations and his offer to the TUC to become partners in the policy process. On his part Heath did not provide additional funds for pensions and school meals. He felt that such a re-ordering of priorities would betray the manifesto on which his party had been elected. Trade unions had also weakened the Labour government's strategy on inflation by withdrawing their support on incomes policy despite the Labour government's commitments on public expenditure and on priorities agreed with the trade unions.

Rose and Peters (1979) asked whether governments could go bankrupt, while Samuel Beer (1982) described the UK political process as entering a period of pluralist stagnation. The impact of strategic groups on governments was leading to a stalemate state.

The political crisis of the 1970s was also associated with the theme of government 'overload'. This argument suggested that citizens were making too many claims on governments; their expectations of what governments would promise to deliver were very different to the reality of what was possible for governments to achieve. This was reflected in public expenditure overload where the rate of growth in public expenditure was seen as outstripping the rate of growth in the economy. In the context of local government the criticism was that local government did not reflect local democracy, but rather local interest groups including public sector trade unions and groups with vested interests in higher local government expenditure.

> The growth of government has involved more people as clients, recognised interest groups, or grass-roots participants. Institutionalised participation is intended to increase the responsiveness of government to diverse interests within society. But this also increases the time it takes government to act. Insofar as participants become veto groups, objecting to proposals of government, as well as to proposals put forward by other participants in consultation, increased participation will limit effective action by government.
>
> (Rose 1980: 18)

The major policy challenge for the first Thatcher government elected in 1979 was how to make Britain governable. This challenge implied the need for strong government not dependent on the consent of sectional interests, which in turn meant pursuing policies that sought to break with the politics of consensus. The central theme was that the major concern of government was the control of inflation and that this was best achieved through the control of an impartial indicator such as the money supply. The Medium-Term Financial Strategy, as outlined by the government in 1980, pointed out that, in future, government economic policy would be conducted within the framework of controlling inflation and government borrowing. Increasing interest rates and the cost of borrowing provided companies with the discipline of containing wage demands – those that compromised found themselves faced with closures and their employees threatened with redundancy. Within this context the government could now break with incomes policy, with the attempt to maintain full employment and with the perceived corporatist structures of the 1970s. The unemployment of the 1980s could not be blamed on the government but on workers pricing themselves out of jobs – the concern for the government was to 'de-regulate' the labour market, to improve competitiveness by reducing wage costs and the tax burden on employees and business.

In addition, it was argued that strong government would seek to control the growth of public expenditure. Government had to push back the frontiers of the state by re-addressing the boundaries between the public and the private sector. The break up of public sector monopolies and the attempt to break with the influence of the knowledge estate of the public sector professionals were seen as essential strategies in dealing with the problems of pluralist stagnation and stalemate. Within this context the politics of interest groups were to be replaced by competition policy and consumer choice.

Privatisation policy was central to the government's strategy in their attempt to break with entrenched interest groups. It was advocated for increasing consumer choice; breaking with the monopoly powers of public sector professionals and public administrators. Competitive tendering for local government services, the creation of internal markets in health and education and the de-nationalisation of public utilities were described as being beneficial to the consumer.

If we look to the 1990s and beyond, the United Kingdom is faced with a series of new challenges. The pledge that the government would arrest long-term economic decline has not materialised. Instead the economy seems to be in a worse shape than when the government first took office in 1979. Manufacturing output is still below the 1979 level; the annual growth since 1980 has averaged 1.9 per cent a year in contrast with growth rates of 2.5 per cent achieved in the 1960s and 1970s. The unemployment rate of the 1980s and the early 1990s has been about 11 per cent of the workforce in contrast with 5 per cent in the 1970s and 2 per cent in the 1950s and 1960s. Despite the recent falls in unemployment, the forecast is that unemployment will remain stuck at over 2 million during the 1990s, in contrast to unemployment rates of 250,00 in the 1950s and 1960s.

The economic context for the 1990s will be qualitatively different to that of the post-war period. The break-up of the Soviet Empire, the emergence of new industrial nations, and problems of public finances and unemployment within the OECD area and also within the European Union (EU) would indicate that the United Kingdom has less options in the 1990s to deal with the problem of unemployment. Within the global economy, remedies that were available in the post-war period seem to be blocked off. The United States and Germany are no longer the locomotives of the world economy and no industrial nation seems capable or willing to accept the role of becoming the anchor to the world economy. In this context it would seem that economic growth would be slow and feeble. Both the OECD and EU are agreed that dealing with unemployment within the industrialised nations would require de-regulation of labour markets, lower wages and declining living standards.

Second, the politics of the 1980s were characterised by the need for strong government which implied increased accountability to the individual citizen and the break with interest group politics. The privatisation of public utilities has transferred public sector monopolies into private sector monopolies. Accountability through Parliament has been replaced with a number of regulators who are supposed to supervise the behaviour of the new monopolies, yet these regulators themselves are not directly accountable to Parliament. Regulators have also tended to 'interpret' their briefs very differently. Ian Byatt, the water regulator, is seen as being in favour of intensive regulation, while Professor Stephen Littlechild has taken a more free-market and 'arms-length' approach to the electricity industry. Furthermore, the previous regulators, including Sir James McKinnon, the former regulator at British Gas, and Sir Bryan Carlsberg at Oftel, were described as being more 'hands-on' and interventionist. The belief that privatisation of the utilities combined with the appointment of regulators would de-politicise the public utilities and make their management a value-free technical exercise seems to be based more on hope than reality. The public utilities continue to be central to the economy and also of major concern to their consumers. The regulators themselves are seen to be under immense pressure from the government to reduce prices since prices are seen by ministers to be the major benchmark for measuring the success of their privatisation policy. Furthermore, since control by the regulators seems to reflect the personality of the regulator, it also seems likely that a change of government would also bring a change of regulators to reflect the political priorities of that new government.

In their attempt to create quasi-markets for public services and to identify consumers and suppliers, the government had to create a series of agencies and quangos which are also not directly accountable to Parliament. The government has in many areas become the major consumer, buying services from various agencies through a series of contracts. The Benefits Agency and the Employment Agency seek to provide a service according to a contract agreed between the chief executive of the agency and the minister. The problem is that these contracts are at present outside the jurisdiction of Parliament. Furthermore, when MPs question ministers about the workings of these agencies, ministers refer their questions to the chief executive, suggesting that the minister is no longer directly responsible or answerable to Parliament in the day-to-day running of these agencies. The agencies are responsible to the minister in the delivery of a contract as agreed between the agency and the minister.

This book is written in two separate parts because the authors feel that there is a real need to provide an accurate and detailed outline of the context and the climate of the policy process. Too often the context has been taken for granted or used as a form of an overall explanation. The attempt of this text is different in that it seeks to use the context as a map on which issues of policy can be located.

In dealing with the twin themes of context and issues there is continuing tension between the macro and the micro, and the extent to which a policy issue can be separated from the context. Two recent examples highlight this tension. The Child Support Agency at one level represents a part of the government's policy on the family, which is to provide better support for lone mothers and make fathers responsible for their children. However, the actions of the Child Support Agency cannot be separated from the government's overall commitment to reduce public expenditure. While fathers are being asked to pay more, children are not directly benefiting from the changes; the Treasury becomes the prime beneficiary by deducting Income Support paid to the mother. The second example has been the blocking of the private members' bill on the rights for the disabled. Rather than seeing the bill in the context of the disabled, the government very quickly provided estimates of the financial costs of the bill and encouraged certain MPs to de-rail the bill.

This text deals with six major policy issues. These include public expenditure, health, pensions, water privatisation, training and employment, reform of the civil service, and issues of ethnicity. The text deals with the context at the level of ideas, as well as the political context, the economic context, Europe and local government. The argument here is that there are a series of interlocking processes and dynamics in policy-making. Policy is influenced by ideas and ideology, but ideas are constrained by the politics of what is possible. The question of what is possible is further constrained by the other contexts such as that of the economy and local government, and also by the United Kingdom being also part of political Europe.

Robert Leach deals with the twin themes of political ideas and the political context (Chapters 1 and 2). He outlines an argument which describes the nature of fragmentation in British politics and how, in the absence of a written constitution, Conservative governments since 1979 have sought to change the nature of politics as established in the post-war period. Leach argues that while the Conservative government dominated British politics during the 1950s there was the held assumption that the government would continue to work within the boundaries of full employment and the welfare state established by the 1945 Labour government. British society of the 1990s is less homogenous; there is less support for the two major political parties and support for the welfare state is less universal. Political parties are concerned with attracting the votes of the contented majorities by promising continued growth and improved living standards, while a growing underclass is left with a future landscape of unemployment, low wages, homelessness and deteriorating public services.

Maurice Mullard deals with the economic context (Chapter 5) and decisions for public expenditure (Chapter 6) for the 1990s. His arguments are that two major challenges for the 1990s will be unemployment and public expenditure. Taking into consideration both the OECD and EU arguments that unemployment would continue to remain high during the 1990s, there is little scope for the United Kingdom to embark on a strategy that does not take into consideration the wider economic context. At present there seems to be a divergence of strategies and policy options being advocated by the EU and the OECD. The EU seems to want to combine a policy of de-regulation with social protection while the OECD seems to emphasise the need to de-regulate labour markets and to reduce labour costs. The EU is aware of the benefits and successes of having created a welfare capitalism which combines a commitment to market economies and social protection. In contrast the OECD points to the US model and the number of jobs created in the United States during the 1980s in contrast to Europe during the same period. The United Kingdom seems to be moving more towards a US approach to labour markets, with the government arguing that in future Britain will have to compete with the new economies of Asia as well as Europe.

The analysis of public expenditure decisions for the 1990s would indicate that the government is committed to restraining the growth of public expenditure for the remainder of the decade, and that in seeking to secure those reductions the government would target those programmes that are seen as the least politically costly to the Conservative government and Conservative voters. This means that the government would continue to make reductions in programmes that are directed towards vulnerable groups. Reductions will therefore continue to be sought within the social security programme including housing benefits, invalidity benefits, unemployment and pensions. Furthermore, the government continues to make reductions in capital expenditure programmes while it seeks to continue to constrain public sector pay. During the previous three years the pay of public sector workers has continued to fall behind that of the private sector. The government argue that during the recession private sector has also been faced with hardships, including the threat of unemployment, and that public sector workers have been protected from the threat of unemployment. Finally the government also know that winning a future election very much depends on their ability to hold down public expenditure and make finances available for tax reductions.

Dealing with the European context (Chapter 3), John Kingdom argues that Britain is a country that has been peculiarly involved in the wider world. The militaristic empire became a giant trading emporium for a newly dominant class. After two world wars the idea of a special relationship with the most powerful nation in the world dominated the psyche of the political class. Although ancestral voices still echo, both these sources of influence have dwindled and today debate within Britain's political class centres on the issues of European integration. Few governmental and political institutions remain untouched by a European dimension and the 1990s will see an increase in this. This chapter examines the impact of the European dimension on the core executive, the Whitehall network, Westminster and the state institutions beyond the central government complex.

Chapter 4 looks at the major areas of the policy during the years of the Thatcher governments and how these have sought to bypass local government and take more power towards the centre. Although the UK system of government has always tended to be centralist, it would seem that during the years of the Thatcher governments the process has accelerated. Within this centralising process, however, the government have sought to de-politicise certain aspects of public provision. The reforms in education now mean that it is governing bodies that are responsible for the running of local schools, yet schools are not really managing but administering budgets on behalf of central government.

If parents complain, their channel is either limited to the chair of the governors or the minister in Whitehall. In the meantime, when the ministers answer questions on education they always point to deficiencies as emanating from mis-management at the level of either the local authority or the governing body.

Tom Burden (Chapter 9) argues that the political context of health-care policy during the 1980s has been strongly influenced by the ideas of the New Right. Health care has been one of the most controversial arenas in which the ideas of Thatcherism have been implemented. Health care forms a major item of govern-ment expenditure which has been growing due to increases in the cost and complexity of medical provision and also for demographic reasons. This chapter looks at the process of how the NHS was established and charts the shift from an organisation structure based on a combination of bureaucratic and professional control to a more market-led structure.

The clash of ideology in terms of either an emphasis on the market or on provision based on need appears nowhere more manifest than in water privatis-ation (Chapter 8). John Dickens argues that the development of privatisation programmes needs to be seen alongside the general political context of the Thatcher years. The underlying theme of the chapter is one of accountability. Regulation and control are at the heart of the matter, whether associated with issues of subsidiarity in the EU in complying with environmental directives or with domestic social policy.

The analysis of training policy outlined by John Konrad (Chapter 11) points to the gaps between the rhetoric of government policy statements and the reality of policy in terms of public resources. The author has pointed out that the issue of training policy has two major political limitations. The first limitation is that there is a lag between embarking on a policy and governments being able to claim the benefits of the policy. Most training programmes need a number of years of sustained commitment before they start to show benefits. Second, there is the problem of resource constraints and, like all other programmes, training has to compete for resources alongside healthcare, social security and taxation. While there is much to be applauded in the sentiments outlined in government policy statements, the question is whether the government is willing to commit the resources to make the policy a success.

Richard Common (Chapter 7) points out that the 'Next Steps' reforms of the UK civil service reflect wider shifts in the political and economic context of policy-making as demands for public expenditure restraint have increased over the last twenty years. While the reforms have been shaped by public choice theory and managerialism, the chapter seeks to assess the radical nature of the reforms and questions whether they constitute a real departure from the traditional Whitehall model of service delivery.

Kirk Mann (Chapter 10) addresses some of the key policy and political issues that relate to pension provisions. The assumptions of the 'Beveridge model' based on National Insurance contributions and the alternative of private market-based insurance are both questioned. In contrast, it is argued that the British could learn a great deal from Australia. It is also suggested that the prospects for pensioners in the next century are closely tied to fiscal policy, the investment strategies of fund managers and the willingness of politicians to address patterns of social exclusion apparent prior to retirement.

Ian Law (Chapter 12) examines the issue of immigration posed for modern territorial states and associated political policy questions. The chapter examines the extent to which immigration policy in Britain is driven by electoral and authoritarian populism and also seeks to explain the changing character of Conservative and Labour party political discourse on race. Finally, the 'weak' management of racism and the 'strong' management of immigration is identified in the analysis of European policy.

The analysis of the various policy outcomes discussed in this text would suggest that the governance of Britain today is qualitatively different to that of 1979. However, it can also be argued that little has changed: the government still spends about 40 per cent of national income; health services and education are still financed through the tax system; most social security programmes including pensions and child benefit remain intact. The de-nationalisation of public utilities has turned public monopolies into private monopolies: there has been no discernible expansion in the number of gas or electricity suppliers, and consumers do not have more choice between their suppliers of gas, electricity, water or telecommunications. The public sector milch cows have become private sector companies making large profits, each paying large dividends to their shareholders.

The governments of the 1980s have introduced competitiveness and quasi-markets for public services, which in turn has meant that crucial areas of public provision have been shifted from the public service to the private sphere. Contracts between agencies and the government outline a number of performance criteria to evaluate the effectiveness, efficiency and value for the money of these agencies. Agencies are therefore only responsible to the minister in the context of delivering a contract. The HEFC and FEFC are now responsible for the delivery of higher and further education – the government, as the client, buy education through these agencies and the agencies on their part buy education through colleges and universities for a certain amount of money. The agencies are also responsible for ensuring quality of provision and securing value for money. In the meantime, colleges of further education and the new universities are now independent corporations, no longer accountable to their local authority or local community.

Hannah Arendt describes the distortion of democracy and public space as 'false politics' (Hansen 1993). Her main argument for democracy is that democracy offers people the opportunity to find their dignity. Within Arendt's framework people find their freedom in politics in being involved in the public sphere in order to bring about change. The move during the past fifteen years has been to make freedom a private issue, to minimise the role of politics and for individuals to find their freedom in the private sphere. In this context, expectations of government are those of consumers. The recently introduced Citizen's Charters are consumer charters. People pay taxes to buy services through government and they evaluate these services as the consumers of these services. The expectation is that government gives value for money.

While it might be argued that the government has succeeded in breaking with interest group politics, it would seem that this has been replaced with what can be called the politics of trusteeship. According to this new politics, governments are elected as the trustees of public services. As the trustees, they contract agencies to deliver services. They appoint chief executives and regulators and devolve funding to these agencies. In between elections, Parliament is reduced to an audience rather than a participant in the policy process. Ministers are longer directly accountable to Parliament – it is the chief executives of the new agencies who are accountable but they are not elected and their accountability is restricted to the delivery of a contract to the minister and not Parliament. Parliament has no say in making appointments to these agencies. In the meantime the trustees will seek an electoral mandate every four or five years from an electorate which is asked to endorse that mandate rather than being asked to participate as democratic citizens.

REFERENCES

Beer, S. (1982) *Britain Against Itself: The Political Contradictions of Collectivism*, London: Faber & Faber.

Hansen, P. (1993) *Hannah Arendt: Politics, History and Citizenship*, Cambridge: Polity Press.

Rose, R. (ed.) (1980) *Challenge to Governance*, London: Sage.

Rose, R. and Peters, G. (1979) *Can Governments Go Bankrupt?*, London: Macmillan.

Part I

The context of public policy-making

1   Political ideas

Robert Leach

IDEAS, GOVERNMENT AND PUBLIC POLICY

The importance of political ideas to a study of government and public policy might be thought almost too obvious to require emphasis. Politics is often presented in terms of a conflict of ideas, for example between socialist planning and the free market. Public policy is frequently linked to specific ideas. Thus the economic policy of Margaret Thatcher's first administration in 1979 was associated with monetarism.

Yet there are perspectives on politics that tend to downgrade the importance of ideas. Traditional Conservatives in Britain, before the advent of Thatcher, emphasised that their approach to politics was based on common sense rather than theory, a practical response to pressing problems of the day (Hogg 1947, Oakeshott 1962). Ideas were suspect. Pragmatism was the hallmark of this traditional conservatism.

To some Western political scientists in the post-war era it seemed that politics involved essentially a competition for votes and influence, in which a pragmatic search for the middle ground was more important than ideological conviction (McKenzie 1963). Market research was employed to enable political parties to deliver what the voters wanted. Image and presentation were emphasised at the expense of ideas. Ideological debate seemed to have little place in a style of politics where the reasoned speech was replaced by the soundbite, and even the soundbite by the wordless photo opportunity.

However, the importance of political ideas has increasingly been re-emphasised, even in such an apparently unpromising context. What came to be called 'Thatcherism' was a new style of conservatism which derided consensus, compromise and pragmatism, and emphasised the importance of ideas and principles. The main opposition parties in Britain desperately sought for their own 'big idea' to counteract the free-market message of Thatcher's Conservatives. Other political movements, such as the Greens and feminists, presented their own alternative value systems which challenged dominant orthodoxies.

Moreover, even before this apparent rediscovery of the importance of ideas, it was always the case that even the most resolutely untheoretical parties, movements and politicians implicitly reflected concepts, assumptions and principles.

J.M. Keynes pointed out that 'Practical men, who believe themselves to be quite exempt from any intellectual influence are usually the slaves of some defunct economist.' People are not always aware of the influences on their own ideas and behaviour, which may be more readily identified by others. Thus one should not necessarily accept at face value the traditional Conservative's rejection of ideas and principles. Some fairly consistent principles can be inferred from Conservatism in action over the years, as well as from the admittedly relatively thin written sources (Eccleshall 1990).

Public policy proceeds on the basis of ideological assumptions, even though these may not be clearly articulated, or even consciously recognised. Public policy problems are not 'given'. The way in which problems are identified and interpreted reflects preconceived ideas. The search for solutions similarly reflects prior assumptions – some possible remedies may be rejected out of hand or not even considered. The ways in which policy is made and implemented will also involve essentially ideological notions, over, for example, the degree of consultation deemed desirable, or the scope for compromise. Finally, the ideas that people hold will influence the acceptance of policy, whether it is enthusiastically supported, grudgingly obeyed, or actively resisted. Indeed the stability of the whole political and governmental system ultimately rests on what the mass of people think about politics, even if, most of the time, the masses seem to give little conscious thought to politics (Leach 1991).

The relationship between political ideas and public policy is complex and often two-way. Ideas constrain and in some senses determine public policy, yet public policy may in turn influence the ideas that people hold. Thus a change in the law, for example legalising homosexual relations between consenting adults, or making illegal discrimination on grounds of race or gender, may help to change public attitudes. The policy of privatisation pursued by the Thatcher governments clearly reflected a belief in government circles in the virtues of the free market and private ownership, but it can also be assumed that the sale of shares to the public on favourable terms helped the acceptance of 'popular capitalism'.

WHAT IDEAS?

The ideas that influence government and public policy are not just the ideas of major political thinkers or even leading politicians, but ideas held at every level in society. The study of political thought has traditionally involved the detailed examination of the texts of a handful of great thinkers, such as Plato, Aristotle, Thomas Hobbes, John Locke, Jean-Jacques Rousseau, J.S. Mill and Karl Marx. Yet some of these thinkers are scarcely known to a wider public, and their direct influence on politics has been fairly minimal. Even Marx had a very limited impact in his own lifetime. Indeed, modern politics has often seemed to reflect the ideas of leading economists rather than essentially political thinkers – Adam Smith, Thomas Malthus, David Ricardo, Keynes, Friedrich Hayek and Milton Friedman. Yet even these names, well known to political leaders, top civil servants and academics, may be scarcely familiar to ordinary voters, although some of their ideas, perhaps in modified or vulgarised form, may have percolated through into popular consciousness.

The concern here is not so much with traditional political theory, but with values, ideas and political ideologies, held at a variety of levels, from the sophisticated to the relatively crude or even unconscious. Unfortunately the term 'political ideology' is one that remains highly contentious, and is still often used in a limited, negative or pejorative way. Here the term is employed in the relatively comprehensive and neutral way in which it has been used recently by Seliger (1976) and other writers (McLennan 1976) to mean any loosely linked ideas, values or perspectives that inform political judgements and behaviour.

The use of the term does not imply any judgement on the worth or truth of the ideas discussed. Conservatism, socialism and liberalism might all be considered ideologies; so might fascism, feminism, nationalism, anarchism and ecologism. Moreover, each of these ideologies has its own subcategories. There are thus varieties of conservatism, socialism and feminism which indicate various tensions and contradictions within each ideology. Furthermore, ideas are held at different levels by different sections within society. Thus there may be considerable differences between the elite and popular versions of an ideology, such as Thatcherism. At one level it may involve the thought of Smith and Hayek. At another it may embrace ideas of the free market, privatisation and national sovereignty. At the lowest level it may amount to little more than slogans which have entered popular consciousness – the 'Nanny State', or 'Up yours, Delors!'

One problem with some of the more familiar political ideologies is that they are closely identified with particular political parties. Some ideologies thus appear to be party ideologies, while other ideologies (for example, feminism) may not be closely associated with a particular party. Yet even where an ideology is popularly associated with a party or movement, it is often discussed in more general or abstract terms. Thus liberalism is commonly analysed in terms that have little relation to the record of the British Liberal Party, or the modern Liberal Democrats. Critics have often castigated Conservative governments for being insufficiently Conservative, while it is sometimes suggested that the Labour Party, popularly associated with socialism, is not a socialist party at all. This implied distinction between political ideologies and the ideas, programmes and records of political parties with which the ideologies are popularly associated is undeniably confusing to anyone embarking on a study of political ideas. It does, however, underline the complexity of the relationship between political ideas and political behaviour.

LIBERALISM, NEO-LIBERALISM AND COLLECTIVISM

Most modern political ideologies have a long pedigree, and it is impossible to discuss contemporary political ideas without reference to the past. This is particularly the case with ideas associated with the governments of Thatcher and John Major. A common term for these ideas is 'neo-liberalism'. This implies that modern conservatism, as articulated by Thatcher or Major, is essentially a restatement of nineteenth-century liberalism. Both government rhetoric and opposition critics suggest that present-day conservatism involves a return to 'Victorian values'. At the same time, some Conservative critics like Sir Ian Gilmour (1978, 1992) have persistently denied that 'Thatcherism' is true conservatism. The ideological tensions within modern conservatism can only be understood with reference to the competing Liberal and Conservative political traditions (Eccleshall 1986, 1990; Greenleaf 1983).

Liberalism of one form or another was the dominant ideology in nineteenth-century Britain. What has come to be called 'classical liberalism' derived its political theory from the Whig opposition to royal absolutism in the seventeenth and eighteenth centuries, and its economic theory from the free-market ideas of Smith, Malthus and Ricardo. Both strands of thought indicated the need for strict limits to be placed on government. Both were built on the assumptions of individualism – on the notion that society is nothing more than the sum of sovereign individuals who are each the best judge of their own interests. Practical implications involved toleration and freedom of thought in the religious and political spheres, and *laissez-faire* (or non-intervention) by governments in the economic sphere (Arblaster 1984, Gray 1986). For many critics, the ideology of liberalism was inseparably involved with the development of industrial capitalism, and the associated interests of the bourgeoisie.

It is this classical liberalism, and more particularly the economic ideas associated with it, that has been revived by neo-liberal or New Right theorists, such as Hayek and Friedman, publicised by think-tanks such as the Institute of Economic Affairs, the Adam Smith Institute and the Centre for Policy Studies, and taken up by Conservative politicians such as Keith Joseph, Thatcher and Nicholas Ridley, and more recently by Michael Portillo and John Redwood. Yet ironically, nineteenth-century conservatism, as articulated by Benjamin Disraeli and others, involved a sharp reaction against the fundamental tenets of liberalism. It was Disraeli's 'one nation' conservatism that provided the inspiration for a later generation of Conservatives, including Harold Macmillan, Rab Butler and Iain Macleod in the post-war era (Beer 1982). Thatcherism was, in turn, a reaction against the paternalistic social reform of this strand of conservatism.

Political ideologies frequently contain competing strands and tensions, and even contradictions. This is as true of liberalism as conservatism. It was always clear also that there were manifest tensions within nineteenth-century liberalism – between, for example, on the one hand the strictly limited aspirations of the Whigs, and on the other hand the reforming radicalism of the utilitarians, who developed liberal principles to embrace representative democracy. This serves to remind us that liberalism, in the eyes of its own spokespersons and supporters, was essentially a political rather than an economic creed. Moreover, religious concerns also loomed far larger for the bulk of the Victorian electorate than is often realised. Nineteenth-century liberalism was more obviously the political voice of religious nonconformism than of industrial capitalism. Towards the end of the century many liberals were consciously rejecting *laissez-faire* ideas in favour of active state intervention. Yet to an extent this apparently revolutionary

'New Liberalism' involved little more than a rationalisation of the actual practice of Liberal governments and Liberal councils, and an updating of Liberal theory to take account of Liberal public policy.

Indeed, to many contemporary observers and subsequent historians the nineteenth century involved, as it progressed, the growth of collectivism (Greenleaf 1983). The individualist assumptions behind early nineteenth-century liberalism, although highly influential, had never been universally accepted. On the one hand there were old-style Tories who had always been suspicious of liberal rhetoric about freedom, rights and equality. The liberal challenge to traditional values and institutions involved a rejection of authority and order which was ultimately damaging to the whole fabric of society, which Tories tended to see as a complex web of interdependent parts, involving mutual obligations. On the other hand, working-class radicals also emphasised the importance of social forces against which the individual was relatively powerless. High-sounding Liberal freedoms meant little to those who were constrained by economic pressures outside their control. Some Tories, like Shaftesbury or Michael Sadler, preached reform and state intervention from a sense of paternalist obligations to those who were in no position to help themselves. Working-class radicals demanded reform in the name of social justice. Such pressures reinforced growing collectivist tendencies within liberalism itself. Thus by the late nineteenth century all the major political ideologies in Britain – Toryism or conservatism, liberalism and a nascent socialism – were moving towards collectivist solutions to public policy problems.

The prospects for a Conservative Party apparently wedded to a declining landed interests appeared poor in the second half of the nineteenth century. Disraeli had helped conservatism to come to terms with the expansion of the franchise, and Randolph Churchill used the term 'Tory democracy' to indicate the new Conservative interest in the mass electorate. The Tory Party contrived to win working-class votes by a two-pronged strategy – appealing to patriotic and imperialist sentiment, but satisfying some of the demands for social reform at home. This strategy succeeded to such an extent that the party was in power for nearly the whole period from 1886 to 1906, despite the dramatic expansion in the working-class vote which might have been expected to spell the party's doom. The Liberal Unionist politician, Joseph Chamberlain, and his sons Austen and Neville, then contrived to convert the Conservative and Unionist Party to the cause of protection, which was never apparently very popular with the electorate.

Liberalism was marked off from conservatism after 1886 by its association with religious nonconformism, its support for Irish Home Rule, its generally more internationalist and anti-war stance, and its continued adherence to free trade. Yet faith in free trade abroad was not matched by a similar faith in market forces at home, and under the influence of thinkers like T.H. Green, D.G. Ritchie, L.T. Hobhouse and J.A. Hobson, the party moved a long way from the *laissez-faire* creed which had been theoretically dominant in the early part of the nineteenth century. The 1906–14 Liberal government helped to lay the foundations for the welfare state with the introduction of old-age pensions, school meals, state unemployment and health insurance, and labour exchanges. Moreover, while both the older parties had competed for the support of organised labour in the period before the First World War, it was the Liberal Party that was the more prepared to meet the demands of the trade unions and the infant Labour Party.

Socialist ideas had been propounded in Britain in the early part of the nineteenth century, most notably by Robert Owen, but made little apparent impact again until the 1880s. Even then what was to prove the major strand of British socialism owed little to Marx, and from the outset favoured gradual reform through existing institutions, rather than revolution. Some would argue that the Labour Party, effectively founded in 1900, was never really a socialist party, and that the term 'labourism' is a more accurate description of its ideas than socialism. It was essentially founded and funded by trade unions, to protect the interests of unions and the working class. It only adopted a socialist programme in 1918, but even then doubts remained over the extent of its commitment to that programme. The socialists who supported the Labour Party from the beginning included the middle-class Fabians, committed to gradual reform, and the more evangelical Independent Labour Party, which employed religious imagery to depict the future socialist millennium, but remained committed to the parliamentary, gradualist strategy in practice. Marxist and anarcho-syndicalist ideas had some support in the early years of the twentieth century, but mainstream British socialism rejected the language of class war, and tended to identify socialism with the growth of state intervention or collectivism. In terms of practical policy, there was little to mark off this British socialism from radical liberalism, beyond its close association with trade unionism (Foote 1986, Crick 1987, Callaghan 1990).

This was clear when the British economy faced crisis between the wars. There was no radical alternative on offer from the British Labour Party, which was apparently as wedded to the dominant economic orthodoxies as the Liberal and Conservative parties. Labour politicians routinely blamed the crisis on capitalism, but as they lacked the power and the will to transform the economic system, they were reduced to attempting to manage the existing capitalist system as best they could. Indeed less orthodox ideas came from the other parties. The Liberal Lloyd George was more prepared to introduce public works to reduce unemployment, while the Conservatives placed their faith in protection. After 1931, the Conservative-dominated National Government, led by the former Labour leader Ramsay MacDonald, abandoned free trade and promoted the rationalisation of British industry and agriculture (Beer 1982).

POST-WAR CONSENSUS

It is often reckoned that there was little fundamental disagreement in economic and political ideas in the period after 1945, so much so that it has become conventional to talk of a post-war consensus, although there is a minority view that questions the extent of that consensus (Beer 1982, Kavanagh 1990). For example, was it just a consensus among the political elite – the front benches in Parliament and the higher civil service – or did it extend through society generally?

One might equally well question whether the consensus in British politics, in so far as it existed, dated only from the Second World War. As we have seen, there was little fundamental disagreement on the essential issue of the handling of the economy, either in the inter-war period, or even in the period before the First World War, although there were considerable divisions over Ireland and foreign affairs.

The ideas behind the consensus had, however, changed. The new consensus was closely associated with the economic analysis of Keynes and the social security system proposed by William Beveridge. Keynes had apparently demonstrated that governments need no longer be passive spectators of recession, unemployment and misery but could so manage aggregate demand in the economy to maintain full employment and stable growth. Beveridge had designed a comprehensive system of state insurance to provide security from the cradle to the grave.

Keynesian economic management and the principles of the welfare state were consistent with all the mainstream British political ideologies. Both Keynes and Beveridge were Liberals, and their ideas could be seen as the natural culmination of the New Liberalism which the Liberal Party had accepted over the previous half century. For the Conservatives it was electorally essential to distance the party from the economic failures of the inter-war years, but the new ideas did not involve a complete revolution in thinking. Previous leaders like Disraeli, Arthur Balfour and Neville Chamberlain had accepted the need for social reform. Moreover, as post-war Conservative politicians like Anthony Eden pointed out, the party had never been wedded to *laissez-faire*. For the Labour Party, Keynesianism provided planning of a sort, and a philosophy that was consistent with their centralised state socialism. It also apparently removed the need for detailed planning at the level of specific industries, which meant that the Labour government could restrict its nationalisation proposals to the commanding heights of the economy.

The extent of the consensus from 1945 should not be exaggerated. Although there was all-party support for Keynesian demand management and for the new National Insurance system, the 1945–51 Labour government's proposals for the National Health Service and the bulk of its nationalisation programme were bitterly opposed by the Tories. However, the Conservative governments of 1951–64 maintained and expanded the NHS and only de-nationalised steel and road haulage, thus preserving what might be described as a 'mixed economy'. Moreover, the same Conservative governments pursued a markedly conciliatory industrial relations policy.

Indeed, under Macmillan, prime minister from 1957 to 1963, the Conservative Party was as closely identified with collectivism as in any time in its history. Macmillan had published a book in 1938 in which he had proposed a 'middle way' between capitalism and socialism. He provocatively declared that Toryism had always been a form of paternal socialism. It might be claimed that his government attempted to follow such a middle way. In 1958 Macmillan was prepared to accept the resignation of his entire Treasury team of ministers rather than accept the financial cuts they thought necessary. Later, he introduced an incomes policy and moved still further in the direction of a form of economic planning when he established the National Economic Development Council in 1962.

Within the Labour Party there was a parallel attempt in the 1950s to devise an ideological middle way between capitalism and socialism. In truth there had always been a gulf between the fundamentalist socialist rhetoric of the party and its cautious reformism in office. In opposition, some on the right of the party concluded that the commitment to nationalisation, and even the party's name, were electoral liabilities. The leading revisionist text was Anthony Crosland's *The Future of Socialism* (1956). Crosland suggested that capitalism had been transformed by the divorce of ownership from control of industry, the development of the welfare state and a progressive system of taxation. Thus the old socialist goal of common ownership of the means of production was now irrelevant, and should be replaced by the pursuit of equality. Hugh Gaitskell, as party leader, tried to remove the commitment to common ownership, represented by Clause IV in the party's constitution. This provoked bitter opposition from the parliamentary left, associated with Nye Bevan, and a prolonged split within the party, which was only superficially healed when the former Bevanite, Harold Wilson, succeeded Gaitskell as leader after the latter's death. The ideological cleavage within the party remained through to the 1980s, although in retrospect the division between Gaitskellism and Bevanism seems more a question of emphasis rather than substance.

There was little marked change of direction, and little in the way of new ideas when Labour returned to power under Harold Wilson in 1964. Both Labour and the Conservatives were then committed not only to Keynesian demand management and the welfare state, but also to incomes policy and a form of indicative economic planning. This required the involvement of business and union leaders in the policy process, and what have been called corporatist institutions and processes reached their height under Wilson and the Conservative premier, Heath.

Corporatism is a slippery concept which has been variously defined. It is most commonly associated with what is called 'tripartism', by which policy was supposed to emerge as a result of tripartite negotiations between government, business (represented by the CBI) and the unions (represented by the TUC). It was also closely linked with new institutions on which employers and unions were represented. Some commentators suggested that it represented a new economic system, others that it involved a shift in power within the political system. Left-wing critics of corporatism suggested that it involved trade unions abandoning their traditional free collective bargaining and real industrial power, for the shadow of involvement in national policy-making, while right-wing critics suggested that governments were surrendering too much power to the unions.

The only other essentially new idea in British politics in this period was Europe. This also might be considered part of the consensus, in that it cut across party lines and drew support from leading politicians on both sides of the party divide, although it inspired, as it continues to inspire, fierce controversy within both major parties. British governments had been broadly sympathetic to the movement towards closer European union from 1945 onwards, but the international role associated with pretensions to world power status and the British Empire and Commonwealth, coupled with the special relationship with the United States, ensured that Britain held aloof from the developments that led to the establishment of the European Economic Community. The Suez débâcle of 1956, coupled with the rapid decline in the British Empire, provoked a fundamental rethink of Britain's role in the world. Thus the bulk of the Conservative Party, which had been pre-eminently the party of the empire, followed Macmillan and subsequently Heath in ultimately successful attempts to join the European Community. The commitment, however, was essentially only to closer economic union rather than the political union desired by the more enthusiastic Euro-federalists. Moreover, a minority within the Conservative Party bitterly opposed the implicit threats to national sovereignty.

The Labour Party was initially more deeply divided over Europe. While the Bevanite left was in general more hostile to Europe, regarding the Common Market as a capitalist club, and the right more enthusiastic, the issue of Europe largely cut across the usual left–right split. Thus opponents included the right-wing revisionist Douglas Jay and eventually the party leader Gaitskell, whose forthright condemnation of membership at the 1962 party conference provoked a rapprochement with the left before his death in 1963. Wilson, as prime minister of a Labour government, eventually decided to pursue British membership of the Community in 1967, but in opposition pragmatically bowed to the anti-European tide within his party to accept a commitment to renegotiation and a national referendum on Britain's continued membership. Subsequently, enthusiasm for Europe was closely associated with the social democratic wing of the party, and it was a critical issue in leading to the establishment of a separate Social Democratic Party in 1981.

By this time, however, the post-war political consensus appeared to be definitely over. The values associated with that consensus indeed now seemed to be rejected by both the major parties, and only maintained by the new SDP and their Liberal allies.

OUTSIDE THE CONSENSUS

There had always, of course, been people outside the consensus. To the right there were those who regarded the abandonment of the British Empire as a betrayal, and who deplored the compromises with what they saw as socialist and trade unionist ideas. To the left there were, besides the Bevanite wing of the Labour Party, various fragments of the extra-parliamentary left, among which orthodox Communists were outnumbered by different brands of Trotskyism.

Perhaps the first anti-establishment political movement with a significant following in the post-war period was the Campaign for Nuclear Disarmament, which made a major popular impact in the late 1950s. In the 1960s the peace movement broadened to include opposition to the Vietnam War and the American alliance, and provided an initial education in political activism for a whole generation of radicals. It was later to become closely linked with sections of the women's movement and with the Green movement.

The peace movement also provided a model for a new politics of protest outside the mainstream party ideologies – where direct action took the place of more conventional political processes. Much of this community or workplace activism took place around single issues outside the party mainstream. Examples would include the squatters confronting the problem of homelessness, claimants' unions to assert the claims of those dependent on state benefits, and later the protest movement against the poll tax.

During the 1960s what has been described as a second wave of feminism also came to prominence. The first wave of feminism had established votes for women and various formal legal rights in the early twentieth century, but fifty years after obtaining the vote, women remained second-class citizens, excluded from certain spheres altogether, and with only a token involvement in others. Thus a second wave of feminist writers sought a more profound and lasting transformation of the position of women (Friedan 1963, Greer 1970). Distinctions are often drawn between different forms of feminism, although it should be emphasised that there are no hard and fast divisions. Thus it is suggested that liberal feminism is largely concerned with further progress towards formal legal equality, involving equal pay and equal opportunities legislation, and effective implementation. Liberal feminists are sometimes criticised for being largely concerned with securing greater opportunities for middle-class professional women (Friedan 1963). Socialist feminists see the bulk of women as effectively exploited twice over, by the capitalist economic system and by men (Mitchell 1971). They emphasise the need to organise women in the workplace, and secure childcare facilities and wages for housework. Radical feminists suggest that women's exploitation has little to do with capitalism and the economic system, but everything to do with men. A key concept here is patriarchy (Millett 1977). Everywhere men dominate and exploit women. Some radical feminists are less concerned to pursue equality for women in what they regard as a man's world, but instead promote women's issues and values through exclusively female organisations. Partly because of their greater involvement in child-rearing and home-making, women, it is argued, are by nature caring and sharing, rather than violent, acquisitive and competitive. That explains why there has been some considerable overlap among radical feminism, the peace movement and latterly the Green movement. Rape and all forms of violence against women (under which heading some feminists would include pornography) are key concerns of radical feminists (Brownmiller 1975). Indeed, some now regard the greater sexual permissiveness with which feminism was associated in the 1960s as leading to a different kind of exploitation of women.

Anti-racism is often bracketed with feminism, in that both involve attempts to counteract prejudice and discrimination, and both have led to similar legal and institutional measures to outlaw discrimination. Black militancy came to public notice around the same time as militant feminism, and both were associated by the tabloid press with left-wing politicians and certain Labour councils. Yet the black movement essentially has different origins, being substantially a consequence of the white backlash against immigration from the so-called 'New Commonwealth' in the post-war era. In the late 1960s, riots partly sparked by racial tension led Enoch Powell to make a provocative series of speeches in which he predicted 'rivers of blood' and advocated 'repatriation'. He was promptly sacked from the Shadow Cabinet by the Tory leader, Heath, but this expression by a mainstream politician of views previously associated with the far right appeared to legitimate racial prejudice.

Powell thought he was the victim of an establishment consensus that was determined to ignore popular hostility to black immigration. Among mainstream consensus politicians the public policy solution was seen initially in terms of assimilation and integration, supported by anti-discrimination legislation, but coupled with stronger controls over new immigration, which seemed to concede part of Powell's case. To the black community, racism was a white problem, not a black problem. Experience of white racism also perhaps helped to stimulate a greater sense of their own cultural identity among some ethnic minorities, which gave some impetus to policies of multi-culturalism rather than assimilation (Saggar 1992).

Ethnic tensions raised in acute form issues of national identity and sovereignty. The rapid run-down of empire and the new pressures towards closer European integration placed a question-mark against the notion of Britain and the future of the union. Hitherto nationalism had been seen through British eyes as an alien creed affecting other countries, although Irish nationalism had been a persistent problem for UK public policy. The problem of Ireland flared to life in 1968 after a period of comparative quiescence. The nationalists in Northern Ireland, of course, challenged the whole basis of the UK state, and continue to pose critical problems for UK public policy. Similar fundamental issues of allegiance and the boundaries of the state were also articulated, less violently, but with increasing support, by Welsh and Scottish nationalists. Attempts by the 1974–79 Labour government to assuage nationalist demands in Scotland and Wales by conceding a measure of devolution failed with Labour's defeat. The politics of nationalism, like the politics of race and gender, cut across the old class-based politics associated with the mainstream political ideologies (Nairn 1981, Smith 1991).

Environmentalism and the Green movement only began to make much of an impact rather later, in the 1970s and 1980s, yet like other political movements described in this section, it was essentially a reaction against the post-war Keynesian or social democratic consensus. Economic growth was seen as one of the prime goals of Keynesian policy. The pursuit of growth was bound up with mainstream political ideologies. Growth enabled Macmillan to boast 'You've never had it so good.' It enabled revisionist socialists like Crosland to believe that greater equality could be achieved by distributing the product of growth rather than by making anyone worse off. Wilson's programme of social reform without tax increases was based on the premise of a substantial rate of annual growth. While some questioned the feasibility of the 4 per cent per annum growth rate, few questioned its desirability. Yet by the 1970s there was wider concern that there were limits to growth, and to human exploitation of the environment (Porritt and Winner 1988).

The ecology movement involves a radical alternative political agenda, with far-reaching public policy implications, which provides the most fundamental challenge yet to the materialist assumptions behind the post-war consensus. However, while Green pressure groups and parties have certainly stimulated greater awareness of environmental issues, they have not forced any fundamental reassessment of priorities. All that has happened is that some Green issues, like lead-free petrol, have since been incorporated into the political mainstream.

To a degree, the same point may be made about the other perspectives discussed in this section. Elements from them all have been absorbed into the political mainstream. To some extent, attitudes have changed. There is a wider acceptance of multi-culturalism, for example. Yet the more radical versions of feminism, anti-racism and ecologism remain politically marginalised.

Indeed, one may question whether any of these radical challenges to the mainstream political consensus had much lasting impact. The 1950s and 1960s apparently inaugurated some highly disrespectful questioning of establishment values, from the 'angry young men' of the 1950s through the satire boom of the early 1960s to the campus revolution of 1968. Yet many of the new rebels were soon comfortably absorbed into the establishment from which they had made their reputation by attacking. As far as disadvantaged groups in society were concerned, there were some largely symbolic gains in terms of equal pay and anti-discrimination legislation for women and ethnic minorities, but pay and employment statistics still indicate substantial inequality. Those who discovered that they were outside the consensus in the 1960s have thus largely remained outside it. If the various radical challenges had any significant impact on the post-war consensus, it was only to weaken it in the face of a far more formidable onslaught from the right.

THE NEW RIGHT AND THATCHERISM

The post-war consensus was to be destroyed, not by any of the radical alternatives apparently on offer, but from the right of the political spectrum, by ideas that had appeared to be dead and buried.

Perhaps too much power should not be ascribed to ideas. Thatcherism was in one sense a reaction against policy failures. Keynesian demand management had apparently failed, producing simultaneous increases in unemployment and inflation which theory had suggested was impossible. The old remedies no longer appeared to work. It was James Callaghan, a Labour prime minister, who sadly concluded that it was no longer possible to spend your way out of a recession. The other main pillar of the post-war consensus – the welfare state – also appeared to be in deep trouble. A range of indicators demonstrated that it was failing to provide security from the cradle to the grave – child poverty, inner-city deprivation, homelessness, and scandals in long-stay hospitals. Yet ever-rising costs provoked hostility to increasing levels of taxes and resentment against 'scroungers'. The corporatism of the Heath and Wilson era had also apparently failed, with its most obvious symbol, incomes policy, breaking down in disorder. Governments had promised to do too much and had manifestly failed to deliver. Some critics saw a wider malaise in society, created by 'permissiveness' and the weakening influence of religion and family values.

Conservatism has only survived so successfully as a political creed because of its flexibility. At one level, the party responded to an altered climate (just as it had done after 1945). Thatcher's election as leader of the Conservative Party in 1975 owed little to her lightly aired ideological convictions. She won because she was not Ted Heath, who was too closely associated with policy and electoral failure. However, the apparent discrediting of Keynesianism left something of an ideological vacuum, and there were hitherto largely neglected thinkers who could be employed to fill that vacuum (Hayek 1976).

What came to be called 'Thatcherism' emerged over time. It has been so extensively and variously interpreted that it is a somewhat problematic concept, but it is too handy a label to be discarded now. Thatcherism is best seen as a politically effective blend of two strands of thought: free-market values associated with old-fashioned liberalism, and traditional Tory values – a mixture of what might be termed neo-liberalism and neo-conservatism (Levitas 1986, King 1987). The combination was not entirely new – Powellism might be regarded as the precursor of Thatcherism (Gamble 1974). But Thatcher proved to be a more successful politician than Powell, and her more flexible combination of old liberal and Tory values had a much greater impact on both popular thinking and public policy. Some would argue that she effectively created a new political consensus to replace the old social democratic consensus. Certainly it involved a profound revolution of thinking within the Conservative Party, away from the Tory collectivism and paternalism that had characterised the Macmillan era.

The neo-liberal sources of Thatcherism are well known: the classical free-market economists, and their modern counterparts, Hayek, Friedman, the Institute of Economic Affairs, the Adam Smith Institute (Green 1987). Their analysis apparently demonstrated that government intervention was the cause of most of the country's economic ills. The solution was to rein back the frontiers of the state, cut public spending and taxation, and stimulate market competition.

The public policy implications of this agenda have included the privatisation of the former nationalised industries, the sale of council houses, the de-regulation of transport, the introduction of internal markets into the NHS and education, and compulsory competitive tendering over much of the public sector. In a relatively short period of time the boundaries and characteristics of the public sector, established through the post-war consensus, have been completely transformed.

How far it has produced a commensurate change in public attitudes, justifying talk of a new consensus, is more doubtful. While the sale of council houses and the early public flotations of shares in former nationalised industries seem to have been popular, they do not necessarily amount to a new enterprise culture of popular capitalism. Other market-inspired reforms in transport, health care and education have met with a more mixed response, while the poll tax, which reflected New Right public choice theory, was so unpopular as to help precipitate Thatcher's fall. Yet she has apparently succeeded in changing some public expectations. Most people no longer believe that governments can do much about unemployment. This throwback to thinking between the wars is a marked shift from the assumptions in the Keynesian heyday.

Many early commentators emphasised the neo-liberal, free-market aspects of Thatcherism (Bosanquet 1983, Keegan 1984), while neglecting the extent to which Thatcher also drew on traditional Tory themes – nation, family, authority, law and order (Cowling 1978, Scruton 1980). Such themes had found a ready response among a large section of the working class in the past, and what radical analysts characterised as 'authoritarian populism' was seemingly equally popular in the 1980s (Hall and Jacques 1983). It was the Falklands, a robust defence and foreign policy, and subsequently Thatcher's vehement defence of British interests in the Community that created the image of the 'Iron Lady' and 'Battling Maggie'. None of this had much to do with the free market.

Thatcherism always involved some contradictions. It was strange that a government apparently committed to market forces and reining back the frontiers of the state should be so persistently interventionist and centralist. In part this could be justified in terms of intervention to make the market work, with the implication that once the new market mechanisms were in place, there would be less need for government to do so in future. It could also be argued that major vested interests had to be taken on and defeated to free up competition. Monopolistic practices by local councils and the professions had to be challenged. Indeed the Thatcher governments did have some problems in securing the implementation of key policies, which led to more legislation, the establishment of new agencies and the bypassing of elected local authorities.

Pragmatic considerations were sometimes more important than ideological convictions. Critics on both the right and left have suggested that the privatisation of the former nationalised industries has not led to a significant increase in competition – rather, state monopolies have been effectively replaced by private monopolies. Yet an important byproduct of the privatisation programme is that this sale of public assets has significantly reduced the public sector borrowing requirement, and enabled the government to avoid painful alternative fiscal policies.

The neo-liberal and neo-conservative aspects of Thatcherism had some mutually consistent policy implications. Neo-liberals, critical of state intervention and high public spending, naturally found a ready target in large areas of welfare provision. Yet neo-conservatives like Roger Scruton and Peregrine Worsthorne were also critical of the 'dependency culture' involved in the welfare state and its undermining of traditional values and institutions.

However, sometimes the neo-liberal and neo-conservative elements of Thatcherism have been at cross-purposes. A good example is Sunday trading.

Abolition of the restrictions on Sunday trading reflects free-market values, but impinges on the traditional Tory respect for the sabbath as a day for religion and the family. Significantly this was one issue on which Thatcher's government suffered a rare defeat (effectively reversed since during John Major's period in office). Europe offers another issue with more serious implications for the Conservative Party. The European Union appears at one level to favour the further extension of free-market ideas which the Conservative Party now champions at home, which is why Thatcher found little difficulty in signing the Single European Act. But the Union also carries with it federalist implications that threaten the national sovereignty which Tories hold dear, which is why Thatcher, Norman Tebbit and many who share their views in the Conservative Party have become so hostile to the Maastricht Treaty. The problem over Europe lies at the heart of Thatcherism, and leaves a dangerous unresolved legacy for Thatcher's successors.

ALTERNATIVES TO THATCHERISM

Thatcher was fond of pronouncing 'There is no alternative.' Electorally this seemed to be true in the 1980s, although it reflected more the divisions among the opposition and the effects of the British electoral system than the overwhelming dominance of Thatcher's Conservative Party, which never attracted more than 43 per cent of the votes cast, a smaller proportion than Sir Alec Douglas Home secured when he lost in 1964. However, in ideological terms it also seemed that there was little obvious alternative to the shrill certainties of Thatcherism.

The initial response within much of the Labour Party to the collapse of the Keynesian consensus was a return to more fundamental socialist orthodoxies. As the Conservative Party moved to the right under Thatcher, Labour moved to the left. Some of the major battles within the party were not fought on major issues of ideological principle but over apparently arcane matters of organisation – control of the manifesto, the election of the leader, and the reselection of candidates. Yet these issues were critical for the power struggle within the party and had considerable implications for its future ideological direction. It seemed for a time as if Labour's radical left, loosely led by Tony Benn, would take complete control of the party (Seyd 1987).

An early product of the party's leftwards shift was the Alternative Economic Strategy (AES), essentially a mixture of updated Keynesianism and socialist planning. Some critics suggested that the AES was based on outdated assumptions on economic growth and was concerned with promoting largely male employment in traditional industries. Such an approach was ill-suited to appeal to other elements on the radical left, such as feminists and Greens.

Particularly in some Labour local councils there was an attempt to meet the concerns of some of the interests that had been largely excluded from the post-war consensus – peace campaigners (through the establishment of 'nuclear-free zones'), feminists, ethnic minorities and Greens. This was linked to the notion of 'local socialism', reviving a more decentralised, participative socialist tradition as a counter to the top-down state socialism that had been dominant within the Labour Party (Hodgson 1984, Boddy and Fudge 1984). Yet this 'rainbow coalition' of interests was not always mutually compatible, and ran counter to the traditional labourism and trade-unionism of the male manual working class which had provided the core of Labour's active support. Moreover, it did not constitute a coherent 'big idea' to counter the free market and Thatcherism.

There was some ideological ferment within the ranks of the newly formed SDP, to which each of the members of the original gang of four (Roy Jenkins, David Owen, Shirley Williams and Bill Rodgers) contributed, although perhaps the most influential new work came from David Marquand (1988). Yet the SDP programme involved little more than a restatement of familiar ideas on the Labour right – support for the European Community, Nato, incomes policy – coupled with some borrowings from their new Liberal allies – proportional representation and a professed interest in devolution and community politics. The only new element, derived from German experience, was the concept of the social market, but the policy implications of this were far from clear.

The debate over the nature of social democracy has scarcely survived the absorption of the new party into the post-merger Liberal Democrats. Ironically, if social democracy is alive it is within the Labour Party which the founders of the SDP abandoned in despair. Yet social democracy has been weakened by events both in Britain and the rest of the world, and no longer provides clear policy prescriptions. The 'new realism' in the trade unions and the Labour movement has sharply reversed the leftward trend of the 1970s and early 1980s. Under Neil Kinnock, John Smith and Tony Blair the party has abandoned most of the policy commitments with which it was previously associated. Much of the Thatcherite agenda has been tacitly accepted, and it is no longer clear that Labour offers a clear alternative.

POST-THATCHERISM?

The resignation of Thatcher in 1990 involved the end of Thatcherism in the literal sense, and certainly marked a change in the style of government, but did not lead to any immediate shift in the ideological climate. While faith in the certainties of the New Right may have diminished, creating something of a vacuum in political thinking, few if any new ideas have come to fill that vacuum.

As earlier with Keynesianism, faith in the prescriptions of the New Right has been eroded by failure. There was a period in the mid-1980s when even radical opponents of Thatcherism were beginning to wonder whether there was not something in the claim of an economic miracle. The first recession in the early 1980s was partially excused as the painful price of longer-term recovery. The prolonged second recession has tarnished the record, apparently demonstrating that New Right economics has been no more successful than Keynesian economics, indeed rather less successful, in securing efficiency, growth and prosperity. There were also more specific policy failures. Controlling the money supply proved of marginal relevance in the control of inflation. Increasing unemployment made it impossible to reduce public spending. Privatisation of the former nationalised industries has not involved a significant increase in competition, and the benefits to consumers are at best contestable. Even one of the government's apparent successes, the encouragement of home ownership, has gone partially sour with the collapse in the housing market and the repossession crisis, part of a wider debt crisis which the prevailing economic philosophy did nothing to discourage. While it is too soon to assess the attempts to introduce more competition into health care, education and transport, it is already clear that the changes are beset with difficulties.

Of course any judgement of the record itself is contestable, and the explanation for the record is even more contentious. Just as Keynesians might claim that policy failure was the consequence of misunderstanding Keynes, or allowing political exigencies to override economic analysis, so the Institute of Economic Affairs would claim that its prescriptions have never been properly or fully applied. Yet the record, however difficult it is to interpret, has taken the gloss off New Right solutions. The answers no longer seem so simple.

Yet if the gurus of the New Right think-tanks have been latterly directing their advice to the transitional economies of Eastern Europe rather than Britain's Conservative government, significantly no new gurus seem to have displaced them in John Major's confidence. Moreover, although there has been some talk of 'Majorism', assisted by some shift in rhetoric, there has been little to mark off Major's Conservative government from its predecessor in terms of performance. The hated poll tax has been abandoned – but that had become a political necessity, and Thatcher's successor has been rather more European-minded. Beyond that, however, the privatisation programme has been extended, the health and education reforms have been maintained, and coal pits closed.

There is little indication here of any real departure from the Thatcherite agenda. The only new initiatives with which Major is associated are the Citizen's Charter and the more recent 'Back to Basics' campaign. The Citizen's Charter (Major 1991) appeared to involve a new concern with the quality of public services, which at first sight seems to be at odds with the Thatcherite tradition of hostility towards state provision. Yet much of the emphasis in practice is on improving services through competition and market testing, which is thoroughly consistent with the agenda of Thatcher. Essentially John Major's Conservatives have tried to capture from Labour the concept of citizenship and redefine it in terms of consumer interests.

'Back to Basics' has been variously interpreted and has notoriously become the source of some internal party tension. At one level it clearly involves a reaffirmation of traditional Conservative themes: the family, law and order, discipline and standards in school. Embarrassingly for the leadership and the parliamentary party, it has been enthusiastically interpreted by constituency activists to involve a return to strict standards of personal sexual conduct. This is more reminiscent of the moral and religious strands of the American right than the free-market ideas of British New Right. However, Thatcherism was always a blend of traditional Conservative themes and neo-liberal ideas, and the record of John Major's government to date seems thoroughly consistent with that mixture.

At another level, both the Citizen's Charter and 'Back to Basics' seem more concerned with presentation than substance, which tends to confirm that the new administration is to be distinguished largely in terms of style rather than under-lying philosophy, even if that underlying philosophy no longer commands the same confidence.

There has been little in the way of effective ideological challenge from the official opposition to the still prevailing, if tarnished, Thatcherite philosophy. Electoral failure prompted a new realism in the Labour Party and led to a policy review which abandoned much of the programme under which the party had fought the 1983 election. Under the leadership of Kinnock, Labour effectively abandoned opposition to the European Community, renationalisation, unilateral-ism and most of its public spending commitments. The socialist left, which the right had feared had captured the party in the early 1980s, was in full retreat after 1987. Moreover, while Western European socialists had always distanced them-selves from the practice of socialism in Russia and Eastern Europe, its collapse in 1989 has left them more demoralised. Dahrendorf's verdict (1990: 38) was blunt. 'The point has to be made unequivocally that socialism is dead and none of its variants can be revived.' Although such a judgement seems premature on a resilient and popular ideology, it has to be admitted that the future direction of democratic socialism appears problematic.

If the Labour Party is now only questionably socialist, it is also distancing itself from old-style labourism and trade unionism (Minkin 1991). Under Kinnock's successors, Smith and Blair, the party has gone further in the pursuit of respectability, promoting constitutional reform and distancing itself from the unions. Yet if Bennite socialism and old-fashioned labourism have been rejected, it is not clear what new philosophy, if any, has emerged in their place.

There has admittedly been some attempt by Hattersley (1987), Gould (1985) and others to reformulate a social democratic ideology within the Labour Party, involving a qualified acceptance of market forces, balanced by a reassertion of the principle of social justice (derived from the work of Rawls 1971). Hattersley has been concerned to recapture from the right the importance of freedom, which socialists are sometimes accused of sacrificing in pursuit of equality. Others have attempted to resurrect the third term in the revolutionary triad, fraternity, seeking to re-emphasise the value of fellowship and community as against the indi-vidualism of the New Right. While much of this work is interesting, it has scarcely caught the popular imagination, partly perhaps because it lacks the simplicity of rival messages.

Outside the mainstream opposition, other radical ideologies have become more internally divided and self-questioning. The old extra-parliamentary left is demoralised, the Greens are split over fundamental issues of philosophy and strategy, and feminists are fragmented. The ferment of ideas of the 1960s and 1970s has provided new perspectives, but has not totally transformed the old ideological confrontation between individualism and collectivism. It is the basic divide that still seems likely to dominate political debate for the immediate future.

CORE READING

Eccleshall, R., Geoghegan, V., Jay, R. and Wilford, R. (1984) *Political Ideologies: An Introduction*, London: Hutchinson.
Gamble, A. (1988) *The Free Economy and the Strong State: The Politics of Thatcherism*, London: Macmillan.
Heywood, A. (1992) *Political Ideologies*, London: Macmillan.
Kavanagh, D. (1990) *Thatcherism and British Politics: The End of Consensus*, 2nd edn, Oxford: Oxford University Press.
Leach, R. (1991) *British Political Ideologies*, London: Philip Allan.

ADDITIONAL READING

Arblaster, A. (1984) *The Rise and Decline of Western Liberalism*, Oxford: Basil Blackwell.
Beer, S.H. (1982) *Modern British Politics*, 3rd edn, London: Faber & Faber.
Boddy, M. and Fudge, G. (eds) (1984) *Local Socialism?*, London: Macmillan.
Bosanquet, N. (1983) *After the New Right*, London: Heinemann.
Brownmiller, S. (1975) *Against Our Will*, Harmondsworth: Penguin.
Callaghan, J. (1990) *Socialism in Britain*, Oxford: Basil Blackwell.
Carter, A. (1988) *The Politics of Women's Rights*, London: Longman.
Cowling, M. (ed.) (1978) *Conservative Essays*, London: Cassell.
Crick, B. (1987) *Socialism*, Buckingham: Open University Press.
Crosland, C.A.R. (1956) *The Future of Socialism*, London: Jonathan Cape.
Dahrendorf, R. (1990) *Reflections on the Revolution in Europe*, London: Chatto & Windus.
Eccleshall, R. (1986) *British Liberalism: Liberal Thought from the 1640s to the 1980s*, London: Longman.
Eccleshall, R. (1990) *English Conservatism since the Restoration*, London: Unwin Hyman.
Foote, G. (1986) *The Labour Party's Political Thought*, London: Croom Helm.
Friedan, B. (1963) *The Feminine Mystique*, New York: Norton.
Fukuyama, F. (1989) 'The end of history', *National Interest*, Summer.
Gamble, A. (1974) *The Conservative Nation*, London: Routledge & Kegan Paul.
Gilmour, I. (1978) *Inside Right*, London: Quartet.
Gilmour, I. (1992) *Dancing with Dogma: Britain under Thatcherism*, London: Simon & Schuster.
Gould, B. (1985) *Socialism and Freedom*, London: Macmillan.
Gray, J. (1986) *Liberalism*, Milton Keynes: Open University Press.
Green, D.G. (1987) *The New Right*, London: Harvester Wheatsheaf.
Greenleaf, W.H. (1983) *The British Political Tradition*, vol. 1, *The Rise of Collectivism*, vol. 2, *The Ideological Heritage*, London: Methuen.
Greer, G. (1970) *The Female Eunuch*, London: Granada.
Hall, S. and Jacques, M. (eds) (1983) *The Politics of Thatcherism*, London: Lawrence & Wishart.
Hattersley, R. (1987) *Choose Freedom: The Future of Democratic Socialism*, London: Michael Joseph.
Hayek, F. A. (1976) *The Road to Serfdom*, London: Routledge & Kegan Paul.

Hodgson, G. (1984) *The Democratic Economy: A New Look at Planning, Markets and Power*, Harmondsworth: Penguin.

Hogg, Q. (1947) *The Case for Conservatism*, Harmondsworth: Penguin.

Keegan, W. (1984) *Thatcher's Economic Experiment*, London: Allen Lane.

King, D.S. (1987) *The New Right: Politics, Markets and Citizenship*, London: Macmillan.

Levitas, R. (ed.) (1986) *The Ideology of the New Right*, London: Polity Press.

McKenzie, R.T. (1963) *British Political Parties*, London: Heineman.

McLennan, D. (1976) *Ideology*, Milton Keynes: Open University Press.

Major, J. (1991) *The Citizen's Charter*, London: HMSO.

Marquand, D. (1988) *The Unprincipled Society*, London: Fontana.

Millett, K. (1977) *Sexual Politics*, London: Virago.

Minkin, L. (1991) *The Contentious Alliance: Trade Unions and the Labour Party*, Edinburgh: Edinburgh University Press.

Mitchell, J. (1971) *Women's Estate*, Harmondsworth: Penguin.

Nairn, T. (1981) *The Break-Up of Britain*, London: NLB and Verso.

Oakeshott, M. (1962) *Rationalism in Politics and Other Essays*, London: Methuen.

Pimlott, B., Wright, T. and Flower, T. (1990) *The Alternative Politics for a Change*, London: W H Allen.

Porritt, J. and Winner, D. (1988) *The Coming of the Greens*, London: Fontana.

Rawls, J. (1971) *A Theory of Justice*, Harvard: Harvard University Press.

Saggar, S. (1992) *Race and Politics in Britain*, London: Harvester Wheatsheaf.

Scruton, R. (1980) *The Meaning of Conservatism*, London: Macmillan.

Seliger, M. (1976) *Ideology and Politics*, London: Allen & Unwin.

Seyd, P. (1987) *The Rise and Fall of the Labour Left*, London: Macmillan.

Skidelsky, R. (ed.) (1988) *Thatcherism*, London: Chatto & Windus.

Smith, A.D. (1991) *National Identity*, Harmondsworth: Penguin.

Tivey, L. and Wright, A. (eds) (1989) *Party Ideology in Britain*, London: Routledge.

Vincent, A. (1992) *Modern Political Ideologies*, Oxford: Basil Blackwell.

2 The political context

Robert Leach

POLITICS, GOVERNMENT AND PUBLIC POLICY

This chapter is concerned with the political context in which public policies emerge. However, the relationship between political activities of various kinds and public policy is not entirely unproblematic.

Public policy itself is not easy to define. Sometimes it is simply equated with the outputs of government, but more usually policy is implicitly or explicitly contrasted with implementation or routine administration, although the distinction is not always clear cut, and may critically depend upon the perception of the observer. Thus what may be regarded by central government as a question of detailed implementation may be perceived as an important policy issue by front-line officials responsible for delivering services. Relatively low-level officials may act as gatekeepers to benefits or resources, thus effectively indulging in what is sometimes termed 'street-level policy-making' (Hogwood and Gunn 1984, Hill 1993).

Thus policy may be made at a number of levels. The outcome of the policy process may be formally registered in the shape of a United Nations resolution, or new European Union regulation, or a Cabinet minute, or a law passed by Parliament. But equally it may lead to the approval of a recommendation in a council committee meeting, or a decision recorded in the minutes of a school governing body. While not all such decisions may be regarded as 'policy', some quite clearly are. Indeed some relatively low-level policy decisions – for example, to close a ward in a hospital, or introduce a new subject into the curriculum of a school – may have a potentially significant impact on the communities they affect.

Political activity similarly takes place at a number of levels, from the elite politics of the Cabinet room and the corridors of Whitehall and Westminster, through the internal processes of political parties and major pressure groups, down to the mass level of voting, or the 'grassroots' activities of participation in ward party meetings or local pressure group activities. All this is part of the political context in which public policies emerge, although of course there is considerable scope for argument about the interrelationship between elite and grassroots political activity, and their relative importance in the policy process.

Policies emerge in a variety of ways. Sometimes they seem to result from a relatively closed process internal to government, from the work of civil servants in major departments of state, perhaps aided by a handful of specialist outside advisers, but with little apparent public debate. Examples might include much of defence policy and some of the more technical aspects of economic policy, such as the decision of Nigel Lawson to maintain the value of sterling in line with that of the German mark from 1985. Such relatively technical policy issues often seem to exclude much of what is usually understood by political activity. Indeed, Lawson's policy of shadowing the mark was so little debated in public that even his own prime minister seemed for a time to be unaware of it. Yet even fairly abstruse technical issues may become caught up in a wider political debate, as indeed subsequently happened with Britain's membership of the Exchange Rate Mechanism.

Public policy may be more commonly perceived as the outcome of an overtly political process involving a highly public debate between political parties. Policy proposals may indeed be derived from party principles or ideologies, or connected with formal commitments in party manifestos. The privatisation programme of the Thatcher and Major governments and the introduction of competition and commercial principles into the operation of public services clearly reflect a particular and contested political philosophy.

The role of organised groups may, however, often be more significant than that of the party in the emergence of specific public policies. The debate between rival interests may take place largely in the corridors of power in Westminster and Whitehall, or it may be fought out in the public arena. It may involve the services of specialist consultants operating behind the scenes, influencing or purporting to influence key decision-makers, or it may involve highly visible public demonstrations. The conflict between rival interests may broadly parallel the party divide, or it may cut across party positions, as in the case of Sunday trading where conflicting pressures upon and within the Conservative Party, involving major retailing, trade union and religious interests, persuaded the Cabinet to allow a free vote.

The role of the wider public in the policy process is more debatable. The electorate is often held to give a 'mandate' to the party that forms the government, and this mandate may be cited to suggest public support for specific policies, particularly those included in the party's election manifesto. However, the notion of a mandate raises considerable theoretical and practical difficulties. Public influence may be more obvious in the negative sense, as a constraint inhibiting certain policies. Thus it was long assumed in the post-war era up until the 1970s that a government that abandoned a commitment to full employment would be decisively rejected by the electorate. More recently there has been a widespread assumption that commitments to increased public spending and taxation would spell disaster at the polls. Such assumptions may not always be correct, but if they are held by ministers, their advisers and other influentials, they are likely to have a significant impact.

Clear evidence of public opposition to specific policies has sometimes led to their reversal – the most notable example being the abolition of the Community Charge (or poll tax) only three years after its introduction as the 'flagship' of government policy. Rather more rarely, public opinion may pressurise a government to act, a possible example being the legislation to control dangerous dogs. Such instances frequently raise questions about the media presentation of particular events and issues. 'Public opinion' is often interpreted, and perhaps essentially moulded, by the press and electronic media, pushing issues such as homelessness or child abuse onto the public policy agenda.

So far, UK public policy has been related essentially to political activities and pressures from within the country. Clearly, however, public policy in the United Kingdom is often constrained by pressures and developments outside. The political system is far from closed. Key policy decisions may be abruptly forced on governments by forces beyond their control. Examples would include the devaluation of the pound sterling in 1967, or the United Kingdom's departure from the Exchange Rate Mechanism in 1992. More routinely, policy is clearly constrained by UK membership of various international associations, most obviously the European Union. Large areas of UK policy, such as agriculture and fisheries, trade, energy and transport, are influenced by decisions in Brussels. Beyond that, the term 'globalisation' neatly sums up a number of clear trends, such as the increased importance of multi-national corporations in the world economy; the communications revolution which has ensured an almost instantaneous reaction to movements in currencies, share prices or commodities on the other side of the world; and the development of an increasingly international culture. In this connection it is worth noting that many public policies that are considered essentially British, or described as 'Thatcherist', seem to reflect changes over much of the Western world. In particular the move towards more competition in the provision of public services, and specifically towards contracting, has been widespread. The timing of these initiatives suggests that other governments are not just copying the Thatcherite agenda, but rather the existence of common causal factors across national boundaries.

Thus public policies may emerge in many different ways. Categorisation is not easy, as many policies have complex origins, and are subject to diverse influences as they progress. For example, the 1994 Criminal Justice Bill involved some relatively technical issues emanating from within the Home Office, and elements of a party and a populist agenda. Thus the initial proposals for a diminished role for elected councillors was consistent with recent Conservative Party policy towards local government, while the abolition of the right to silence might be interpreted as a quasi-populist measure to satisfy perceived public demands to be tough on criminals. Established pressure groups, such as the police, local authorities and the legal profession, seem to have had a relatively marginal influence on the genesis of the bill, but have subsequently modified some of its provisions markedly.

Policy-making in a particular sector can also change significantly over time. Roads policy, for example, seemed in the past to be a product of a decision-making process that was largely within government, with a narrow range of pressure groups exerting some influence behind closed doors, and the public largely confined to token and ineffectual participation through public inquiries. More recently, environmental groups of various kinds and groups of residents have combined to force policy decisions on road-building into the public arena.

Behind the analysis of specific case studies, there are more general questions about the distribution of power and influence in British society which are fundamental to any interpretation of the public policy process. An explicit assumption of much New Right thinking is that individual consumers and producers have real power through the market, and are the best judge of their own interests. Thus ordinary citizens can be given more effective power by removing obstacles to market forces, and by introducing market mechanisms into the management of public services. From a slightly different perspective, much analysis of pressure group activity tacitly or explicitly assumes that influence is widely dispersed through the effective participation in the policy process of a large number of conflicting interests. Marxists and other left-wing radicals assume by contrast that power is very unevenly distributed to the clear disadvantage of ordinary citizens as workers or consumers. Individuals are not necessarily conscious of their own real interests, as they are conditioned by their experience of the existing economic and social system, reinforced by the concentration of media ownership in the hands of the wealthy few. Thus in a capitalist society where the ownership of productive wealth is highly concentrated, the ability of business interests to shape public policy far exceeds that of the masses. In between these sharply differentiated positions, there are significant arguments about the real power and influence of public sector bureaucrats, political parties, organised interests and the wider public. Some interpretations assume that power is fairly widely dispersed, with many groups and individuals able to exercise an influence on the public policy process. Other interpretations assume that opportunities for involvement are rather more restricted (Dunleavy and O'Leary 1987, Ham and Hill 1993).

It is possible only to identify such questions, not to resolve them, but merely to list some of them is to indicate how widely it is necessary to interpret the political context within which the public policy process takes place, encompassing the system of government, parties, pressure groups, the public and a range of external constraints.

PUBLIC POLICY AND THE BRITISH SYSTEM OF GOVERNMENT

Public policy is created within the framework of established political institutions, and formal and informal rules of procedure. In most countries the formal rules that outline the responsibilities of particular offices and institutions, which determine the interrelationship between parts of government, are contained in a written constitution. Such a document provides an authoritative statement of the 'rules of the game', although invariably they are subject to conflicting interpretations and have to be supplemented by subsequent custom and practice. The United Kingdom lacks such an authoritative statement of the rules of government because of the unwritten, or at least uncodified, nature of the British constitution. Its imprecision has sometimes been regarded as an advantage, offering flexibility and the capacity to change with the times. Moreover that constitution, although variously interpreted, has been widely admired, both at home and abroad (Jennings 1941). Indeed some of its real or imagined features have been reproduced in other systems of government.

More recently, the British system of government has attracted considerable critical comment, both as a whole and with regard to some of its key elements, from across the political spectrum (Hillyard and Percy-Smith 1988, Institute of Public Policy Research 1992, Mount 1992). Some of its principles are regarded as inoperative, unrealistic or out of date. The unitary state, parliamentary sovereignty and Cabinet government were all once regarded as key features of the British constitution, but all, to varying degrees, are now subject to qualification or are open to question. The role of some of the most ancient and venerable institutions in British government, such as the Crown, the Commons and the Lords, have been exposed to critical scrutiny. Optimistic assumptions concerning the democratic nature of the modern system of government or the rights extended to individual citizens or minority groups have been challenged. The previously vaunted flexibility of the British constitution is interpreted by some critics as offering only confusion, and potential for abuse. Thus there have been demands for a modern 'Bill of Rights' or a full-scale written constitution (Institute of Public Policy Research 1992).

Both enthusiasts for the British system of government and some of its more ardent critics would largely agree that there has been little in the way of real constitutional change in recent years. That indeed is the problem for the critics – the system urgently needs an overhaul, and has not received it. Certainly there have been only minor modifications of the way in which some of the core institutions of the British state operate. Parliamentary processes and the Cabinet system have not been fundamentally altered since 1979. There was a significant extension of the parliamentary select committee system soon after Margaret Thatcher took power (Norton 1993), and John Major later broke with precedent in providing details of the responsibilities and membership of Cabinet committees in the interests of more open government. Neither of these developments, although important, have really transformed the way in which British government operates. The criticisms of executive dominance, legislative overload and abuse of parliamentary procedures which have been expressed during the Thatcher and Major years have been frequently voiced in earlier periods, and involve little that is essentially new (King 1985).

Yet despite little apparent alteration in the traditional institutions at the centre of the British system of government, there have also been fundamental changes in the Civil Service (Hennessy 1990), local government (Butcher *et al.* 1990, Cochrane 1993) and other parts of the state bureaucracy which amount to a virtual revolution in the delivery of public services. The changes here have had some clear constitutional implications. Thus assumptions of ministerial responsibility and Civil Service anonymity and impartiality have been challenged (Dowding, in

Dunleavy *et al.* 1993). The introduction of the linked policies of compulsory competitive tendering, market testing and commercialisation through internal markets have fundamentally altered the relationship between elected politicians and state officials, and perhaps also between state officials and service users or customers (Self 1993). The implications for public policy in the future are also profound. Key questions of policy are clearly involved in drawing up framework agreements for executive agencies or contracts for competitive tendering, but with significantly reduced scope for subsequently changing policy through a political process during the timescale of the agreement or contract. Thus appointed officials have increased formal responsibilities and power of decision, with reduced scope for intervention in service delivery by elected politicians. The changes have also led to some significant shifts in influence among professionals, and between professionals and managers, which are particularly important at institutional level (Dunleavy 1991).

At another level, major changes have become manifest in the relationship between the United Kingdom and what is now the European Union, although in truth the changes here are more in terms of the realisation of the implications of UK membership rather than significant changes of substance. Both the Single European Act, approved by Thatcher in 1988, and the Maastricht Treaty, signed by Major in 1992, were part of a progression towards closer union already implicit in the Treaty of Rome and subsequent developments. The debate over British membership in the 1960s and more particularly the 1970s concentrated on the economic arguments, while the political and constitutional implications were ignored or played down by most participants. Arguably, those implications were always there, and have only been highlighted by Maastricht. Involvement in a quasi-federalist association of states inevitably provokes some questioning of traditional assumptions about parliamentary and indeed national sovereignty, as well as massive implications for public policy, particularly agriculture, fisheries, trade and energy, but increasingly perhaps with regard to taxation, industrial relations and social policy (Arter 1993).

Yet while changes have been only too evident in these aspects of government, there have been other areas where change has stalled or been actively resisted in the period since 1979. This is perhaps most obvious with regard to the devolution of power, which was a major preoccupation of the 1970s, but has been clearly off the immediate political agenda since the change of government in 1979. Thus while over most of Europe there has been a marked trend towards giving more power to regional and local government, in the United Kingdom proposals for national and regional devolution have been abandoned, while local authorities have faced a loss of functions, an erosion of their operational responsibilities and tighter central control of their spending and levels of provision. Of course, Conservative governments since 1979 would argue that many of the changes to local government have not involved centralisation, but a transfer of power downwards to institutions, to professionals, and ultimately to service users, but from a local government perspective what is more obvious is the bypassing of elected local representative institutions in favour of appointed bodies with little effective accountability to local communities. In Scotland and Wales in particular, traditional assumptions of representative and responsible government are even more open to challenge. Public policy is determined by a party that only enjoys minority status in those countries, while much public spending is in the hands of massive quangos, whose members are appointed by ministerial patronage, and whose decisions are subject to little public scrutiny and no democratic control.

It could be argued, however, that minority government, while most clearly manifest in Scotland and Wales, is actually a feature of the United Kingdom as a whole. The other constitutional change that has been fairly extensively debated, but not implemented, is electoral reform. The UK simple plurality, or 'first past the post' electoral system, is now unique in Western Europe, with dramatic implications for parliamentary representation, government and public policy (Bogdanor 1984).

PARTY POLITICS AND PUBLIC POLICY

The most immediately obvious aspect of British politics and government since 1979 has been the long dominance of the Conservative party. In winning four consecutive general elections from 1979 until 1992, the Conservatives have enjoyed a longer continuous period of office than any party has previously managed since the early nineteenth century, with obvious implications for public policy. Yet this Conservative dominance in Parliament and government has rested on a fairly stable 42–3 per cent of the popular vote. Sizeable shifts in the size of the government's Parliamentary majorities have reflected changes in the distribution of votes among opposition parties rather than any significant shift in support for the Conservative Party.

While the United Kingdom is often described as having a two-party system, this has been more the exception than the rule over the last 150 years. Only since 1945 have two major parties dominated representation in Parliament and monopolised control of government, and even in this period the two-party system has been to some degree the product of the electoral system. This has been particularly the case since 1974, when the support for the Liberals, the Alliance and the Liberal Democrats has ranged from a low of 13.8 per cent in 1979 to a high of 25.4 per cent in 1983, and has averaged around a fifth of the vote over a twenty-year period. This would have secured them substantial parliamentary representation in any other Western European state, and probably a significant role in government. The obvious comparison is with the Free Democrats in Germany who have never matched the Liberals' post-1974 share of the vote, but have been strongly represented in the German Bundestag and continuously involved in government since 1969. Yet it is not just the Liberals and their successors who have been penalised by the electoral system. The UK Green Party failed to win a single seat in the European Parliament in 1989, despite winning 15 per cent of the vote, while the Scottish Nationalist Party might also claim to be under-represented in Parliament, and more obviously in the government of Scotland.

At the level of the electorate, the United Kingdom seems to have been moving from a two-party system to an essentially multi-party system, yet this is less apparent in Parliament. A multi-party system exacerbates the distortions inherent in the UK electoral system (as it did in the 1920s). Partly because of the fragmentation of opposition, the trend towards a multi-party Britain has para-doxically produced one-party government, and, more contentiously, perhaps even a one-party state.

Such a claim might seem exaggerated. After all, there have been previous periods of Conservative dominance. The party's hold on office since 1979 has not persisted much longer than that from 1951 until 1964, and there are obvious similarities between the two periods. Yet there are also some obvious differences. The long period of Conservative dominance since 1951 involved strong elements of continuity with the past. Conservative administrations under Winston Churchill, Anthony Eden, Harold Macmillan and Sir Alec Douglas Home did not seek to reverse much of the work of their Labour predecessors. In 1951 Crossman predicted that the new Conservative government would involve, like Attlee's Labour government, 'a coalition policy on a party basis' (Crossman 1981: 30), and so it largely proved. Thus while Labour was out of office, the Labour legacy on the shape of much public policy remained. Moreover, appointments to public corporations, royal commissions and other public bodies were also generally made on a bipartisan basis, so that Labour politicians were not without a voice even within the formal institutions of government. Since 1979, there has been a government determined to reverse much of the socialist legacy, and Labour has been largely excluded from influence as well as from power.

Moreover, there were also in the 1951–64 period significant centres of counter-vailing power within the UK political system, including local authorities with sufficient independence to pursue policies sometimes markedly different from those favoured by central government, a Civil Service with a strong ethos of neutrality and enjoying the confidence of most politicians across the political spectrum, and substantial interests, including prestigious professional bodies and a powerful trade union movement, who were regularly and routinely consulted by government. These checks on the dominance of the governing party have largely either been removed or at least substantially attenuated since 1979.

Increasingly after 1979 the leadership of the Conservative Party has effectively controlled not only Parliament and the Cabinet, but appointments to an increasing number of non-elected public bodies, such as health authorities, hospital trusts, training and enterprise councils, development corporations and agencies, and a host of others, controlling together more than a third of total public spending.

Yet perhaps the changes are even more significant in the informal processes of government. It is difficult to quantify changes here, but there is a widespread perception that major interests which were previously central to the policy process have been ignored or marginalised. Since 1979 Conservative govern-ments have preferred to take advice from their own party or ideologically sympathetic sources, such as friendly academics or the flourishing New Right think-tanks. Even groups that have previously enjoyed the ear of the Conservative Party, such as doctors, lawyers and the police, have sometimes found their advice ignored or spurned.

GROUPS AND PUBLIC POLICY

The role of organised groups in the public policy process has long been recognised, and raises some important value questions (Richardson and Jordan 1979, Grant 1989). Some early critics saw group pressures as a rather sinister interference with the democratic process, but, by contrast, political scientists both in the United States and the United Kingdom in the 1950s and 1960s placed group activity at the centre of an updated pluralist democracy. Many more people were enabled to participate in the policy process through the activities of countless groups pressing on each other, Parliament and government. Thus government consultation with groups was legitimated as an essential part of the democratic system. In some versions of pluralist theory, government was perceived as an essentially neutral agency, converting the sum of group pressures into legislative and executive action, or as a referee, only intervening to see fair play between the conflicting interests (Dunleavy and O'Leary 1987).

Critics suggested that there were significant sections of the population not represented by organised groups, that there were massive differences between the resources and influence of groups, that group spokespersons were not necessarily representative of, and generally unelected by, those they claimed to represent, and that government was far from neutral in response to group pressures. In effect, some groups were trusted and regularly consulted, while others were ignored. The cosy relationship between some government departments and group interests (such as road interests and the Department of Transport, or the National Farmers Union and the Ministry of Agriculture, Fisheries and Food) was sometimes perceived as involving an unhealthy exclusion of other interests and ideas. Radical critics from both the left and right of the political spectrum perceived the entrenched role of certain established interests in the policy process as contributing to the maintenance of the *status quo*.

In the 1970s the UK governmental system was fashionably described as tripartite or corporatist, although corporatist practices have been identified in British politics much earlier by some commentators (Middlemas 1979). Corporatism has been variously defined, but is perhaps most easily understood through comparison with pluralism. Pluralist theories implied countless groups freely competing for the ear of an essentially neutral government. Corporatism suggested, by contrast, that only a few powerful groups (often umbrella or peak groups), perhaps enjoying a virtual monopoly in their policy field, really counted in the policy process. Government was not a neutral arbiter, but an active player in the game, with a close relationship with certain groups, which might be specially recognised, licensed or even created by government. Instead of the fairly clear boundary between government and groups implied in most pluralist theory, corporatism implied a close interrelationship between government and powerful interests, which might be involved not just in influencing policy but in executing it (Ham and Hill 1993).

The term 'tripartism' suggested that important areas of policy were essentially determined through a bargaining process involving three principal actors – the government, business interests represented through the CBI, and trade union interests represented through the TUC. Economic planning in the 1960s and 1970s, successive forms of incomes policy and the 1974–79 Labour government's social contract all involved, and indeed required, business and trade union involvement. Tripartism was given institutional recognition in the composition of a number of new state bodies, including the National Economic Development Council, the Equal Opportunities Commission, the Commission for Racial Equality, and the Health and Safety Executive.

Tripartism or corporatism may be seen as a practical way of implementing consensus politics, and breaking down the barriers between the two sides of industry. Indeed it might be viewed as an appropriate antidote to class conflict or the perceived adversary nature of the British political system (Finer 1975). In Austria and Scandinavia it has been suggested that corporatist policies have been more successful in promoting planned economic growth without industrial conflict or inflation. Thus there are some commentators who argue that Britain still requires an essentially corporatist policy process, and that past failures reflect institutional and societal weaknesses which need correcting.

It is easier to identify critics than advocates of corporatism. Critics have taken various positions, some diametrically opposed. Some have suggested that corporatism involves an undemocratic bypassing of the parliamentary democratic process. On the radical and Marxist left, the objection was more that the participation in the policy process it apparently offered to labour interests was illusory. Corporatism was capitalism's response to crisis and falling profits. The interests of labour and capital were not reconcilable. Incomes policy was a means to restore profit margins. Union leaders who agreed to limits in wage rises were betraying the interests of those they represented. The social contract introduced by the 1974–79 Labour government was a social 'con trick'. The New Right objections were very different. Corporatism was the consequence of governments intervening in areas of policy that should be left to market forces. But if corporatism involved governments attempting more than they could or should deliver, it also paradoxically involved an abdication of state authority because corporatist processes involved conceding too much power and influence to producer groups, particularly trade unions, at the expense of the mass of individual citizens and consumers.

Theoretical objections to corporatism from advocates of the free market were accompanied by a widespread (if not necessarily accurate) popular perception that trade unions were too powerful, and bitter Conservative memories of the role of the unions in undermining and finally bringing down the Heath government of 1970–74. This established the ground for the successful assault on trade union power from 1979. The consequence of this has not only been a reduction of the ability of trade unions to influence wage levels, but their virtual elimination from involvement in the broader policy process. Thus tripartism was rejected in practice as well as theory.

The continuing role of business interests in the policy process is a more contentious issue. For some radical left critics who never took seriously the involvement of trade union interests in policy-making, nothing much has changed. Corporatism was always a cloak for effective business influence. Business interests continue to be massively influential in government policy-making, without the token involvement of the TUC. Significantly perhaps, some commentators have identified a 'local corporatism' at the level of urban policy-making, involving council–business cooperation, without, generally, a significant trade union input. Thus corporatism is identified with 'bipartism' rather than tripartism.

Other commentators have suggested that the Confederation of British Industry (CBI) has also lost some influence, perhaps to rival business interests such as the Institute of Directors. Business is not homogeneous, and there are actual or potential conflicting interests between, for example, financial and manufacturing interests, manufacturers and retailers, and large and small firms. Government may favour some interests at the expense of others. The broad-based CBI may sometimes be perceived as too wedded to the *status quo*.

It might also be argued that Thatcherism has sometimes appeared to involve an assault on almost all sectional interests. Not only the major trade unions but the state bureaucracy, the legal, medical and teaching professions, and even the police, have all been 'taken on' at one time or another by Conservative governments since 1979. Government rhetoric suggests that the state is reasserting its authority on behalf of individual customers or citizens against powerful vested interests. This implies the state's withdrawal from pluralist group politics, yet governments since 1979 have not systematically turned their backs on established processes of consultation. Rather, much like previous governments, they have consulted when it suited them and, where appropriate, used the views of established interests and outside experts and professionals to buttress their own arguments. The relative decline of some interests is offset by the growing significance of others.

Corporatism is (or was) concerned with the central policy-making process. A fashionable concept among academic commentators in the 1980s and 1990s has been the notion of 'policy networks' (Rhodes 1988). One assumption here is that policy-making is essentially segmented, with different policy areas, such as education, health care or transport, involving different departments, public agencies, professional bodies and interest groups. Each involves a distinctive policy community or policy network. In each case it is possible to 'map' the actors involved and their interrelationship, which may throw some light on the policy-making process. Yet critics have suggested that the concept lacks explanatory power. Policy networks may indicate who is involved, but the distribution of effective influence within networks is rather more problematic. The new terminology of policy networks may in fact mask familiar pluralist assumptions. Certainly the whole debate re-emphasises the importance of the relationship of government institutions with groups outside government, and indeed the shadowy dividing line between government and non-government, typical of much neo-pluralist and corporatist analysis. The rhetoric of Thatcherite individualism has not banished sectional interests from the political process.

THE ELECTORATE

So far this account has focused on what might be regarded as elite rather than mass politics. Yet the rhetoric of Thatcherism implied a return of power to the people and some interpretations have emphasised its populist elements. The tabloid press version of Thatcherism was not primarily an esoteric economic theory which by a series of accidents captured one of the major British parties, but a radical anti-elitist crusade which evoked a ready response among ordinary people, including the manual working class. This may owe more to propaganda than reality, but, at the very least, some explanation is required for the continuing electoral success of the Conservative Party, even if it is acknowledged that this success has owed something to the electoral system and a divided opposition.

Interpretations of British politics and more particularly voting in the twentieth century have, until recently, placed particular emphasis on the importance of social class. Thus, with pardonable exaggeration, Peter Pulzer declared in 1967, 'British politics is about class: all else is embellishment and detail.' It is not a generalisation that could be repeated with any confidence today. In the first place it is suggested that divisions within classes and cleavages cutting across class have considerably complicated the analysis of contemporary British society. Second, it is argued that the connection between social class and party allegiance have been significantly weakened (Denver 1989).

Thus the old manual working class which provided the bedrock of Labour's electoral support had declined from 58 per cent of the workforce in 1961 to 45 per cent in 1981. There were always important divisions within the working class between skilled, semi-skilled and unskilled workers, and these have been supplemented by increasingly significant divisions based on age, gender, race, housing tenure, union membership and geographical location. There are more old people, more working women in proportion to the total workforce, significant ethnic minorities, fewer council house tenants, fewer union members, and fewer people living in the old industrial heartlands. These differences have considerable implications for party allegiance, and most of them work against Labour. As Ivor Crewe (in Dunleavy *et al.* 1993) has observed, 'Unionised council tenants in the North remain solidly Labour, but they are increasingly outnumbered by the "new working class" of non-union homeowners in the South, who are much more inclined to vote Conservative.'

More significant divisions may be between those who work for the public sector and those who work for the private sector, and more fundamentally between those in work and those out of work. Those who work for the state, or those substantially dependent on state benefits, have an interest in public spending and taxation not necessarily shared by those who work for the private sector, and who resent deductions from their take-home pay. This is a cleavage that cuts across the old division between white-collar and blue-collar workers. Just as Labour has lost some support from manual workers employed in the private sector, so the Conservatives have lost support from those among their traditional professional middle-class constituency who are employed by the state.

Also important for party allegiance may be what Dunleavy (1980) has called consumption cleavages. The relevant division here is between those who make extensive use of state-run or state-financed services, in areas such as health, education, housing and public transport, and those who chiefly rely on private provision. While there is clearly some correlation in each case with occupational class, these consumption cleavages can cut across that normal class divide. Better-off manual workers will probably own their own house and, as car owners, make little use of public transport, and may even have private health insurance and send their children to private schools, while some indubitably middle-class professionals may be committed users of public transport, state health and education services, even if they could easily afford to 'go private'.

Much of the traditional analysis of voting behaviour emphasised the links between social structure and party allegiance, but some analysts have attributed rather more importance to issues and ideologies. The notion of consumption cleavages does raise the question of where social determinants end and issue voting begins, as much of the analysis of issues focuses on such services as health and education. What does seem clear is that electoral behaviour has become much more volatile, and party identification correspondingly weaker.

This suggests that all the determinist assumptions based on projecting social trends may be challenged by new policy agendas that catch the public mood. Conservative victories at the polls from 1979 to 1992 may not have been due to demographic changes inexorably working against Labour, but to an electoral appeal that chimed in with growing public concerns over high taxation, declining British influence in the world, rising crime and perceived trade union power. Labour, by contrast, lost support because it was perceived to be deeply divided and was associated with unpopular policies and interests. Such old-fashioned political explanations for changing party fortunes do imply that there is an electorate out there to be wooed and won, and challenge notions of inexorable Labour decline and Conservative hegemony. Opposition parties may benefit from one of those mysterious periodic swings in public opinion such as brought Thatcher to power in 1979, and earlier benefited the Conservatives in 1886, the Liberals in 1906 and Labour in 1945.

A problematic issue here is the role of the mass media in shaping public opinion. A feature of media in Britain is domination by national (largely London-based) press and television, and the concentration of ownership in relatively few hands. Thus Rupert Murdoch's New International group owns the mass-circulation *Sun* and *News of the World*, the mid-market *Today* and the quality *Times* and *Sunday Times*, as well as extensive broadcasting interests, including *Sky* Television. The political influence of the media has been the subject of much debate. The political coverage of television and radio is constrained by laws that require balance between the treatment of parties and candidates. Indeed television is often perceived as non-partisan, although it has been criticised for reflecting an establishment or sometimes consensus perspective. National newspapers, by contrast, are under no obligation to show balance, and are generally blatantly partisan. The party bias of the national press is now more one-sided than it was, with a strong bias towards the Conservative Party in recent elections. The impact of this bias on political attitudes and, more specifically, voting, is more contentious. 'It was the *Sun* wot won it,' boasted the biggest mass-circulation tabloid after the 1992 election, and some academics are now more ready to concede a significant press influence on voting behaviour and political attitudes generally, although others remain more sceptical (Butler and Kavanagh 1988, 1992).

An essentially national media would seem to reinforce a national political culture. Yet the national electorate now seems more fragmented than it was. The near-universal electoral swings of the 1950s and 1960s, symbolised by Robert McKenzie's 'Swingometer', have been replaced by markedly different swings in different parts of the country. The cumulative effect has to been to transform the electoral map, marginalising the Labour Party in most of the country south of a line from the Bristol Channel to the Wash (excluding London) and reducing the Conservatives, who held a majority of parliamentary seats in Scotland in 1955, to minority-party status north of the border as well as in many northern industrial cities where they once challenged for power.

A notion that has received some media and academic attention is that of an alienated underclass. As political parties compete for the support of those who are relatively prosperous and contented, there is less incentive to look after the interests of the sizeable minority of the poor and unemployed, who in any case are less likely to be registered to vote, or to use their vote if they are registered. Thus it is suggested that particularly in inner urban areas there are whole communities effectively alienated from normal politics, although vulnerable to extremists, such as racist or neo-fascist groups, and potentially prone to violent disorder. Riots have been an intermittent feature of the politics of inner urban areas, and a catalysing issue, such as was provided by the Community Charge, might make such abnormal political activity more general.

In the 1960s British political culture was described in terms of homogeneity, consensus and deference (Almond and Verba 1963, Kavanagh 1990). All these descriptions are now more questionable. A homogeneous British political culture has been arguably replaced by a series of distinctive subcultures, based on perceived national or ethnic identity. The political consensus of the post-war period from 1945–70 has been broken, although some would argue that it has been replaced by a new Thatcherite consensus. The deference that some saw as the basis of British political stability had given way to the politics of protest. However, it is possible to exaggerate the changes that have taken place within the British political community. Compared with many other political systems, the United Kingdom, with the significant exception of Northern Ireland, continues to display stability and continuity.

BRITAIN, EUROPE AND THE WORLD

Yet of course Britain is not a closed community, immune from developments outside its frontiers, but is increasingly subject to constraints and pressures from without. These have clear implications for domestic politics. In the latter nineteenth century British imperialism was a major issue in electoral and party politics, while perceptions of national decline and loss of great power status have been a marked feature of late twentieth-century British politics. Indeed the restoration of British pride was an important element in the appeal of Thatcherism, and in the patriotic rhetoric surrounding the Falklands and Gulf wars. The assertion of British national interests is part of the explanation for the growing 'Euro-scepticism' shown earlier by Thatcher, and more recently by Major, and a substantial section of the Conservative Party, although this seems unlikely to reverse the growing importance of the European Union as a factor in British public policy.

Although political activity still centres primarily around and within the nation-state, increasingly it transcends national boundaries. This is most obvious at the formal level in the politics of the European Union. In a hierarchy of established institutions, heads of government, ministers and civil servants from the United Kingdom and other member states meet on a routine basis to shape policy. Elections for the European Parliament have become a familiar element in the political calendar.

However, there is also an increasing level of less formal political activities which operate across state boundaries. One aspect of this is the growing power of transnational corporations to influence and constrain the economic policies of national governments. Another is the development of pressure groups such as Amnesty International and Greenpeace which derive their support and active membership from many countries and operate in an international sphere. Already, cross-border alliances have been formed by communities and groups with common interests. Towns in different countries with similar problems, industries across frontiers facing similar threats, pressure groups with similar aims, are increasingly combining for the purpose of political action. Individual local authorities, business firms and trade unions often choose to lobby Brussels direct, although they may also work through national government and representative institutions, and their own umbrella organisations. Political activities are thus acquiring an increasingly European or even global focus.

These activities tell us something about the public policy process and the location of power in the modern world. Political lobbying will take place wherever power is perceived to be, and although power in Britain still predominantly resides in the corridors of Westminster and Whitehall, it also and increasingly resides elsewhere. This is reflected in the growing significance of political processes operating across state boundaries.

48   *Robert Leach*

CORE READING

Denver, D. (1989) *Elections and Voting Behaviour in Britain*, Hemel Hempstead: Philip Allan.
Dunleavy, P., Gamble, A., Holloway, I. and Peele, G. (1993) *Developments in British Politics 4*, London: Macmillan.
Grant, W. (1989) *Pressure Groups, Politics and Democracy in Britain*, Hemel Hempstead: Philip Allan.
Ham, C. and Hill, M. (1993) *The Policy Process in the Modern Capitalist State*, 2nd edn, Hemel Hempstead: Harvester Wheatsheaf.
Hogwood, B. and Gunn, L. (1984) *Policy Analysis for the Real World*, Oxford: Oxford University Press.
Jones, B., Gray, A., Kavanagh, D., Moran, M., Norton, P. and Seldon, A. (1994) *Politics UK*, 2nd edn, Hemel Hempstead: Harvester Wheatsheaf.
Richardson, J.J. and Jordan, A.G. (1979) *Governing Under Pressure*, Oxford: Martin Robertson.

ADDITIONAL READING

Almond, G. and Verba, S. (1963) *The Civic Culture*, Princeton: Princeton University Press.
Arter, D. (1993) *The Politics of European Integration in the Twentieth Century*, Aldershot: Dartmouth.
Bogdanor, V. (1984) *What is Proportional Representation?* Oxford: Martin Robertson.
Butcher, H., Law, I., Leach, R. and Mullard, M. (1990) *Local Government and Thatcherism*, London: Routledge.
Butler, D. and Kavanagh, D. (1988) *The British General Election of 1987*, London: Macmillan.
Butler, D. and Kavanagh, D. (1992) *The British General Election of 1992*, London: Macmillan.
Cochrane, A. (1993) *Whatever Happened to Local Government?*, Milton Keynes: Open University Press.
Crossman, R.H.S. (1981) *The Backbench Diaries of Richard Crossman*, ed. J. Morgan, London: Hamish Hamilton and Jonathan Cape.
Dunleavy, P. (1980) 'The political implications of sectoral cleavages and the growth of state employment', *Political Studies*, 28 (3 and 4).
Dunleavy, P. (1991) *Democracy, Bureaucracy and Public Choice*, Hemel Hempstead: Harvester Wheatsheaf.
Dunleavy, P. and Husbands, C.T. (1985) *British Democracy at the Crossroads*, London: George Allen & Unwin.
Dunleavy, P. and O'Leary, B. (1987) *Theories of the State*, London: Macmillan.
Finer, S.E. (ed.) (1975) *Adversarial Politics and Electoral Reform*, London: Anthony Wigram.
Grant, W. (1993) *Business and Politics in Britain*, 2nd edn, London: Macmillan.
Hennessy, P. (1990) *Whitehall*, London: Fontana.
Hill, M. (ed.) (1993) *The Policy Process: A Reader*, Hemel Hempstead: Harvester Wheatsheaf.
Hillyard, P. and Percy-Smith, J. (1988) *The Coercive State*, London: Fontana.
Institute for Public Policy Research (1992) *A New Constitution for the United Kingdom*, London: Mansell.
Jennings, W.I. (1941) *The British Constitution*, Cambridge: Cambridge University Press.
Kavanagh, D. (1990) *Thatcherism and British Politics*, Oxford: Oxford University Press.
King, A. (ed.) (1985) *The British Prime Minister*, 2nd edn, London: Macmillan.

Middlemas, K. (1979) *Politics in Industrial Society*, London: Andre Deutsch.

Mount, F. (1992) *The British Constitution Now*, London: Heinemann.

Norton, P. (1993) *Does Parliament Matter?*, Hemel Hempstead: Harvester Wheatsheaf.

Pulzer, P.G. (1967) *Political Representation and Elections in Britain*, London: George Allen & Unwin.

Rhodes, R.A.W. (1988) *Beyond Westminster and Whitehall*, London: Unwin Hyman.

Schmitter, P. and Lehmbruch, G. (eds) (1979) *Trends Towards Corporatist Intermediation*, London: Sage.

Self, P. (1993) *Government by the Market: The Politics of Public Choice*, London: Macmillan.

3   The European context

John Kingdom

The extent to which what is now referred to as the European Union will feature in British politics as the 1990s unfold remains something of an imponderable. The break-up of the Soviet Union, the reunification of Germany and the crisis of the European Exchange Rate Mechanism (ERM) are but some of the factors influencing a development that only the foolhardy would attempt to predict. Nevertheless, if we are to complete a picture of the context of British politics as we move through the 1990s we must try to consider the implications of events. There can be little doubt that the opening of the decade has witnessed a debate capable of generating considerable heat. Although in substantive terms there are various strands to this, it has centred on the Treaty on European Union signed at the Dutch town of Maastricht in 1992 and the subsequent process of ratification.

In addressing the European context of British politics in the 1990s this chapter opens with a brief account of the long journey that led to the Maastricht Treaty. Next it sketches the actual institutions of the European Union, noting the way in which the Treaty modifies them. This leads to a twofold analysis of the effect of the European dimension on British government and politics. The first part of this considers the impact of membership on both government institutions and the political process. The second considers the presence of European issues as part of domestic debate. Here the focus is on key aspects of the Maastricht debate: monetary union, social policy and the question of sovereignty.

SLOW TRAIN TO MAASTRICHT

We cannot discuss the present and future position without reference to the past. The United Kingdom has long performed a kind of stately square dance towards Europe; advancing with apparent enthusiasm, pausing before the promised embrace only to withdraw to turn aside to another partner, the United States or the Commonwealth.

During the Second World War Winston Churchill appeared to enthuse over the idea of a United States of Europe, envisaging the great powers accepting government through a joint council backed by a court and an army. However, when in 1948 the Congress of Europe decided to establish a Council of Europe the negotiations revealed a fundamental difference between Britain and the rest of Europe.

In June 1948 sixteen West European countries established an Organization for Economic Co-operation and Development (OECD) to coordinate the post-war recovery strategy, but any hopes that it might develop into a permanent supranational institution were dashed by British and Scandinavian opposition.

The United Kingdom also stayed out of the European Coal and Steel Community (ECSC) formed by Italy, France, West Germany and the Benelux countries in 1951 and remained cool when, in November 1954, Jean Monnet resigned the presidency of the ECSC to help found an action committee for a United States of Europe. Although taking part in early negotiations, when the Treaty of Rome establishing the Common Market was signed on 27 March 1957, Britain stood aloof, thereby relinquishing any claim to a major leadership role in Europe.

The first decade in the life of the new Community saw substantial political and economic achievements and envious neighbouring states expressed interest in joining. In 1959 Britain combined with Norway, Denmark, Sweden, Switzerland, Austria and Portugal to form another free-trade area but without the aspirations to political union. This European Free Trade Association (EFTA) expressed interest in trade links with the six but this suggestion met with a frosty response from France's General de Gaulle who returned to power in 1958. He viewed the move as an opportunistic ploy to secure the free-trade advantages of the community without the political obligations of full membership.

EFTA was no rival to the Community and in 1961 Prime Minister Harold Macmillan finally announced that the United Kingdom would apply for membership. Although he received encouragement from the United States, he moved with characteristic languor and seemed more interested in the idea of the 'special relationship' that was believed to exist with the United States. When he spoke of Europe it was in terms of economic union, with little mention of the political union built into the Treaty of Rome and logically implicit in the Common Market ideal. De Gaulle, still doubting the United Kingdom's commitment and suspicious of US intentions, remained frosty and vetoed the application. He did the same with a second application by the Labour government. Only after his resignation in 1969 did the United Kingdom get a sympathetic hearing.

Hence, in 1973, Edward Heath, clearer in his European intentions than his predecessors, managed to take Britain into the Community. However, British scepticism died hard; Labour had opposed the entry terms and, upon returning to office in 1974, held a promised referendum on continued membership once these had been renegotiated. A 'yes' vote duly came with a 65 per cent turnout and a two-thirds majority on 5 June 1975.

The career of the European Community (EC) has itself been fitful, with periods of stagnation (or *immobilisme*) and of dynamism when the drive has been towards greater integration. Although many aspects of the Rome Treaty remained paper promises; the initial decade was one of dynamism. It was, however, followed by four years of stagnation beginning with de Gaulle's first veto of UK membership in January 1963, during which the 'Luxembourg Compromise' of 1966 emerged which curtailed the ability of the Community to make decisions by majority vote. De Gaulle's retirement heralded a more fruitful period; the goal of advancing political union was affirmed at the Hague summit of 1969 and plans were made to coordinate foreign policy. In 1970 the Werner Plan argued for harmonisation of economic, fiscal and budgetary policy and 1979 saw the establishment of the European Monetary System. In 1974 the European Council, bringing together the heads of state in regular summit meetings, was given legal recognition. In 1979 democratic elections were introduced for the European Parliament.

However, a further period of tension began in 1979 when a new head of state, as nationalistic as de Gaulle himself, took a place on the European Council. The United Kingdom was again to reveal itself as 'an awkward partner' (George 1990). Echoing her 'no such thing as society' sentiment on the domestic front, Margaret Thatcher was to declare: 'There is no such thing as a separate community interest; the community interest is compounded of the national interests of the ten member states' (Urwin 1989: 369). She began with an acrimonious campaign to secure a reduction in the size of the UK contribution to the community budget. Given the gross inequality in this, the goal was not unreasonable and Labour also favoured such negotiations. However, the strategy entailed a denigration of the Common Agricultural Policy (CAP), regarded by the six original members as their greatest achievement, and the Thatcher style did little to enhance the United Kingdom's Euro-credentials.

ARRIVING AT MAASTRICHT

Yet in spite of the negative tone of much Thatcher rhetoric, the lead-up to the accession of Portugal and Spain in 1986 saw considerable re-invigoration of the integrationist spirit. In June 1985 the European Commission, under the presidency of avowed integrationist Jacques Delors, produced a White Paper, *Completing the Internal Market*. The following year saw the Single European Act, with its programme for a genuine internal market, free of all trade barriers, by the end of 1992. This promised a number of significant institutional, social and economic repercussions and the year 1992 became a symbol of progress. Delors used the single market as a springboard for a wider vision of integration, including something that particularly alarmed the UK government: a social dimension. In 1989 all EC states except Britain accepted a Charter of Fundamental Social Rights of Workers. This 'Social Charter' gave the EC competence to pursue social goals in employment-related matters. In addition there had been progress towards monetary union with the establishment of a European Monetary System (EMS) in 1979 to which Britain had given only half-hearted support.

The Treaty

The Treaty on European Union was formally signed in the previously little-known Dutch town of Maastricht on 7 February 1992. In its 61,351 words it went further than any other EC agreement in promoting the cause of integration. This major development did not come out of the blue; its provisions consolidated much that had gone before and marked the conclusion of the intergovernmental conferences on economic, monetary and political union (opposed by the UK government) which had opened in Rome on 15 December 1990. The European Parliament had requested such talks ever since the signing of the Single European Act in 1986. The Maastricht summit assumed additional significance because of its momentous historical conjuncture which included the end of the cold war, the reunification of Germany and the collapse of the Soviet Union. There was an urgent desire within some member states for a quickening of the pace of integration. In the year leading up to Maastricht, first Italy and then Holland produced radical plans for federal union.

The use in the Treaty of the term 'Union' was significant in that it made the EC part of a wider association comprising three pillars. One of these was the EC itself, the other two being the Common Foreign and Security Policy, and Cooperation in the Field of Justice and Home Affairs. (In discussions the UK government initially chose ostentatiously to eschew the term 'Union', although some Cabinet members, such as Chancellor Kenneth Clark, did not do so.) In declaring that member states should seek a common foreign and defence policy, the West European Union – a defence association comprising the original EEC members plus Britain – was seen as playing an integrational role in implementing Council decisions with defence implications. The international situation would be monitored by a specially created political committee. The justice and home affairs pillar would see cooperation in various areas previously left within national competence, including asylum policy, crossing of borders, immigration policy, drug addiction, fraud and judicial cooperation in civil matters. There would also be cooperation in police matters.

Significantly, the second and third pillars were not to fall within the competence of the EC legislative and judicial institutions. They were to depend upon cooperation between states rather than supragovernmentalism. This provision, preserving the legal sovereignty of member states, was one of the proclaimed successes of the UK government in the negotiation stage. Broadly, the Treaty can be seen to address the two principal themes of the intergovernmental conferences: political union and economic and monetary union. Among its most important features were the following:

- *EC citizenship* Of symbolic as well as practical significance was the concept of EC citizenship which had received little publicity before. This allowed all nationals of member states to enjoy certain rights. They were to be able to reside and move freely throughout the Community, vote and stand in municipal elections, and stand for the European Parliament in their country of residence regardless of nationality. When abroad, EC citizens, if without consular representation from their home country, would enjoy access to the services of any member's embassy.
- *Policy competence* In addition to the defence and security and home affairs matters encompassed within the broader Union, the policy remit was extended

to cover aspects of education, culture, public health, industrial policy and consumer protection.

- *The institutions*   The decision-making procedures were reformed to allow majority voting in the European Council over a wider range of areas. The Council and Commission would be assisted by two advisory bodies, an Economic and Social Committee and a Committee of the Regions. The powers of the Parliament and the Court were increased.
- *Subsidiarity*   An inelegant neologism became much used and abused in the debate. It related to the competence of the Community institutions *vis-à-vis* those of member states and was regarded by the UK government as a vital bulwark against centralisation and loss of national sovereignty. Essentially it established a form of devolution: in areas that did not fall within their direct competence the Community institutions should act only if the objectives could not be better met at a lower level of government. However, a tantalising ambiguity remained in the idea. For the UK government it meant as little power as possible to Brussels and as much as possible to Westminster. Yet the term could also mean devolution to regional and local governments, an inter- pretation quite at variance with trends in Britain since 1979. Moreover, there remained grounds for dispute as to which is to be deemed the most appropriate decision-making level for any particular item of policy.
- *Social policy*   The objectives of the agreement on social policy, which be- came known as the Social Chapter, were to promote employment, improve living and working conditions, instigate social protection and develop human resources with a view to lasting high employment, and equal pay and condi- tions for men and women. The United Kingdom opposed these provisions and negotiated an effective opt-out by allowing the other members to sign a special Treaty protocol on social policy.
- *Economic integration*   In economic terms the Treaty placed great emphasis on the open market economy, the convergence of economic indicators and monetary union. Member states were enjoined to avoid budget deficits and the Commission was empowered to monitor performance in this respect. Economic harmonisation called for a three-stage process leading ultimately to the establishment of a single currency. Member states were to regard their economic policies as matters of common concern and to coordinate them through the Council. Economic policy in the Council would be determined by qualified majority voting so that no single country would be in a position to exercise a veto. Again the United Kingdom negotiated an opt-out of the third stage towards monetary union.

Ratifying Maastricht

Once signed, the Treaty required ratification by the national assemblies and, in some cases, the courts. The process was not as smooth as might have been expected. The Danish people made themselves the unexpected heroes in the eyes of Euro-sceptics when, in a referendum, they narrowly voted 'no'. Subsequently referendums in Ireland and France gave support, although only the first was decisive. The French embarrassed President Mitterrand with an equivocal 'oui'. Although prominent British Euro-sceptics journeyed to Denmark to add their voices to the debate, the 'no' vote was subsequently reversed in a second referendum of 18 May 1993. Despite calls so to do from Thatcher, such events gave little encouragement to Major to adopt the same method of resolving the debate within his own country. Finding himself in the most turbulent waters of his premiership he was forced to ask the House of Commons for a vote of confidence as Labour and the Liberal Democrats made unlikely bedfellows with the right-wing Euro-rebels in the Prime Minister's own party.

What next? The variable geometry thesis

There are grounds for anticipating that future integration will take place according to a principle of 'variable geometry' which will permit states, and groups of states, to proceed at different speeds. Indeed this idea is built into the very architecture of the Union. The Maastricht Treaty itself enshrined a multi-speed ideal with its schedule for achieving a single currency. Here was a clear statement of the principle that no member would be forced along with the others, and its corollary that no state could hold the others back.

The 1992–93 collapse of narrow-band ERM provided another example of the variable gearbox in operation. The present ERM, in a new etiolated form, contains only nine of the twelve. Moreover, home affairs, defence and foreign policy see different European groupings looking for intergovernmental cooperation in different ways. The variable principle is also seen in the willingness to allow Denmark to opt out of future EU defence policy. The Western European Union, viewed as the eventual defence arm of the Union, contains only ten of the twelve. France's moves towards a 'Euro-corps' could embrace Germany, France, Belgium, Luxembourg and Spain. The Schengen Agreement to drop border controls is signed by only nine of the twelve. The development of immigration and asylum rules may leave out Britain, Ireland and Denmark.

The imminent membership of three Scandinavian states plus Austria could give the impetus to a Green grouping from which Italy, France, Spain, Portugal and perhaps Britain may wish to exclude themselves. Again, the widening of the Union to perhaps sixteen, and later to around twenty, must add to the pressure for variable geometry. It is recognition of these realities that leads the French to think in terms of a hard core of the original six proceeding at a pace different from that of a surrounding penumbra of the less committed.

This principle of a multi-track Europe has proved particularly attractive to the British government, but whether it offers the best route to integration remains to be seen. An important Maastricht review conference is scheduled for 1996 and this will be a time to consider that question.

THE EVOLVING INSTITUTIONS

The institutional structure of the European Community is more than a collection of ornate modernistic buildings and offices in Brussels (and Strasbourg and Luxembourg). It is the physical embodiment of the values that underpin the ideals of integration. The great issues of debate, such as democratic accountability and sovereignty, are ultimately understood and resolved in institutional terms. Four key bodies dominate the institutional landscape: the Council of Ministers and its offshoot, the European Council; the Parliament; the Commission; and the Court of Justice.

The Council of Ministers

Meeting in Brussels, the Council stands as the political head of the Union. It comprises a general council made up of the foreign ministers of member states and a number of technical councils made up of ministers for particular policy areas such as trade, finance, social security and so on. Associated with the Council is the Committee of Permanent Representatives (COREPER). COREPER I consists of national ambassadors to the Union and COREPER II comprises their deputies who are national civil servants. The system is held together by a dense web of committees, subcommittees and working parties, some permanent and some set up on an *ad hoc* basis staffed by national civil servants. Policy decisions emerge as regulations (having immediate force of law), directives (which are binding, but in practice leave member states with leeway in interpretation) and recommendations and resolutions (which are qualitatively different in that they are not compelling).

The Rome Treaty laid down a system of weighted voting so that decisions could be reached on the basis of a majority rather than unanimity. However, strains in this system resulted in the French boycotting the Community. To resolve this deadlock the 'Luxembourg compromise' was reached in 1966, permitting any state a veto if a proposal was thought to threaten its vital national interest. Since it was for the state concerned to decide what was indeed vital, the system was a severe inhibition. The Single European Act allowed qualified majority voting, requiring fifty-four votes out of seventy-six. Yet this is a high threshold and decisions continue to be dominated by complex bargaining with national interest to the forefront. Britain under both Thatcher and Major has been blatant in this respect.

The European Council

In one major development illustrative of the evolving nature of the Council, heads of state and foreign ministers have, from the early 1970s, come to play a dominant role through 'summit meetings'. These were formalised at the Paris summit of December 1974 as regular European Council meetings held in different member countries. Heads of state hold the presidency on a rotating basis. The run-up to such meetings sees protracted negotiation and speculation and they provide major foci for media attention. This development shows the increasing importance of the Union in the political lives of member states although it also betrays the persistence of nationalism.

The European Commission

In the demonology of Euro-sceptics the Brussels-based Commission features as the greatest *bête noir*. It is the institution most removed from democratic influence and the one most redolent of Kafkaesque faceless bureaucracy. Effectively the civil service of the EC, it is not really faceless, being open to consultation at various levels. Headed by seventeen commissioners nominated by member states, it is serviced by legions of civil servants organised in twenty-three directorate-generals (departments) for various policy areas.

The Commission is charged with responsibility for implementing Council policy and also has the function of initiating legislation which it does by forwarding proposals to the Council. Given the relative weakness of the other institutions its position contains much potential power. However, the nationalistic bargaining tendencies of the superior institutions (the Council of Ministers and European Council) have tended to curtail its authority, reducing its leadership role to one of mediation and compromise seeking. Hence, it may be seen as the more supranational institution.

The European Court of Justice

The existence of the Court is a further challenge to the idea of national sovereignty. Its role is to ensure adherence to the Community treaties and the laws that flow from them. The Court sits at Luxembourg and comprises one judge from each member state. Decisions, which are made by a majority verdict, are binding upon member states. EC laws become supreme over domestic laws, challenging the British principle of the sovereignty of Parliament. Moreover, the Court has a responsibility to consider the constitutionality of any laws passed by a domestic legislature, a power not possessed by the British courts. The existence of the Court to enforce its decisions makes the EC almost unique among international associations.

The European Parliament

Central to any debate about democracy within the EC must be the position of the European Parliament (EP), its most obviously democratic institution. Initially members (MEPs) were appointed by governments but this was changed to direct election in 1979. Unlike the other member states, the United Kingdom (except Northern Ireland) retains its 'first past the post' voting system, a feature that distorts the representative nature of the assembly. At the Edinburgh summit of 1992 it was agreed, as a result of German reunification, to increase the number of seats from 518 to 567 in the 1994 elections. The UK representation rose from 81 to 87. The single-chamber assembly meets for one week every month in Strasbourg. In addition it does much serious detailed work through committees which, significantly, meet at Brussels.

The MEPs have party allegiances and form groups which cut across national boundaries. After the June 1994 elections these were: Socialists (221), European People's Party (204), Liberal Democratic and Reformist (28), Greens (23), European Democratic Alliance (27), Rainbow (8), European Right (12), Left Unity (28) and a residual group of non-attached members (34). UK Labour MEPs (62) sit with the Socialists. Conservatives (18), since Spring 1992, have sat with the European People's Party, two new Liberal Democrats sit with the Liberal Democratic and Reformists and two Scottish Nationalists with the Rainbow Group.

A major debate over the Parliament concerns its powers, which were very limited. It is true that it can dismiss the Commission and reject the budget, although a two-thirds majority is required. The real legislative authority lies with the Council. In reality the Parliament has been seen largely as a talking shop, its main influence coming through the publicity of its debates which may bring pressure to bear upon national governments and the other EC institutions.

Its powers were extended in the Maastricht Treaty. Most important was the principle of co-decision with the Council, enabling it to reject certain categories of proposals (on the internal market, research and development, trans-European networks, training and education, culture, health care and consumer affairs) by an overall majority. In addition the Commission can be asked to submit any proposal where the EP decides by overall majority that new legislation is required, although the extent to which the Commission will comply remains to be seen. Power was also granted to investigate citizens' complaints of maladministration in the implementation of Community law and to appoint an ombudsman to assist in this.

The Economic and Social Committee

Another body with a quasi-democratic function is the Economic and Social Committee (ESC), which brings together representatives of employers and unions to discuss industrial policy. As a consultative forum it has no executive powers although its presence represents a nod in the direction of corporatism, a style of government more prevalent in continental Europe than in Britain. The ESC has been viewed with misgivings by British governments since 1979, with their avowedly anti-union and anti-consultative domestic policies.

The institutional debate

This is not a static world, and the institutional architecture of the Union can be expected to evolve continually to reflect developments in thought and practice. Various aspects remain subject to debate. There is the issue of the 'democratic deficit', focusing on the perceived lack of accountability and responsiveness to

European citizens. A further important debate is that over deepening (more integration) or widening (extending membership to other countries including those of Eastern Europe) the Union. In either case, important institutional implications will have to be faced.

One can also expect some working out of a tension between the ideals of nationalism and supranationalism. Essentially the EC, including its precursors, is a supranational association but within it the Council of Ministers and the European Council have produced a nationalising force with bargaining in national interest replacing the search for some overarching Community interest. The Common Foreign and Security Policy, and Cooperation in the Field of Justice and Home Affairs pillars of the post-Maastricht Union again point towards cooperation rather than supranationalism. The impact of UK membership has favoured the nationalistic trend.

IMPACT UPON UK GOVERNMENT AND POLITICS

How will the government and politics of the United Kingdom be affected by Europe in the 1990s? We begin with an examination of the core executive, the Whitehall network, Westminster and the world beyond the central government complex. This is followed by an analysis of the more informal faces of political power; the political parties and pressure groups. However, throughout this section it must be remembered that the structure of state power is infinitely malleable and any description can only be a snapshot in time. We are as interested in trends as we are in particular snapshots. What we broadly find is that institutions and practices are being insidiously permeated by the European Union at all levels. The trend is one that will probably continue and become more overt.

The core executive

The core executive of British government has become well integrated into the institutions of Europe and can be expected to become more so. Ministers operate at the very heart of the decision-making process on the Council of Ministers and the prime minister sits on the European Council, sometimes assuming its presidency. At home ministers most involved in European matters sit on a special Cabinet committee chaired by the foreign secretary. The Cabinet Office is at the heart of all European policy deliberations and its officials attend interdepartmental meetings on European issues. Their role in establishing compromise solutions that enable ministers to present a unified front to the Council of Ministers affords considerable influence.

Whitehall

Government departments closely involved in formulating UK policy towards Europe (the Treasury and those concerned with agriculture, food and fisheries; employment; trade and industry; and energy) have established special European sections. Policy towards Europe is coordinated formally and informally through an interdepartmental network permeating Whitehall. *Ad hoc* committees dealing with areas of special concern are set up at the instigation of the department most involved. Although it is the Treasury and Cabinet Office that are the traditional coordinating forces within the system, in the internal Whitehall power struggle it is the Foreign and Commonwealth Office (FCO) that has probably gained most through EC membership, thereby arresting its declining importance. At the highest level, senior civil servants also meet to take a long-term strategic perspective on the UK position within the Union. Above all is the EC Committee which coordinates European policy and oversees the preparation of briefs for the UK Permanent Representation and the Council.

At Brussels, UK civil servants are heavily involved in the operations of the COREPER network. In addition there are those forming the UK Permanent Representation to the European Community. About one-third come from the FCO with the remainder seconded for two-year terms by other departments with which they remain in contact. However, once they breathe the heady air at Brussels they develop strong links with their opposite numbers from other countries and Euro-sceptics express fears of them 'going native' and becoming arrogant and isolated from the real world. Treasury mandarins become particularly powerful as they become interlocked with their counterparts from other governments, preparing for summits, IMF meetings and European Councils (Sampson 1992: 40–1).

Westminster

The position of the UK Parliament will continue to be a key feature of debate. The fact that policy decisions of the Council can have the immediate force of law in member states means that the UK Parliament can no longer lay claims to absolute sovereignty in the domestic sphere. Hence, if it is to have any policy impact it must rely on its ability to influence the negotiating position of the government. However, its powers in this respect are severely limited.

In May 1974 a sixteen-member committee on European secondary legislation was established with a right to examine draft proposals submitted to the Council by the Commission. However, the committee is not empowered to consider the merits of a proposal; it can only recommend that it be submitted to a standing committee or to the House. Even if the proposal is so debated it cannot be amended. The House can only debate it as a 'take note' motion in the hope that the government will modify its position. Moreover, the parliamentary timetable is not coordinated with that of Europe, so that a proposal may escape scrutiny by surfacing in a recess. In practice the committee has not proved popular with MPs. The House of Lords also has a scrutiny committee. Larger than that in the Commons, it works through seven specialist subcommittees. Unlike its Commons counterpart it may debate the merits of a proposal and can call upon expert witnesses. Debates are again confined to 'take note' motions.

However, rather than testifying to the dominance of the European institutions, Parliament's weakness is more a reflection of the might of the British executive. In Denmark, for example, the Folketing has secured far greater powers to influence its government's negotiating position.

Beyond the Whitehall/Westminster complex

The United Kingdom is a highly centralised state but the concept of subsidiarity, highlighted in the Maastricht Treaty, might seem to offer a lifeline to local government and perhaps even add vitality to the etiolated UK regions. However, although it played a leading role in establishing the principle in the Maastricht negotiations, there is little evidence that this has been the intention of the UK government. The 1980s saw an unprecedented weakening of democratic local institutions in favour of outright centralisation or governance by non-elected, centrally appointed boards and agencies.

UK local authorities have not themselves made a uniform response to Europe. Some have appointed special officials and units to relate to the EC, and some have even established a representative presence in Brussels for lobbying purposes, but others have done little. Yet UK local authorities cannot afford to ignore this dimension since, as the body of European legislation grows, they will increasingly be drawn in through their responsibilities to implement regulations, monitor standards and conform to requirements (consumer protection, environment, competitive tendering and so on). Moreover, there are incentives for links with Europe such as the European Social Fund (ESF) and European Regional Development Fund (ERDF) offering grants for certain projects (although the value of these is undermined if the UK government makes pro-rata cuts in its own grant). Generally, the squeeze put upon them by the centre since the late 1970s gives good reason for authorities to look increasingly to Brussels for support. It may even be possible to argue the subsidiarity case in an effort to hoist Westminster with its own petard.

In the United Kingdom, where English political and administrative domination has for long been the main historical thrust, the regional dimension of the state remains strikingly underdeveloped. Calls for greater autonomy by Wales and Scotland are stoutly resisted and, in dealing with the EC, these countries have been obliged to conduct their affairs through the single UK Permanent Representation.

However, this pattern could come under threat. The regional dimension has greater vigour in some of the other member states and the EC has often looked to this level as a basis for development. This can be in the interests of federalism in that it weakens the nation-state. Some see a vision of the future in terms of a Europe of regions, and the Maastricht Treaty made provision for an advisory Committee of the Regions. Hence, without a genuine regional level of government the United Kingdom may be fundamentally disadvantaged. Wales and Scotland have managed to establish offices in Brussels where they may lobby in the manner of pressure groups. The uneven economic development seen within Britain could also encourage the regions in the north of England to seek to defend their interests via Europe. Again the ERDF offers an incentive. However, this will almost certainly meet with opposition from the centre; in its present review of local government, the government has rejected a regional dimension (although the cause is now espoused by Labour).

The parties

Although racked by ambivalence, the main political parties have been forced to make organisational changes in response to EC membership. European elections have necessitated larger constituencies which has brought adjacent party organisations together. However, the Westminster-based MPs have not been entirely warm in their embrace of their MEP cousins, reflecting the suspicion that the EP will erode the much-cherished sovereignty of Parliament. For their part, the MEPs will, *ipso facto*, espouse the integrationist ideal, a tendency increased by pressures to go native in the communitaire climate of Strasbourg.

Both Labour and Conservative parties entered the 1990s with considerable Euro-scepticism within their ranks. Indeed, the antipathy of Thatcher meant that Conservative MEPs (to whom she had shown little warmth) were denied entry into their appropriate grouping until 1992, after her departure. It was, in considerable part, rampant anti-Europeanism that led to the fall of this most dominant of post-war leaders, splitting the party between the euphemistically named Euro-sceptics and those willing for one reason or another to support the new leader, John Major. Major was obliged to fight the general election of 1992 with Thatcher as a sword of Damocles; would she or would she not raise the European issue?

In her memoirs, the deposed leader was to label her opponents 'treacherous' but Major was to find language even more unparliamentary, referring in an unguarded moment to the Euro-sceptics dogging him from the front and back benches as 'bastards'. Yet the negative attitude of the UK government in the Maastricht and post-Maastricht negotiations was testimony to the Euro-sceptics' continuing power within the party.

On 22 July 1993 the Speaker was forced to exercise her casting vote when government rebels had produced a tie in a vote on a Labour amendment to include the Social Chapter in the UK version of the Treaty. Minutes later, amidst great excitement, a government motion to take note of the policy on the Social Chapter was defeated by 316 votes to 324. The premier, described in the media as 'ashen-faced', rose to announce nothing less than a confidence motion the next day. If the rebels persisted, they would not merely lose the Treaty, but they would also lose their seats since he would call a general election. Although enough of the recalcitrants fell into line, a stern warning had been delivered to the government. Major, or any other leader of the party, could only face the coming decade with trepidation.

Signs of Major's unease continued to show in various concessions to the Euro-sceptics. Thatcher had warned of the insidious threat of socialism through the back door and, in a speech at Ellesmere Port on the eve of the 1994 European elections, Major echoed the sentiment: 'Trying to make every country conform is a socialist way of thinking: it is not for us.' In what was proclaimed as a new vision of Europe he argued that 'the functions of the Community should be carried out in different ways, often involving different groups of states'. We have seen above that the idea of a multi-track Europe is by no means new, but it might seem a particularly useful concept to a leader of a split party. 'Variable geometry', 'multi-track', 'multi-layered' and 'multi-speed' can be custom-built terms to appease as many shades of opinion as there are Heinz varieties.

Certainly the vision seemed to be music to the ears of the Conservative right. The harmony was enriched by the exercise of the veto at the Corfu summit of June 1994 to thwart the appointment as president of the Commission of Jean-Luc Dehaene, a federalist and the preferred choice of France and Germany. Talk of a 1994 autumn challenge to the Prime Minister receded. Yet, to critics, he appeared a desperate man wishing to forestall a leadership challenge rather than a visionary. Concessions to the hard right may only prove of short-term value and did not mask Major's weakness within his party.

The eve of the 1994 Euro-elections saw the opinion poll gap separating Labour and Conservatives greater than at any time since the great poll tax débâcle. Fears of a Tory rout were high. In the event, they lost nearly half their seats. The longer term may see the pro-Europeans becoming more vociferous. Edward Heath saw the vetoing of Dehaene as a crisis for the Union. Douglas Hurd sought to assure the Conservative Positive European Group, a pro-European group within the party, that there had been no sell-out to the Euro-sceptics. Chancellor Kenneth Clark fought hard to keep Britain in the mainstream at Brussels although the Euro-sceptics were accusing *him* of threatening unity.

For a considerable time the Labour Party opposed the EC on the grounds that it would be a club for businesspeople to grow fat at the expense of others. Their 1983 manifesto actually contained a pledge to take the United Kingdom out. However, the Kinnock leadership, with its taming of the left, reversed this. At the same time, the stress by integrationists on the EC's social dimension, together with a necessary tendency to oppose the Conservatives, saw Labour's conversion to the integrationist cause. Hence the party entered the 1990s with a friendly face towards its MEPs, making the leader of the European Labour Party an *ex officio* member of its National Executive Committee, permitting MEPs to attend Westminster back-benchers' meetings and making them part of the electoral college choosing the party leader.

The Liberal Democrats are largely united in their espousal of Europe. Their basic goal of proportional representation is, of course, well established in Europe, as is the principle of coalition government, which they see as their key to power.

Pressure groups

Formal institutions can never provide a complete picture of the policy-making process. It is vital to go beyond the formal trappings of state to a more shadowy world of power and influence. The same proviso applies to the European Union.

Generally this is an area seriously neglected in accounts of the processes and power relationships at Brussels, although it is one that should see much greater study in the future.

Although never going to the corporatist lengths of some other European countries, Britain, during the post-war era, can largely be portrayed as a pluralist democracy affording interest groups a legitimate place in political life. However, the Thatcher era saw much retrenchment of the consultative front in an effort to release the country from what had been seen by critics as 'pluralist stagnation' where government was believed to have forfeited the power to govern. However, the EC, drawing on more corporatist traditions of other European states, places emphasis on the idea that employers and unions are 'social partners'. This approach is institutionalised in the existence of the ESC. Hence the community offers a new focus for British interest groups. It may offer a more receptive ear than their own government.

There are other reasons for the welcoming embrace from the European institutions. Much Brussels legislation is highly technical in nature and could not be made without external know-how. There is also a great need for cooperation in the implementation of policy, much of which sets standards for private companies. Again, the Commission at Brussels is generally anxious to combat the criticisms that it is faceless and undemocratic; an open-door policy can help legitimation. Finally, it cannot be forgotten that many of the private corporations that move on the European and indeed the world stage possess immense political power. With the might to undermine national economies their voices cannot go unheeded.

It is fear of this corporate power that has driven much left-wing criticism of the EC. On the other hand, for post-1979 Conservative governments developments have smacked of corporatism through the back door, an idea as repugnant as the more loudly trumpeted fear of socialism through the same entrance.

There are many hundreds of groups lobbying at Brussels concerned with trade issues, agriculture and food, commerce and the service industries. Indeed, interests go beyond the industrial to include human rights, consumer interests and the environment. As the flow of directives from the Commission increases in number, more and more associations are drawn into the process.

Pressure groups interested in influencing the making and implementation of European policy have two broad avenues: they may either approach the EC's institutions or they may seek support on the home front (most profitably the relevant Whitehall department) in the hope of influencing the government's bargaining stance. The first of these suggests supranationalism while the latter falls back on nationalistic bargaining. However, they are not alternatives; if a matter is deemed of sufficient importance both may be utilised.

The direct approach

In the direct line to Brussels there are two further alternatives; a group may speak on its own behalf or may act through one of the many federations of national interest groups which have formed at European level, such as the Association of

Plastics Manufacturers in Europe or the Federation of European Explosives Manufacturers. There are also peak organisations including the European Trade Union Confederation and the Union of Industries of the European Community.

The second of these alternatives represents a natural evolution with a kind of informal political federalism growing alongside the institutional federalism. The advantage to the groups is that where cross-national interests speak with a single voice, their power is increased. The associations can help to build a consensus and can sometimes even change the policy of one or more governments. Even so, consensus is not always possible and it is still necessary for groups to speak for themselves. In contrast, the very powerful interests, such as the multi-national corporations, use the direct line because they have little need of others. Indeed, with their immense muscle they can sometimes compete with, and undermine, the federal associations.

Groups must also choose an avenue of access. They may talk to the Parliament and the ESC, although neither can deliver much in terms of real influence and it can be a mark of weakness to concentrate much effort here. The key access point at Brussels is the Commission; not the individual commissioners but the bureaucrats operating within the committee network. Here groups will find an open door and be invited to participate at very early stages in the process. As stated above, the Commission needs advice and expertise and can also gain (much-needed) democratic legitimacy from consultation.

As in the case of national politics, policy communities form at EC level through vertical alliances of those concerned in a particular area, including national ministries of member countries, parliamentary committees, bureaucrats, politicians and professional lobbyists as well as the pressure groups themselves (Scharpf 1988: 270). Within these communities much business is transacted informally by telephone, in casual social meetings, and over elaborate lunches, entertainments and mutually enjoyed sporting activities. Close relationships develop between the favoured interest and the relevant directorates and there is even rivalry between directorates in advancing the claims of their clients.

It would be naive to believe that all groups received an equal chance of a hearing. From its inception the idea of a federal Europe has offered a tantalising glimpse of new forms of power to the powerful; the big banks, the international financiers and the mighty multi-national companies (including those with US bases). The vision of a giant market-place like that of the United States was tempting indeed so that today every major company has offices in Brussels. More than other interest groups, these largely bypass the Parliament in favour of the Eurocrats whom they fête with lunches and entertainment. It is the desire to contain this world of transnational power that helps to give rise to the drive to make the European institutions more democratic.

Contacts via national governments

It is symptomatic of the relatively embryonic stage of European federalism that this indirect avenue remains central to the strategy of most groups. This is a result of the nationalistic style of the Council. Thus a pressure group will seek to persuade its own government that what it wants is in the national interest. In this way it can leave the bargaining to ministers and their civil servants. A further advantage of this is that it enables groups to utilise existing channels and avoid an expensive Brussels presence. Business interests tend to prefer this form of representation (Sargent 1987: 228–9). Yet there are risks; the government may be forced to let a group down by making concessions in the Council.

Again, for groups with demands at variance with the political philosophy of the government, it cannot be a promising avenue. Hence under a neo-liberal regime, non-commercial lobbies such as those aiming to protect human rights or the environment have recognised the potential in Brussels. Calls for strict regulation of drinking water and bathing beaches have bypassed national governments and in 1980 brought the British government before the Court at the Hague for its failures.

EUROPE AS A POLITICAL ISSUE

Turning from the political system into the 1990s we now examine the extent to which the EU will itself constitute an issue in British political debate. It has already precipitated considerable political fury, even forcing a break with tradition in the use of a referendum. Indeed, during this period Prime Minister Harold Wilson was obliged to suspend the constitutional doctrine of collective responsibility in order to prevent his Cabinet from splitting asunder. In the 1980s the issue led to the fall of the United Kingdom's most dominant post-war prime minister, endangered the political life of her successor and almost brought down the government. Yet, notwithstanding the referendum, this has been largely a private debate within parties, without the capacity to engage the public.

No Euro-talk please, we're British

When Britain considered entry into the Common Market, debate took place largely in a fog. Harold Wilson declared 'anyone who can claim to understand this issue in simple black and white terms is either a charlatan or a simpleton!' (Sampson 1992: 15). The referendum on the renegotiated terms was motivated more to avert rupture within his own party than to enlighten voters.

Almost twenty years later the same could be said of the Maastricht Treaty, upon which the government was economical, if not miserly, with information. While other Europeans could obtain cheap copies of the Treaty at bookshops, the UK government made it available at a cost hardly designed to encourage popular consumption (£13.30) through Her Majesty's Stationery Office. When it was signed, they were told triumphally that their leader had won the game, but they could have little idea of the rules or indeed the prizes secured on their behalf.

In similar vein the 1992 general election saw the parties seemingly engaged in a conspiracy to obscure European issues. A similar cloak of privacy was draped over the heated ratification debate which was conducted largely within the precincts of Westminster. Unlike the Danes, Irish and French, the people were not invited to voice their feelings in a referendum.

Yet ultimately the Euro-debates are about issues that will affect the quality of life of ordinary people. Why is there not more discussion in the pubs, clubs and launderettes of Britain? Part of the answer may lie in the xenophobic strain in popular culture which sees little that is good across the English Channel. Again there is the deferential political culture which, following the doctrine of Edmund Burke, is content to leave the great issues of state to those believed to know best. Coupled with this is the legendary wall of secrecy behind which Whitehall likes to conduct its affairs. A Whitehall committee is currently preparing the government's position for the next EC intergovernmental conference in 1996. No attempt is made to make clear how central the issues at stake will be for UK foreign policy. Wallace (1993) warns that 'Unless those questions are raised by Ministers outside the secrecy of Whitehall there is no hope that Parliament or the public will agree on how to answer them.' Another factor is the British party system, and the electoral system which cherishes it, revealed as patently incapable of accommodating the debate. The fissures run largely within the two main parties rather than between them; electors can have no choice and the parties no incentive to woo or inform them.

However, the troubles of the Conservative government have highlighted certain crucial issues. One is economic and monetary union, the issue that most inflames the Euro-sceptics and which led to the rift between Thatcher and Nigel Lawson. Another is social policy, a question over which the two main Westminster parties part company. Both issues were central in the Maastricht Treaty negotiations and led to the UK opt-outs. Finally there is the perennial question of sovereignty which haunts both left and right. Discussion of these forms the substance of the remainder of this chapter.

Economic and monetary union

This issue is emblematic of much debate over Europe. It can be argued that the lack of UK enthusiasm for economic and monetary union (EMU) is odd because it is highly conducive to a free market, itself a key feature of the neo-liberal agenda (Grahl and Teague 1990: 97–140). In the halcyon days of Britain's vast trading empire the good ship Britannia ruled not only the waves but the shores upon which they washed; sterling was the wind that filled her billowing sails and also those of the trading partners. The post-war years of economic boom saw a new basis for world monetary stability through the Bretton Woods Agreement, much approved of by Britain, in which the currencies of the capitalist economies were tied with fixed exchange rates to the powerful US dollar.

Yet in 1972 Britain left the EC system known as the 'snake in the tunnel' which had begun only the year before (although, of course, the system ultimately failed). Again, when the European Monetary System (EMS) began operating in 1979 Britain, although allowing sterling to be included in the basket of currencies used to determine the value of the new European Currency Unit (ECU), would not allow it to be part of a joint float against the dollar and for a considerable time stood outside the ERM (which is a means of keeping exchange rates between currencies within a narrow range of each other). This was in large measure in response to Thatcher's 'you can't buck the market' conviction. Sterling was to find its own value.

However, by the late 1980s pressure on Thatcher was building up. Many British businesspeople did not share her sentiments. With other member states in a monetary union, they were at a grave disadvantage on the outside. The City, most economists and the opposition parties also favoured entering the ERM. The Prime Minister was at loggerheads with many within her own party including Chancellor Nigel Lawson and Foreign Secretary Sir Geoffrey Howe. From the late 1980s Lawson covertly pursued a policy of 'shadowing' the Deutschmark in a kind of DIY membership of the ERM. The tension led in 1989 to Lawson's resignation over Thatcher's refusal to sack adviser Alan Walters, who declared the EMS to be 'half baked'.

Thatcher agreed cryptically that sterling would enter when 'the time was ripe'. This meant a time when the UK inflation rate matched that of other member states and when clear steps were being made by Italy and France in the removal of exchange controls. The 'right time' duly arrived under the new Chancellor, John Major, and it appeared to be October 1990, the eve of the Conservative Party conference. However, entry was to be on the basis of extra wide fluctuation bands and doubts about the sincerity of government intentions remained.

In the event the time was to prove quite wrong; the pound entered at an unsustainably high level and subsequent efforts to hold its value proved disastrous to the domestic economy. Tempers in the Conservative Party were running high and the time was not sufficiently right to save the political skin of a prime minister whose Euro-credentials were looking threadbare.

However, the UK stance did not change substantially with the departure of Thatcher. In the Maastricht Treaty leaders agreed on a three-stage programme towards monetary union. This would centre upon three institutions: the European System of Central Banks (ESCB) responsible for implementing monetary policy, exchange rate policy and management of each member state's foreign reserves; the European Central Bank (ECB) with an exclusive right to issue bank notes under a council comprising the governors of the national central banks; and finally the European Investment Bank with powers to grant loans to underdeveloped regions.

Three stages towards monetary union

In the first stage, which was expected to be completed by the end of 1993, governments would exercise strict budgetary discipline to get their economies into shape for further progress. The second stage would entail programmes designed to secure convergence between national economies with respect to certain key variables such as price stability, the absence of budgetary deficits, a position within defined fluctuation margins on the ERM and stable long-term interest rates. This essentially transitional period would also see progress towards the independence of the Central Bank. Developments would be overseen by the European Monetary Institute (EMI). The third stage would see the irrevocable fixing of exchange rates and lead to the introduction of a single currency (the ECU). A meeting of heads of state no later than 31 December 1996 would decide on a qualified majority basis whether a majority of states were ready for the adoption of the single currency. If so, the date for the final stage would be fixed. The EMI would prescribe the regulatory framework necessary for the ESCB to work in the third stage, but would be dissolved upon the creation of the ECB. If the date for the third stage had not been set by the end of 1997 it would start regardless on 1 January 1999.

In opting out of the key third stage of the programme towards monetary union, Britain gained agreement that it would not move towards a single currency without a separate decision by its national Parliament. Major claimed the Maastricht negotiations generally as a personal and national triumph ('Game, set and match to Britain').

Though not caused by Maastricht, tumultuous events followed which were to culminate in 'Black Wednesday' with the Bank of England frantically buying sterling in an effort to protect its value against selling by foreign exchange speculators (see Chapter 5). Eventually Britain was forced to withdraw ignominiously from the ERM. Shortly after, the Italian lira followed.

However, this was to be overshadowed by a momentous crisis for the ERM itself. The immediate trigger was a decision by the German central bank (Bundesbank), faced with Herculean currency problems arising from reunification, on 29 July 1993 to resist an expected cut in one of its key interest rates. Such a cut would have signalled rate cuts in other ERM currencies, thereby easing recessionary pressures. The result was turmoil in the foreign exchange markets, with heavy selling of the Belgian and French francs, the escudo, peseta and Danish krone, causing them to slump in value. Yet the crisis reflected much deeper tension caused by the differing economic performances of countries, and an insufficiently recognised time bomb which had been ticking since the fall of the Berlin wall.

Despite lamentations that the ERM was dead, emergency meetings resulted in the instigation of a new system in which the narrow bands (2.25) were replaced by wide ones of plus or minus 15 per cent. Critics argued that such wide bands rendered the system meaningless and Major claimed it vindicated the decision to suspend UK membership, arguing that 'the fault lines in the system have been exposed'.

The voices of the Euro-sceptics were raised in unison to proclaim the death of the ERM. On the other hand, there were also grounds for the alternative view that the fragility of the ERM suggested that the only way forward for the Community was acceptance of a single currency in which destructive speculation was impossible. In the event, countries revealed a continuing commitment to the ideal of EMU by resisting the temptation to exploit the wider bands with beggar-thy-neighbour devaluations. Germany worked hard to restore the battered French franc. British EC Commissioner Sir Leon Brittan was among those arguing that the idea that the ERM could lead to a single currency was doomed to failure. Fundamental convergence by other means should be sought so that 'in due course . . . the move to a single currency can be decided and implemented directly, without the artificial prop of years of narrow-band ERM' (Brittan 1993). Clearly the United Kingdom moves through the 1990s with the monetary union debate still alive, and the case for a single currency still viable in the eyes of its advocates.

Towards a single currency?

There are strong arguments for a single currency in the EC. At an emotional level it is a potent symbol of political union. It also offers members a greater collective weight in world politics. Indeed, a European currency would in all probability develop into a reserve currency rivalling the dollar and the yen. In more practical terms it eliminates the considerable cost incurred in currency transactions, facilitates comparisons between costs and prices in different countries, eases travel between countries, and conduces business confidence, stability and growth over time by removing the temptation of competitive devaluations. Perhaps most importantly in the light of the EMS experience it eliminates the possibility of damaging currency speculation.

The UK government position

The gravamen of the case against a single currency resolved into the holy cow of national sovereignty. Member states must sacrifice autonomy, accepting common objectives such as inflation targets, the exchange rate is no longer available to regulate international competitiveness, and control over monetary and fiscal policy is surrendered. This can result in domination by a leader economy with costs borne largely by the weaker economies. There is also the possibility that economic convergence will lead on to convergence in social policy, justifying the right-wing dread of 'socialism via the back door'.

Reservations go to a deeper emotional level. In a notorious speech at Bruges in September 1988, Thatcher voiced her fear that monetary integration would lead inexorably to political integration. Horrific scenarios have been painted by Euro-sceptics, with talk of a mighty German-dominated central bank and Britain falling under a neo-Nazi regime. Indeed, Thatcher's close confidant, Trade Secretary Nicholas Ridley, was obliged to resign in June 1990 for the intemperance of his anti-German utterances.

Problems with the UK government position

The autonomy argument is open to considerable doubt. With or without a formal surrender of autonomy to European financial institutions, there would be a relentless threat from the Bundesbank and the mighty German economy.

European institutions and full monetary union offered a means for the weaker economies to stem the loss of control which was already occurring. This has been a major reason for the quest for monetary union (George 1991: 188). Moreover, there remains on the domestic front considerable debate as to whether the UK opt-out will in fact be to the benefit of ordinary people, industrialists or the economy at large. An important cost of the low level of commitment to EMU is the sacrifice of the right to participate in major decisions. This includes the appointment of the senior officials and the loss of voting rights on all matters connected with the third stage. In this sense autonomy is lost rather than gained by remaining an EMU wallflower. One long-term possible scenario is of a two-speed development towards integration with the United Kingdom in the slow lane.

The social dimension

Although long known as the Common Market, the EC was always more than this. Rising out of the discord of world war, it enshrined an internationalist idea of world peace and harmony. A political rather than an economic unit, its impact was to be measured in terms of the quality of lives of citizens.

As presently constituted, the EU cannot have a social policy in the sense that a country can. It does not provide schools, houses, health care, social services and so on. Its role is limited to the protection of workers within a largely capitalist economic system. This has been present from the time of the ECSC. The Rome Treaty included provisions for the achievement of the free movement of workers through eligibility to social security, educational exchanges of young workers, harmonisation of working conditions, labour law, vocational training, health and safety at work, rights of association and collective bargaining and equal pay for men and women. It also established a European Social Fund to promote worker mobility and created a framework for a community vocational training policy. At the same time the Euratom Treaty established basic standards for the protection of workers and public against radiation.

Although initially muted, the social dimension was brought more to the fore. As economies did well, there developed a greater awareness of the social costs of growth, including pollution, health and safety problems at work and uneven economic geographic development which saw some areas falling behind others. There was also the essentially political problem of maintaining legitimacy of a dominantly capitalist system which did not distribute the fruits of enterprise evenly. In addition there was a feeling among some that, by the end of the 1960s, the force towards integration was losing momentum. Contrary to expectations, the Common Market was not automatically leading to a common community; a more positive social policy was required.

At the 1972 Paris summit agreement was secured for greater vigour in the social field and the result was a resolution by the Council on 21 January 1974 for a concerted social action programme. However, the reality was to fall a long way short of the aspiration: unemployment was not reduced, little progress was made on training policy and the coordination of labour market policies, regulations on working conditions were not enforced and worker participation was resisted in some states. Reasons for failure included insufficient power available to the Commission in the social field and a lack of commitment from member states (particularly Britain after 1979).

In addition there was the world economic slump from the mid-1970s. This not only precipitated unemployment, but it also produced a backlash against social democracy and saw a resurgence of New Right thinking which espoused monetarism as against Keynesianism and looked with suspicion on government social programmes. To resist this, the 1980s saw renewed attempts to rekindle the social dimension, although the phase was to find the United Kingdom, where under the name of Thatcherism the most hard-nosed variant of the neo-liberal vision was to be seen, increasingly isolated.

Again, a key figure was Jacques Delors who had formerly been a socialist finance minister in France. In his opening speech as president of the Commission, he presented the EP with a vision of a Europe which was more than a gigantic market-place; it was also to be a social community. The programme for the completion of the single market by 1992 and the Single European Act which came into force on 1 July 1987 not only committed member states to the single market and EMU, but there were also a range of social goals to mitigate social disruption caused by the restructuring of industry and services.

On 7 September 1988 the Commission adopted a set of detailed programmes to be completed alongside the single market. After considerable debate, including strong opposition from the UK government, the Community Charter of the Fundamental Social Rights of Workers was adopted by the European Council at the Strasbourg summit in December 1989. The lone dissenting voice was that of the United Kingdom. The Social Charter, as it became known, was probably the most significant of the developments in the EC's social dimension (Gold 1993: 10). It was accompanied by a social action programme comprising forty-seven initiatives to be implemented in different ways and at different levels of government. It guaranteed employees certain rights with respect to working hours, pay levels, rates of social security benefits, trade union activity, worker participation, training, sex equality, child protection and support for the aged. In addition to its substantive policy initiatives the Charter also considered the policy-making process, proposing majority voting in the Council over all social initiatives.

The UK dissent was to carry through beyond the Thatcher era to the negotiations around the Maastricht summit. Apart from the United Kingdom, member states wished to continue along the path laid down by the Social Charter. Heralded as another triumph of diplomacy, Major negotiated a special protocol whereby the United Kingdom effectively opted out of what became known as the Social Chapter.

The UK government position

The position of the UK government owes much to its domestic neo-liberal agenda. Crucial to the Thatcherite vision was a de-regulated labour market, and a fusillade of anti-trade union legislation was among the first of the reforms. It was argued that a reduction in wages and other labour costs would make British products more competitive, thereby creating more jobs. Major was to declare, 'Let them have the social chapter, we'll have the jobs.'

There is also an argument that a social policy at Community level conflicts with the subsidiarity principle. Social policies fall within that area of administration that is best left to national governments. Perhaps the darkest fear of the right comes from the belief that the social dimension equates with socialism and is therefore erosive of Thatcher's achievements. The Bruges speech asserted: 'We have not rolled back the frontiers of the state at home only to see them reimposed at a European level.' Finally there is the fear that accepting the social dimension might strengthen the left in domestic politics and give succour to the Labour Party. This is an area where party conflict does exist, Labour pledging itself to adopt the Social Chapter if returned to government.

Problems with the UK government position

In the first place, the 'we'll have the jobs' argument contravenes the idea of fair competition within the Community. The free movement of labour will be restricted without harmonisation of working conditions, social benefits and so on. There is also the danger of 'social dumping' where companies show predilection for areas where workers' rights are less well protected. If low labour costs in Britain draw jobs from the rest of Europe this will be disruptive of the Community spirit and could be politically disruptive. Moreover, there is a fundamental illogicallity in the UK position in that the principles of the Social Chapter are already present in earlier treaties, in the programme for the internal market and the Single European Act, all of which have been signed by the United Kingdom. Since citizenship normally entails the idea of equality, the policy seems in conflict with the idea of European citizenship in the Maastricht Treaty. Finally, constitutionalists are suggesting that the legal basis for the Social Protocol may be questionable.

On the other hand, the results may not prove to be in the United Kingdom's favour at all. This may be the reason that the other eleven are able to live with the Social Protocol. Britain may become a low-wage economy with an unskilled workforce. This may be undesirable in itself in terms of the quality of life of workers. Moreover, and contrary to expectations, the strategy may lose jobs rather than gain them in an increasingly high-tech economic world. Again, low wages, de-regulated working conditions and weak unions may not be enough to attract investment. Firms also consider factors such as roads, railways, telecommunications and educational costs in deciding where to locate. Much UK policy in the 1980s has questioned the state's role in maintaining these.

Finally, social policy becomes another area where the United Kingdom relinquishes any claims to a leadership role. If a subsequent government decides to opt in (as Labour has promised to do) it will be obliged to accept measures over which the United Kingdom has had little influence.

The great sovereignty debate

A further area of debate which can be expected to echo throughout the 1990s springs from various versions of a basic argument that Britain will lose its national sovereignty through entering wholeheartedly into Europe. Federalism, a system of association in which states relinquish sovereignty to a central power, as in the case of the United States, is a word that hardly dare speak its name. Indeed, it was UK opposition that ensured that the unmentionable 'F word' was expunged from the Maastricht Treaty. However, the concept of national sovereignty is by no means as simple as is implied in much political debate. It may be subject to ethical and practical questioning.

The ethical question

In spite of its dominance in international political discourse the centralised modern nation-state is by no means the only way in which people can live or have lived. It is the outcome of a process of evolution which has its origins in Europe. Whatever its merits (the ancient Greeks saw it as the highest form of association), its values of patriotism and national pride are not far away from racism and fascism. Indeed, it has been associated with the horrors of terrible wars. It was to avert the inhuman excesses of nationalism that the movement for European union arose.

Today we live in a world made increasingly tense and threatening. There is the rabid nationalism of Zhirinovsky in Russia, the rise of the Republicans in Germany and the National Front in France, Islamic fundamentalism in the Middle East, Britain's own troubles in Ulster, the emergence of the strong Hindu nationalist party (the BJP) in India and, of course, the tragedy of former Yugoslavia. Hence, despite the end of the cold war, the proliferation of sophisticated weaponry means that international relations are conducted on a knife edge and it is difficult to see how overt nationalism can resolve world tensions.

Moreover, beyond the threat of war a new ecological awareness reveals the human species as one that can only survive if countries subjugate national interest (acid rain, nuclear dumping and so on) to the greater health of the planet. Communications technology reveals to people a gross maldistribution of world resources which nationalistic competition produces. Increasingly international charity movements find it necessary to erode the state boundaries of the old order. The spread of AIDS is a metaphor alerting people to the internationalisation of sorrow and disaster. As the members of the Victorian bourgeoisie discovered that they could not remain healthy while the poor suffered plagues and malnutrition, so the rich nations ignore the plight of the underdeveloped world at their peril. The idea of state sovereignty increasingly appears ethically outmoded.

The practical question

The reality of sovereignty in the modern world is also highly questionable. We may address this in internal and external terms.

Sovereignty within

We may begin by asking where sovereignty lies within the United Kingdom. Constitutionally it is said to lie with Parliament and hence with the people. However, this is largely illusory. The effective sovereignty of Parliament is hijacked by the leaders of the majority party, the prime minister and the Cabinet. This, combined with the powers of the royal prerogative inherited from the Crown bestows a seigneurial authority. Hence it is not the sovereignty of Parliament that is at stake but that of a party-dominated core executive. However, even this interpretation of sovereignty within the state is unsatisfactory. The answer to the question of where real power lies remains elusive and various schools of thought offer theories. Neo-pluralists argue that power is dispersed between various groups and government is little more than a referee. Neo-corporatists look to closed consultative networks, or policy communities, where government shares power with chosen insider groups. Neo-elitists see the formal machinery of the state as a charade, with real power lying in the hands of a web of elite groups sometimes said to form a stratum of society vaguely termed 'the establishment'. Public choice theorists have seen in the state machinery a large empire pursuing its own interests. For the neo-Marxists the formal trappings of government are but a legitimating cloak for a configuration of power based upon a great edifice of capital and finance upon which the modern economy is erected. These various schools are all united in the view that real sovereignty is no simple matter to be resolved by constitutional lawyers.

Hence the lament for the loss of popular sovereignty is simplistic. It may be more accurately seen as a lament for the decline of some class, group or elite within society. Indeed, it is possible to argue that integration within a Europe-wide polity will actually enhance the power of citizens by undermining other power bases.

Beyond the nation-state

Yet the difficulties with the sovereignty argument go even deeper. Regardless of whose hands hold the tiller, the idea that the ship of state is free to chart its own destiny within the modern world is itself highly contestable. Security alliances such as Nato and the UN limit the hallowed right to wage war. Advanced weaponry decreases rather than increases sovereignty because proliferation promises mutual destruction. Moreover, increased technology also gives weapons to internal non-state actors such as the PLO or the IRA. Another development of profound importance is the emergence in the post-war era of the private international corporation. With wealth greater than that of many countries, these leviathans own over half of the fixed assets in the world and lie at the heart of an international power structure. They operate a world economy in which states, anxious to attract investment and secure jobs for ordinary people, must be beholden.

The growth of the international economy has undermined national systems of control. Governments find it increasingly difficult to stimulate employment, control inflation or regulate the money supply. Black Wednesday provided grim evidence of this state impotence. Similarly national labour agreements are undermined by international competition. Thus, paradoxically, the UK rejection of the Social Chapter can be seen not as preserving sovereignty, but as capitulating before multi-national business. In this world, European integration can retrieve autonomy rather than deny it. It can facilitate the renewal of legal and administrative regulatory mechanisms to give some control over the social disruption threatened by global movements of capital (Grahl and Teague 1990: 15).

CONCLUSION: A DECLINING NATION IN A GROWING EUROPE

There is little reason to anticipate that the remainder of the 1990s will produce a lessening of UK difficulties over European integration. Why does the debate seem so endless? Part of the answer may lie in its great imperial past. Despite a xenophobic political culture, Britain has not been isolationist. Imperialism and a long espousal of free trade has made it open to the world. However, this was a world community to be dominated and led rather than joined on equal terms. It has not been easy for the political class, and indeed ordinary citizens, to come to terms with the fact that, since the mid-nineteenth century and particularly during the post-war era, Britain has been a nation in relative decline. The unwillingness to accept the European embrace in the 1950s was the result of the belief that the United Kingdom remained a great power in its own right. Such connections as were cultivated were those with the United States, where a 'special relationship' was believed to exist whereby the United Kingdom could rise on the US coat-tails in world influence, and the British Commonwealth, from which could be heard the echoes of imperial greatness. As sources of world power, both were to prove illusory.

The United Kingdom moves through the 1990s with the ancestral voices sounding it its ears. The Prime Minister presides uneasily over a party marked by a deep fault line which has already forced him to seek a vote of confidence. If the European issue subsides before a general concern over economic recession, Major can expect to be stronger within his party and hence as prime minister. However, if growth in the EC picks up, new integrationist initiatives can be expected (Hutton 1993). This could mean political fireworks for the Conservative Party and for British politics.

Never has a prime minister appeared so much in hock to a vociferous minority within his party. Under Thatcher, fears of prime ministerial government were rife among constitution watchers. Today, as Major basks in the praise of the likes of Norman Tebbit and Thatcher, those who agonised over the rise of presidential-style government in Britain can at least sleep soundly in their beds. Yet many of these figures behind the throne are no longer burnished with the legitimating patina of popular election. The constitution seems scarcely safer than under Thatcher and a party that traditionally laments the impropriety of trade union influence on any possible Labour government should, *mutatis mutandis*, feel uneasy.

This prospect will not cause a moment's loss of sleep to the Euro-sceptics. It will, however, mean a Britain excluded from the key collective decision-making forums. To the Euro-sceptics, still wedded to a world-view of autonomous nation-states, this does not matter. However, in a real world of aggressive economic penetration across national boundaries, footloose multi-national capital and dangerous global flashpoints, with the United States looking increasingly towards Bonn, and France and Germany locked in a warm embrace, an atavistic, nineteenth-century Britain may find itself increasingly ill equipped for survival.

CORE READING

George, S. (1990) *An Awkward Partner*, Oxford: Oxford University Press.
Sampson, A. (1992) *The Essential Anatomy of Britain*, London: Hodder & Stoughton.

ADDITIONAL READING

Brittan, L. (1993) 'Time to retune to EMU harmony', *Financial Times*, 27 October.
Camilleri, J.A. and Falk, J. (1992) *The End of Sovereignty?*, Aldershot: Edward Elgar.
George, S. (1991) *Politics and Policy in the European Union*, Oxford: Oxford University Press.
Gold, M. (ed.)(1993) *The Social Dimension: Employment Policy in the European Community*, Basingstoke: Macmillan.
Grahl, J. and Teague, P. (1990) *1992: The Big Market*, London: Lawrence & Wishart.
Hutton, W. (1993) 'The European train we must not miss', *Guardian*, 1 November.
Nugent, N. (1991) *The Government and Politics of the European Community*, 2nd edn, Basingstoke: Macmillan.
Sargent, J. (1987) 'The organisation of business interests for European Community representation', in Grant, W., *Business and Politics in Britain*, Basingstoke: Macmillan.
Scharpf, F. (1988) 'The joint decision trap: lessons from German federalism and European integration', *Public Administration*, 66: 239–78.
Urwin, D. (1989) *Western Europe since 1945*, 4th edn, London: Longman.
Wallace, W. (1993) 'Britain's search for a new role in the world', *Observer*, 15 August.

4   Local government as a context for policy

John Williamson

INTRODUCTION

It is important to grasp the way in which changes in the wider economic and political contexts have shaped the policy-making agenda. In the economic sphere, with rising unemployment, slow growth and the United Kingdom's inability to compete in increasingly competitive international markets, successive governments from the 1970s onwards found themselves in a new economic context, demanding new solutions and different economic strategies. Similarly the wider political context, itself bound up with changes in the economic context, also changed during this period in terms of new demands, issues and political alignments. The most dramatic and decisive aspect of these changes was the election in 1979 of a government intent on breaking with the consensus around a Keynesian Welfare State political strategy during the post-war period. It is important to recognise what all this meant for the policy process. Policies are never made in a political vacuum; there are changing demands, new policy issues and new political alliances attempting to shape the political agenda to influence what direction policies should take.

This much may seem obvious. What may not be so obvious is why a chapter on local government as a *context* for the policy process is deemed necessary. We would suggest that just as the economic and political context can, and has, placed constraints on certain policy options across a number of policy spheres, so the system of local government, and intergovernmental relations more generally, can act as a constraint on policy choices and challenge the policy intentions of central government departments. In many areas of policy, central government in the post-war period came to depend on the active cooperation of local government in helping to formulate and implement policies. This allowed the consolidation of institutions, professional bodies and service users with a vested interest in certain kinds of policy options and a bias against other options. What this has meant for a government intent on a programme of radical change, of rolling back the frontiers of the state, such as that of successive governments since 1979, is that they are faced with a local government system as a major obstacle to these changes in policy direction. As Allan Cochrane, writing on these changes during the 1980s, put it: 'Local government sometimes assumed a high political profile because it appeared to be an obstacle in the way of broader political change, rather than because it was always a major focus of government attention in its own right' (Cochrane 1992: 15).

The objective of this chapter is, first, to map out the nature of the local government system as it developed in the post-war period. What was the role of local government in the Keynesian Welfare State political consensus, and how did it help to coordinate the development and administration of policies during this period? This will then set the scene for situating the attempts by successive Conservative governments in their strategy of restructuring, diminishing the role of and bypassing the local government system, in their attempt to implement a programme of policies more conducive to a market-liberal economic and political project. We also need to evaluate what these changes have meant for local government and how local government has responded. Finally, after surveying the changes in local government, we need to look at the options open for the future direction of local government. What are the alternatives?

SITUATING LOCAL GOVERNMENT

The development of local government in the post-war period is inextricably bound up with the development of the Welfare State. Hence, while local government lost responsibilities for local hospitals, electricity and gas in the 1940s, and water in the early 1970s, they acquired responsibilities in the growing social policy areas of education, housing and social services. In this sense the growth of local government was closely allied with the development of the Welfare State. What is important to note here, however, is how these changes in the role of local government were instigated from central government, or more specifically by Acts of Parliament. This implies that the development of policies are decided at Westminster, the relevant departments of state are then charged with their implementation and this they do through departmental and subnational bureaucratic structures. Seen in this light, the role of local government has been merely an administrative arm of central government. They have been charged with the implementation of policies decided elsewhere. As Rhodes points out:

> The conventional picture of Britain is of a unitary state, with a single Parliament, government and civil service, deciding on policy for the whole country and applying it throughout the national territory. Local elected councils . . . exist, but these decide only trivial matters such as bye-laws for the use of parks.
>
> (Rhodes 1985: 33)

How accurate a characterisation is this of central–local government relations? Certainly local governments are only allowed to undertake activities delegated to them by central government. Central government has also become financially important in the running of local government. The implications of these observations reinforce the view that policies are decided nationally and then handed down the hierarchy of command to be implemented unquestioningly by local bureaucrats.

In a strict formal constitutional reading of central–local government relations this may be a reasonably correct interpretation; it is, however, also a gross oversimplification of how this relationship has worked in practice. As Rhodes continues after the above passage, 'Almost every assertion made above is misleading' (*ibid.*), and of course anyone with even a superficial knowledge of local government will recognise it is 'misleading'. It would, for instance, be difficult to explain the well-documented conflicts between central and local government if this were the case. This is not to say that an element of hierarchical coordination has not been present in central–local government relations, only that this needs filling out by other determinants to give a fuller more complex picture.

One way in which we can begin to fill out the above hierarchical characterisation of central–local government relations is to ask, why have local government at all if it is merely a means of implementing policies decided by the centre? Surely the *raison d'être* of local government is to allow it to be responsive to the particular needs of often quite distinct local communities. To do this with any kind of effectiveness requires local government having a degree of autonomy from central government. Hence for much of the post-war period most legislation concerning local government was facilitative, giving local government the power to do certain things, but not determining in detail how they should meet their responsibilities. Rather than seeing central–local government relations in terms of hierarchy then, Rhodes suggests that it is better to see them in terms of power and dependency. Both central and local government have resources that the other needs and can use these resources in bargaining over policies. As Rhodes explains:

> it is clear that central government does not exercise effective, detailed control over local authorities. It is more accurate to describe central and local government as inter-dependent. Central government has resources which the local authorities need if they are to achieve their goals. Conversely, local authorities control resources which central government needs.
>
> (Rhodes 1985: 42)

Thus while central government has ultimate control over legislation, and provides expenditure for local government, it is local government that employs staff, many of them working in professions with expert knowledge in particular policy fields. However, what makes local government stand out from other forms of subnational government is the democratic legitimacy of a local mandate and an independent source of finance (*ibid.*: 43).

However, two things should be noted here. First, to say that central–local government relations are interdependent does not mean that they negotiate on equal terms. It is often central government that set the agenda for policy changes. This is difficult for local government to do, given their fragmented nature and lack of unity due to the different political party control of the different councils. Second, it is debatable whether the power dependency model is universally applicable or whether it is only relevant to a period of consensus politics. In other words, we could argue that this characterisation of central–local government relations in terms of partnership was only applicable to a specific period of UK political history – a period when the economic and political contexts facilitated this kind of relationship. However, with changes in these economic and political contexts, this once symbiotic relationship began to break down as central government throughout the 1980s came to see local government as a major obstacle to their wider economic objectives of controlling social expenditure.

However, before we enter into a discussion of these wider contextual changes and their implications for local government, we first need to make our discussion of central–local relations even more determinant and complex.

So far we have been treating the entities of central and local government rather unproblematically. The dispute has been about how we characterise this relationship. However, the view that central government display a necessary unity in dealings with local government needs to be questioned. Similarly, to what extent are there divisions and conflictual interests within local government? And what does this mean for the picture of central–local government relations that we have painted so far?

First, it would be wrong to assume that central government necessarily display a united front in their dealings with local government. Different departments within central government may, and often do, have conflicting interests and press for alternative policies in their dealings with local government. As Gerry Stoker explains:

> In local government expenditure for example, there are, at least, three axes: the Treasury with its broad concern for budget restraint; the spending departments – such as the Ministry of Defence – with little direct interest in local government who may wish to see local government bear the brunt of any cuts; and finally, there are those spending departments with a major interest in local government – such as the Department of the Environment or the Department of Education and Science – who may advocate and seek to protect local spending.
>
> (Stoker 1991: 141)

Nor should we necessarily even see departments as unified entities. Even within departments there can be divisions of interest promoting competing policy options. In this sense, to portray central government as displaying a necessary unity around common concerns and interests is misleading. As Rhodes argues, 'The terms 'central government' and the 'centre' have to be understood . . . as shorthand for a diverse collection of departments and divisions' (Rhodes 1991: 208).

However, it is not only central government which displays this element of diversity but also in their relationship to local government (and other subnational governments in general) we find that there is a complex web of contacts, connections and networks of interests gathered around particular policy areas and cutting across the central–local government dichotomy. Thus in the area of education we could find that Civil Servants from the Department of Education, teachers' representatives, local education authorities' education officers and various interest groups provide the link between central and local government.

Rhodes refers to these networks as policy communities. These are characterised 'by stability of relationships, continuity of a highly restrictive membership, vertical interdependence based on shared service delivery responsibilities and insulation from other networks and invariably from the general public' (Rhodes 1991: 204).

Rhodes offers a more complex picture of central–local government relations than the one we started out with when discussing the view of the unitary state. What we now need to grasp at this stage is what all this means in terms of local government as a context for this policy process. This complexity and fragmentation of intergovernmental relations, coupled with the crystallisation of policy communities on which governments have come to depend in the post-war period, make it difficult for a government to formulate and implement policies without the cooperation of key institutions and actors in these policy networks. This was to prove a major constraint on a government intent on cutting back and restructuring the state, such as the first Thatcher governments of the 1980s. As Rhodes explains, these policy communities were 'a product of the welfare state, they had a vested interest in, and helped to fuel, its continued expansion' (Rhodes 1991: 210–11).

All this is not to suggest that the intergovernmental relations are necessarily fragmented and conflictual. Indeed for much of the post-war period this was not the case, where epithets such as consensus and partnership were used to describe intergovernmental relations and relations within given policy communities. However, to a large extent this was dependent on the wider economic and political context facilitating this. In this sense it was the success of a given political and economic strategy that provided the foundations for an element of unity in intergovernmental relations. As Jessop notes, 'the state comprises a plurality of institutions (or apparatus) and their unity, if any, far from being pre-given must be constructed politically' (Jessop 1982: 222).

LOCAL GOVERNMENT: CONTEXT AND RESTRUCTURING

So far we have concentrated our investigation on the internal functioning of intergovernmental relations in a rather static and formalistic way. We now need to situate this analysis in its wider economic and political contexts to introduce another dimension which should allow us to understand why the problem of local government took on such a high political profile in the 1980s. To do this requires us to look at how central and local governments relate to their particular political environments and the kind of determinants at work in their respective spheres. Again it needs to be emphasised that we are doing this to allow us to grasp with more accuracy how local government as a context for the policy process can prove problematic for a government intent on making a radical change in policy direction.

At the risk of simplification, I would suggest that the Keynesian Welfare State had by the 1970s led to a bifurcation in the functions of the state. While the central government came to be much more concerned with the politics of production such as negotiating with the organisations of business and unions over policies of how to stimulate economic growth, local government was seen as the provider of major aspects of collective welfare such as education, housing, social services and leisure. Another way of putting this is that central government were concerned with economic growth and policies of production, and local government with social expenditure and meeting local collective needs. In the period of Keynesian Welfare State consensus, a political strategy was followed which saw a symbiotic relationship between the two. While economic growth provided the resources for growing expenditure, this social expenditure was in turn seen as beneficial for production by providing a major stimulus to economic demand. Hence Keynesian economic policies legitimated increased social expenditure, much of it channelled through local government (Saunders 1984).

What we need to be clear about here is the political implications of this bifurcation of the concerns of the central and local government. While the political concerns of central government and the major determinants of policy took the form of negotiations with producer and financial interests with a view to managing the economy, local government politicians, to acquire political support, had different concerns, and a different constituency determined their political agenda. The brittleness of this symbiotic relationship was exposed during the 1970s and 1980s as Keynesianism no longer appeared to work; with low growth and falling tax revenues, coupled with demands for extra social expenditure as unemployment increased, the control of public expenditure became a major concern of central government. To limit social expenditure meant reducing local government expenditure. However, as we have seen previously, the chief concerns of local government were different from those of central government. Local communities as an electorate, as well as various pressure groups in and around local government, were more concerned with meeting the social needs of their locality rather than what was happening down in Westminster or the City of London. This was to prove a major problem in controlling local expenditure. As Cochrane makes the case: 'Local politics is . . . difficult to manage from the centre, because it reflects locally generated demands through local democratic institutions (including political parties, community groups and other local interest groups)' (Cochrane 1989: 115).

Already by the late 1970s that partnership between central and local government referred to earlier, was being undermined as local government opposed attempts by central government to reduce local expenditure. However, with the election of Margaret Thatcher in 1979 this problem of central–local government relations was compounded by the introduction of contradictory political objectives. Notions such as partnership were jettisoned as it became abundantly clear that the New Right's political project was totally incompatible with that of many, usually labour-controlled, councils. Indeed by the early 1980s many on the left of British politics looked to local government as a way of promoting more radical values, supporting minority interests and fighting oppression, as well as developing local economic strategies to combat the worst excesses of the recession on their localities. As Mark Goodwin explains:

For the new government, economic regeneration rested on more than mere control of public expenditure. It also depended on the promotion of the belief that free markets are both economically efficient and socially just – and in crucial respects local government stood in the way of such promotion. It was not only a substantial spender of public money, but also a major provider of public services, often allocated collectively, sometimes even on the criteria of social need. Moreover, in some places these services were explicitly provided, usually by Labour-controlled authorities, to offer protection against the putrefying winds of the market, and to mitigate the cut and thrust of commercial rationality.

(Goodwin 1989: 143)

We have now come a long way from the hierarchical view of central–local government relations with which we started. It should be clear why local government (and subnational government more generally) are so important in the policy process, at least in those areas for which local government have some responsibility. It should also be clear why governments, such as those of successive Conservative administrations during the 1980s, intent on making a dramatic turn in political direction and set on initiating a number of radical policy changes, would need to get to grips with this context in an attempt to weaken and marginalise those institutions and groups likely to oppose these changes, and to restructure the local government system to enhance the power and influence of those likely to be supportive of such a programme. What should also be clear from the discussion so far is that this attempt to reorganise and restructure the local government system to make it more amenable to the New Right's economic and political project is not just about the centralisation of power. Certainly this is part of the process, particularly in the area of attempting to control social expenditure. However, the process, like the picture we have painted so far of the local government system, has been, and is, far more complex. From what we have said so far we can isolate three areas where central government in the 1980s attempted to restructure local government to provide an environment within which New Right policies could flourish.

1. *Central–local government relations* These have taken the form of central government using their legislative powers to reduce the autonomy of local government. Compulsory competitive tendering, the right to buy council houses, and the national curriculum are examples of this process of central government specifying in more detail what local authorities can do.
2. *Institutional and policy network relations* While central–local government relations are concerned with establishing vertical lines of command to make local government more amenable to central control, there have also been attempts by central government to shift power vertically by downgrading certain institutions, policy communities and groups within policy communities, and upgrading the influence of others, who are seen as being more supportive of central government policy endeavours.
3. *Restructuring local government–community relations* The emphasis here is

concerned with changing the parameters of local government relations with their community. First, there is the delivery and administration of services. As we will see, an important element of restructuring here has been to make the providers of services improve their efficiency and make them more responsive to consumers by the introduction of market competition. This is another strand in central government's attempts to prise open what are seen as unaccountable professional networks. Another important area of concern for central government is to transmute the demands coming from local communities. A key strategy here has been to alter the way in which local taxes have been raised. As we will see, one of the major objectives of the introduction of the community charge (or poll tax) was to make the connection between the payment and level of services clearer. In other words, by spreading the tax net wider, more people would come to realise that if they, or others, wanted a service, they would be expected to pay higher local taxes. This, it was assumed, would act to stifle electoral majorities and pressure groups from channelling their demands onto local government. Thus there would be electoral majorities, it was expected, in favour of reducing local taxes and local services, particularly for minority groups and causes, hence undermining the power base of left-wing authorities.

The above is not to assume that the Conservative government elected in 1979 came into power with some well-thought-out strategic plan for local government. Rather, we witnessed during the 1980s a strategic battle taking place as different interests attempted to out-manoeuvre their opponents and tilt the political agenda to their own advantage. Local governments, certain policy communities and sections of policy communities looked for ways to circumvent the radical implications of those policies emanating from the centre, central government in turn looking at alternative tactics to overcome the intransigence of those opposed to their policies.

LOCAL GOVERNMENT AFTER 1979

It would be wrong to say that changes in local government began with the election of the Thatcher government in 1979. During the 1970s, attempts were introduced to reform and modernise local government through the creation of larger authorities and the introduction of corporate management. However, the consequence of these reforms was to make authorities more bureaucratic and impersonal for service users and those employed within them. Then during the mid-1970s in the wake of a world recession, the Labour government turned their energies towards curtailing public expenditure, targeted local authority spending and introduced a regime of cash limits to ensure that spending was kept within tight limits. The above changes, coupled with the government's attempts to maintain a pay policy in the public sector, culminated in the 'Winter of Discontent' as public sector workers went on strike, discrediting the Labour government's supposed partnership with the trade unions and leading directly to a Conservative victory in 1979.

In this sense the claim that 1979 marked a radical watershed in the development of local government could be challenged. After all, it was Labour who made cuts in public expenditure, introduced cash limits and attempted to enhance the influence of policy communities concerned with managerial and financial rectitude. However, there was a major difference between governments prior to 1979 and subsequent Conservative governments: the strong, principled, ideological stance against what Conservative governments believed were the failings of local government as they had developed in the post-war period, a belief they derived from their more general philosophical distrust of the public sector.

The extent of the required reforms to restructure local government were of such magnitude, given the government's belief in the need for structural changes and the entrenched hold of producer interests, meant that any notion of consultations and negotiations seemed pointless. In this sense it was not just what the government did (and it must be said that some of the reforms were radically different), but also how they set about doing it, that sets them apart from previous governments. As Rhodes argues, during the 1980s the consultation style in central–local government relations of the post-war period was replaced by a centralised, hierarchical and authoritarian style. Rhodes says of the 1980s:

> As relations between the two sides have deteriorated so there has been marked changes in behaviour. Successive secretaries of state for the environment have adopted a unilateral style of decision making and the more consultative mode of proceeding has been forsaken.
>
> (Rhodes 1985: 62)

During the 1980s we had a run of Conservative governments in control of central government, committed to a political strategy of breaking with the post-war political consensus around a belief in the efficacy of the Keynesian Welfare State, and this required restructuring a set of institutions and their associated interests which had crystallised and consolidated areas of influence during the post-war period.

What is important for us to grasp at this juncture is that attempts to restructure the local government system were a central and essential aspect of the Conservatives' political project. Only by changing the institutional parameters of the policy process could New Right policies in education, housing and community care be realised, as well as helping to meet their wider concerns in restructuring the economy and building a durable body of support for their reforms.

The success of the Conservatives in winning four successive elections has given them the continuity of office to undertake a sustained strategy of restructuring the local government system. Given the scale and comprehensive nature of the reforms introduced makes it extremely difficult to encapsulate easily the different dimensions of these changes. One way of grasping these changes is in terms of centralisation and privatisation. By centralisation we mean central government curtailing the autonomy of local government in what they are allowed to do. There has been an increase in legislation detailing more tightly the responsibility of local government. The privatisation element is based on the New

Right conviction that, outside the few limited situations of market failure, the private sector is more efficient and user-responsive than the public sector. This does not mean merely transferring assets from the public to the private sector. Privatisation in the sense used here can also mean that, to the extent that private ownership is not possible, the public sector should be made to take on some of the characteristics of the private sector. This may mean introducing management structures and strategies from the private sector, altering the culture of local government to allow it to be run much more on the lines of a business. However, it is an assumption of the New Right that what really has distinguished private from public organisations in the post-war period has been the environment within which they have operated. It is the lack of stimulus provided by market competition that has allowed public monopolies to grow fat, lacking efficiency and becoming unresponsive to users. So another strand in recent reforms has been the political construction of administered or internal markets.

Another dimension of this privatisation strategy has been the increase in business interests in the development and implementation of policies. In some cases this has taken place through the process of transferring power from local government to non-elected quangos where business interests are invariably well represented. In other cases it has meant local authorities forming some kind of partnership with the private sector to realise certain objectives.

Overall, however, what we witnessed during the 1980s was a secretion of power away from policy communities dominated by state professions to policy communities dominated by business interests.

Although we have characterised the reforms introduced into local government during the past fourteen years in terms of centralisation and privatisation, we need to realise that they are moments of the same process. Thus the centralisation of powers has been necessary to implement policies of privatisation. It is also important to re-emphasise that these reforms were not the outcome of some blueprint, some grand design. While the Conservative governments, or more correctly their dominant faction, were committed to a radical restructuring of local government, and it was this that gave these reforms a sense of direction and purpose, the reforms themselves came about through a process of trial and error. They had to be constantly concerned with what was possible, given the political and economic context. This meant garnering support for their reforms while isolating opposition. At least until the introduction of the community charge, governments certainly showed some tactical expertise in this project.

What is important for us to grasp at this point is that attempts to restructure local government were an essential dimension of the broader New Right political project. Only by changing the institutional parameters could radical changes in education, housing, community care and its wider economic concerns be realised.

LOCAL EXPENDITURE

Probably the dominant strand of the first Thatcher government in their dealings with local government was the centralisation of control over local expenditure.

The Local Government Planning and Land Act (1980) introduced a new block grant where the needs of local government were determined by central government. From 1980 any authority that increased expenditure in excess of a centrally imposed target would bring a penalty in the form of a reduction in this central grant. When some councils, despite these penalties, continued to increase rates, central government introduced 'rate capping' in England and Wales in 1984. This again meant a loss of local government autonomy as now central government set a maximum rate for councils and penalised those that tried to increase rates above this level.

There was also during the 1980s an increase in specific grants, that is grants ear-marked for a particular use. As Travers points out:

> In the mid 1970s, specific grants made up 9 percent of central government grants to local authorities: by 1979/80 this percentage had grown to over 16 percent. In the 1987/88 rate support grant settlement, specific grants accounted for about 26 percent of total grants.
>
> (Travers 1987: 20)

Again this can be seen as a further curtailment on local government autonomy in responding to local needs as they deemed necessary. Central government could target resources to areas that they favoured, under terms they defined.

This, of course, is an example of restructuring the relations between central and local government by centralising control over expenditure. The other major strand of the Conservative government's strategy was an attempt to restructure the relations between local government and their communities. The centrepiece of this change was the attempted reform of the rate system by the introduction of a community charge, or poll tax. Under the rates system, local finance was raised by householders paying rates in proportion to the rateable value of their property. This meant that the number who paid rates was limited to the heads of households and generally those in more expensive property paid higher rates.

The main criticism of the rates system from the New Right was that those who paid lower rates, or even no rates at all, were encouraged to elect councils promising extra resources for their particular needs, secure in the knowledge it would be other rate-payers who would have to foot the bill. Hence the poll tax was intended to curtail local government profligacy by making a more direct link between consumption of services and the payments for them. In short, this restructuring of local government–community relations was intended to alter the perception of local government citizens. They were to be transmogrified into consumers rather than citizens expecting services as a right. As Kingdom points out, 'everyone would pay the same for services in the way that they did for cauliflower or bread and it would promote greater local accountability since more voters would be paying for the consequences of their choices' (Kingdom 1991: 182). However, at the same time, presumably in case some local communities did not realise what their best interests were and elected high-spending councils, central government continued with rate capping or, as it was renamed, community-charge capping. This was another example of the centralisation of power, as were the changes introduced into the non-domestic rates (NDR). In future NDR, or business rates, were set by central government, then collected and distributed by central government to local authorities in a formula based on population size.

These reforms of local finance proved to be a tactical blunder and led, it is argued, to the fall of Thatcher. Previous reforms had been introduced by taking sectional interests on one at a time after first isolating them in terms of potential areas of support. For once a reform was introduced that was likely to hurt a majority of the population, including many Conservative voters.

The political backlash against the poll tax led to its replacement by a new council tax. This meant a partial return to the rates system, whereby the tax is levied on property, but then adjusted to take account of the number of people living in the property.

COMPULSORY COMPETITIVE TENDERING

In the financing of local government, central government have attempted to reduce the autonomy of local government. In other areas too, central government have used their powers to restructure local government and weaken those groups that were likely to be hostile to their economic and political project. One such area is the introduction of compulsory competitive tendering (CCT). In place of services being provided by the local authority through their own employees, these services are now put out to competitive tendering, allowing private companies to bid for the contract. By 1989 these services included construction, building and highway maintenance, refuse collection, cleaning buildings and streets, catering, and ground maintenance. Other areas were subsequently added to the list, such as street lighting, management of leisure services, professional and technical services (Elcock 1993: 159).

This was privatisation in at least two senses. First, to the extent that private companies won the contracts, it meant that private organisations would replace public organisations. Second, it introduced an element of market competition. Thus even if the contract was awarded internally to a local government agency, the economic imperatives of market competition would mean a change in its mode of operation. In particular it would mean local government services having to increase their efficiency by reducing costs in areas such as pay and conditions of their workforce. As Walsh argues the point, CCT 'has the virtue of forwarding a number of different government policy objectives. It provides more work for the private sector, it reduces the power of the local authority and it weakens the public sector trade unions (Walsh 1989: 52).

HOUSING

Privatisation was also used to launch an assault on other monoliths of the post-war Welfare State. In housing the most vivid example was the sale of council houses contained in the 1980 Housing Act. This 'right to buy' meant a transfer of assets from the public to the private home-owning sector. By 1990 over a million properties had been sold to tenants, usually accompanied by favourable discounts off the price. While council properties were being sold off, capital expenditure on new public housing was cut, thus ensuring a diminution of the local authority housing stock. In short, local authorities would in future be managing a smaller and generally non-saleable deteriorating stock.

Another strand to this strategy of housing privatisation during the early 1980s was changes in the system of subsidies. Again it was central government that strengthened their role in determining how subsidies were to be calculated. By 1984 this meant, in effect, for a majority of councils no subsidy at all, with the consequence of large rent increases. During the Conservatives' first term of office, rents increased by 64 per cent in real terms.

After their election victory in 1987 the Conservatives, with the 'right to buy' scheme running out of steam, introduced another package of policies in an attempt to make an even greater inroad into public housing. Often referred to as de-municipalisation, it meant a transfer of whole estates from the public to the private sector. The 1988 Housing Act introduced a scheme called the 'Tenants Choice'. This meant that if a prospective new landlord was interested in acquiring a council estate, a ballot of tenants would be held to decide whether they would stay with the council or transfer to the new landlord. The rules governing the ballot procedures, however, again displayed an unusual lack of confidence in what the government felt were the obvious benefits of the private sector. Fifty per cent of those eligible to vote had to vote against for the sale to be thwarted. In effect, abstainees were counted as in favour of the transfer.

This form of privatisation is different from the 'right to buy' strategy. Instead of encouraging home ownership, it rather attempts to stimulate the private rented sector at the expense of the public rented sector. And again, just in case council tenants are reluctant to make the correct decision of leaving council control, the 1989 Local Government and Housing Act introduced a new financial framework preventing councils subsidising rents from the general rate fund, the consequence being rising rents and a further stimulus to prise people out of the public sector. Indeed by the 1990s it is increasingly the case that only people on Income Support are in the financial position to rent council property, and this is because they have their rents paid for them.

What we have witnessed in housing, then, is privatisation in the transfer of assets from the public to the private sector, and second, the attempt to cut back on subsidies in the remaining public sector to introduce market rents. Indeed any new money on housing has usually bypassed local government and has been filtered through housing associations. As Stoker points out: 'Housing associations are the Government's preferred policy instrument for providing housing in the socially rented sector and most new money for housing has been directed towards them' (Stoker 1991: 215).

EDUCATION AND SOCIAL SERVICES

Other areas of local government have similarly seen radical and far-reaching changes. In education the devolution of responsibilities to schools through local management of schools, schools opting out of local authority control and the attempts to promote city technology colleges have all undermined the ability of local education authorities to plan the delivery of education to their community. The introduction of a national curriculum has also, albeit in a different way, curtailed local authorities' and the teaching profession's autonomy. But these reforms are not just about transferring power, they are also about changing the culture of those who work in public organisations. Hence the introduction of devolved budgets to schools and the size of these budgets being determined by the number of children that the school attracts, means that school heads have found themselves increasingly taking on the mantle of managers concerned with financial flows and marketing their products.

Similarly in the social service departments following the introduction of the 1990 Community Care Act, some social workers have become social care 'managers', again making use of devolved budgets to buy packages of welfare through entering contracts with various providers of services in the public, commercial and voluntary sectors.

We could multiply these examples, but enough has been said to give a flavour of recent changes in and around local government to realise that these reforms are attempts to change the culture and ethos of local government institutions to bring them more into line with private organisations.

THE FUTURE OF LOCAL GOVERNMENT

From even this relatively brief overview we can see that there have been major changes in the structure and role of local government since the 1970s. Indeed the changes are so fundamental that the language, concepts and ways in which we have previously characterised local government may be theoretically redundant. Even the use of the term 'local government' may no longer be suitable as more and more policy decisions and modes of implementation at local level are channelled through non-local government agencies.

So where are local governments going? What shape are they likely to take in the future? Or have they a future at all? To conclude this chapter we will attempt to answer these questions by critically evaluating some possible scenarios.

The enabling authority

To the accusation that the changes in local government during the last decade have meant a virtual end to local government responding to their communities' needs, has come the response that although local governments have changed, they may have changed for the better; or at least recent reforms promise a golden opportunity for local governments to take on a wider strategic governmental role. Local governments will no longer be the sole providers of services in a locality. They will increasingly have to work through other agencies, either through contracts or some form of partnership. But where is the harm in this? As long as the services are provided, does it really matter which organisations provide them?

Indeed, for supporters of an enabling authority this will free local governments from these responsibilities and allow them to take on a more overall strategic role in responding to the changing needs of local communities. In short, community needs may be met in a number of ways, making use of a plurality of organisations, but local governments would still have an important coordinating governmental role (Brooke 1989).

One problem with this vision of an enabling authority is that it tends to downplay the devolution of power which many recent changes in local government were supposedly intended to bring about. It suggests that there will be a strategic elite of key decision-makers with little space for public participation.

A more public-participatory form of an enabling authority has been widely advocated by John Stewart (1989). He too feels that some of the recent changes occurring in local government could provide new opportunities. However, Stewart tends to stress the devolution of power and the need for structures that will facilitate more active participation in the form that services will take in an attempt to avoid the more hierarchical mode of coordination which was a hallmark of local government–community relations for much of the post-war period. For Stewart then, the more strategic role of local government, when wedded with structures that encourage more service-user participation, is an option that local government could, and in his view should, take.

While supporters of an enabling-authority future provide a welcome antidote for those pessimistic determinists who have been forecasting the demise of local government, it could be argued that they suffer from an excess of the other extreme – optimistic idealism.

There are few signs that local governments are likely to have the power, resources or political space to undertake the role of an enabling authority, certainly as envisaged by John Stewart. Central government have over the past decade curtailed the functions, cut the resources and constrained the decision-making powers of local government. This merely highlights the fact that local government cannot be seen in isolation from the wider structures of social and economic change. This problem of over-optimism is given particular credence if we look at the changing role of local government in relation to collective consumption.

Local government and the Welfare State

As we have had occasion to mention, the development and recent changes in local government have been inextricably bound up with changes in the Welfare State. Many of the recent changes we have discussed in relation to local government have also been examples of restructuring the Welfare State. So what are the changes likely to mean for local government and the communities they serve? One view promoted by supporters of these reforms is that they will promote more efficient, consumer-responsive services, offering greater freedom of choice in terms of how individuals and families meet their needs.

The introduction of internal markets, devolution of agency budgets and the decentralisation of decision-making will ensure more flexible, user-friendly services.

To opponents of these reforms, the above characterisation is to view these reforms through rose-tinted spectacles. What these reforms will actually introduce is a two-tier Welfare State. Those who have the money, the contacts and the right credentials will have some choice, while those lacking these attributes will not. And as the quality of public services deteriorate, or those public institutions that are 'unsuccessful' in internal markets find their resources dwindling, those consumers who have the choice will increasingly opt out of the public sector, or at least out of local government control. The consequences are likely to be that local authorities will be charged with controlling marginalised sections of society who do not have these choices. Politically, Jessop (1982: 244) has referred to this as a two-nation strategy, producing a two-thirds/one-third society.

However, while the strategy of a two-nation politics of support may have had some success in maintaining the Conservatives in power during the 1980s, it could be argued that it is doubtful whether it can do this through the 1990s. As more and more areas of society come under the vicissitudes of markets, unemployment, the threat of unemployment, deteriorating working conditions and general anxiety about the future affect more and more people. This is not the foundation for carving out an enduring body of support for future governments.

Local government and private enterprise

At the same time that local governments are being stripped of many of their welfare functions, some authors see them taking on a rather different role in relation to economic policies. As Alan Cochrane argues:

> if the post-war settlement was one which sought to incorporate the working class and its organisations, that of the 1980s, arising from the crisis of social democracy which characterised the 1970s, is one which starts from the needs of business and its organisations. At the local level it implies the arrival . . . of business as an active participant in the political process.
>
> (Cochrane 1991: 292)

The impetus for the increasing involvement of business has a number of sources. A central government committed to nurturing an enterprise culture has been important. But local authorities, often Labour-controlled at that, have also taken the initiative as they have attempted to combat the worst effects of recession and the accompanying industrial restructuring. Indeed in much of the discourse around social problems it is increasingly argued that the problems are related to the decline of local economies; to tackle this decline requires economic regeneration, and the best institutions to lead this regeneration are those representing business interests.

A host of bodies representing business interests in the community have burgeoned forth during the 1980s. In education and training, business interests have become more involved in curriculum matters and resourcing; the governing bodies of the independent new universities and colleges have business interests well represented. The local training and enterprise councils which channel public funds into education are made up largely of business interests. In planning and economic renewal we have a host of bodies representing business interests taking over responsibilities from local councils. The urban development corporations, 'Business in the Community' and other initiatives, often in partnership with other public bodies, have come to predominate in local economic policies (Eisenschitz and Gough 1993). This has been facilitated by the fact that dialogue between public and private management has become much easier with the adoption of a more managerial culture in local authorities, which has its root in private management initiatives.

In a sense there is also an economic imperative at work here. As markets become more central to economic coordination, and as public resources dry up, local authorities themselves, if they are to continue providing for their communities' needs, have to enter into competition to attract businesses and investment to their locality by creating a welcoming environment.

If we link the above changes with our earlier observations we could make a case that, in future, local governments will be less concerned with providing universal welfare services and more concerned with coping with a residualised Welfare State and controlling a potentially disruptive underclass. Second, it will be the case that business interests will play a far more active and structural role in local politics.

CONCLUSION

This chapter has argued the case for seeing local government as a context for the policy process. This context, however, should not be seen in isolation from the changes in the wider economic and political contexts which are the concerns of other chapters. In particular we have seen during the 1970s a fragmentation of the consensus politics of the post-war Keynesian Welfare State and the institutions associated with it. Subsequent governments through the 1980s and into the 1990s have attempted to use this opportunity to restructure local government to make it more amenable to a market-liberal political economy.

As we have seen, the restructuring has had a number of dimensions. In central–local government relations, central government have become more assertive in their strategy of curtailing the autonomy of local government. This centralisation of power has then been used to restructure local politics by shifting power away from certain institutions and their associated policy networks which had their roots in the post-war political consensus, towards institutions and policy networks more supportive of a market-liberal political project. Often this has meant new non-elected bodies outside local government control. To a great extent this means that local governments will have to learn to live with an increasing number of non-elected public and private bodies. In short, local politics has become more fragmented. This restructuring in turn has meant changes in local government–community relations in an attempt to move away from a democratic collectivist form of service delivery and accountability and its associated values of community and citizenship. In its place, service delivery and accountability through markets have become more central. Citizens are viewed much more in terms of individual consumers than they are as members of local communities.

The above characterisation is not intended to undervalue the many initiatives introduced by local governments in their attempts to forge more democratic participatory institutional networks between local authorities and community groups. But the terrain, in terms of broader economic political changes, means that they are often doing this in an increasingly difficult environment. However, this terrain is not set in concrete; the future of local government is not predetermined. There are other alternatives where local government could play a more pro-active role in meeting social needs and in restructuring local economies. Indeed it could be suggested that Britain is very much out of step with most other industrial countries where more responsibility for responding to social needs are being devolved to local communities (Cooke 1990: 116) and where they are taking on a more pro-active and strategic role in economic rejuvenation (*ibid.*: 163–8).

Finally, and to return to an earlier theme, in future, as local politics becomes more fragmented and pluralistic, we may need to invent new concepts in our analyses of local government: in short, a new language for local politics in 'new times' (Hall and Jacques 1989).

CORE READING

Butcher, H., Law, I., Leach, R. and Mullard, M. (1981) *Local Government and Thatcherism*, London: Routledge.

Cochrane, A. (1991) 'The changing state of local government: restructuring for the 1980s', *Public Administration* 69(3).

Cochrane, A. and Anderson, J. (eds) (1989) *Politics in Transition*, London: Sage.

Farnham, D. and Horton, S. (eds) (1993) *Managing the New Public Services*, London: Macmillan.

Kingdom, J. (1991) *Local Government and Politics in Britain*, London: Philip Allan.

Stewart, J. and Stoker, G. (eds) (1989) *The Future of Local Government*, London: Macmillan.

Stoker, G. (1991) *The Politics of Local Government*, 2nd edn, London: Macmillan.

ADDITIONAL READING

Bennington, J. (1976) *Local Government Becomes Big Business*, London: Community Development Project.

Boddy, M. and Fudge, C. (eds) (1984) *Local Socialism*, London: Macmillan.

Brooke, R. (1989) *Managing the Enabling Authority*, London: Longman.

Cochrane, A. (1989) 'Restructuring the state: the case of local government', in Cochrane, A. and Anderson, J. (eds) *Politics in Transition*, London: Sage.

Cochrane, A. (1992) 'Running local government', *Running the Country*, D212 Unit 20, Milton Keynes: Open University.

Cockburn, C. (1977) *The Local State: Management of Cities and People*, London: Pluto Press.

Cooke, P. (1990) *Back to the Future*, London: Unwin Hyman.

Eisenschitz, A. and Gough, J. (1993) *The Politics of Local Economic Policy*, London: Macmillan.

Elcock, H. (1993) 'Local government', in Farnham, D. and Horton, S. (eds) *Managing the New Public Services*, London: Macmillan.

Goodwin, M. (1989) 'The politics of locality', in Cochrane, A. and Anderson, J. (eds) *Politics in Transition*, London: Sage.

Gyford, J. (1991) *Citizens, Consumers and Councils*, London: Macmillan.

Hall, S. and Jacques, M. (eds) (1989) *New Times*, London: Lawrence & Wishart.

Hoggett, P. (1991) 'A new management in the public sector', *Public Administration* 69(4).

Jessop, B. (1982) *The Capitalist State*, Oxford: Martin Robertson.

Offe, C. (1984) *Contradictions of the Welfare State*, London: Hutchinson.

Rhodes, R.A.W. (1985) 'Intergovernmental relations in the United Kingdom', in Meny, Y. and Wright, V. (eds) *Centre–Periphery in Western Europe*, London: George Allen & Unwin.

Rhodes, R.A.W. (1991) 'Policy networks and sub-national government', in Thompson, G., Frances, J., Levacic, R. and Mitchell, J. (eds) *Markets, Hierarchies and Networks*, London: Sage.

Saunders, P. (1984) 'Rethinking local politics', in Boddy, M. and Fudge, C. (eds) *Local Socialism*, London: Macmillan.

Stewart, J. (1989) 'A future for local authorities as community government', in Stewart, J. and Stoker, G. (eds) *The Future of Local Government*, London: Macmillan.

Travers, T. (1987) 'Current spending', in Parkinson, M. (ed.) *Reshaping Local Government*, Hermitage: Policy Journals.

Walsh, K. (1989) 'Competition and service in local government', in Stewart, J. and Stoker, G. (eds) *The Future of Local Government*, London: Macmillan.

5   Economic policy options

Maurice Mullard

INTRODUCTION

There are a number of general statements that can be made about the state of the UK economy and the options that will be available for the UK governments during the 1990s. The Chancellor Kenneth Clark implicitly accepted in both his budget speeches of November 1993 and 1994 that UK unemployment will not fall below 2.7 million for the foreseeable future and that the prospects for economic growth and increases in living standards will be slower than those experienced in the mid-1980s. Unemployment will continue to be of major concern for most of the industrialised world; unemployment in the OECD area has now reached 35 million (8.5 per cent), while in the EU there are now 18 million people unemployed. Reducing UK unemployment will in future years depend on the prospects of the wider international context. Second, the decision to leave the ERM and the subsequent devaluation of sterling might have reduced the costs of exports but a best-hope forecast for a growth rate of 2 to 3 per cent during the 1990s is not likely to have much impact on unemployment and living standards. Furthermore, the competitive advantage gained through devaluation might only be of a short-term duration – improved competitiveness in future years will depend more on long-term investment in capital goods, education and training.

Alongside the problem of unemployment is the concern of how to deal with the UK budget deficit. Although the chancellor, during the November 1993 budget, did outline a strategy that seeks to balance the budget by the year 1998, unemployment is likely to persist, which means that the government will continue to have a problem in funding the public sector deficit through reductions in public expenditure. The prediction is that the social security budget will continue to increase at 3 per cent per annum and that it is likely to increase from £76 billion to about £93 billion by the year 2000. The proportion of GDP going to social security will increase from 12.3 per cent to 13.5 per cent (HMSO 1993). On the basis that the global sum for public expenditure will not change (£260 billion) because of the constraint of the deficit, the government will only be able to fund the increases in social security by higher taxes, by reducing expenditure elsewhere or by reforming the social security system itself. Bill Robinson, a former director of the Institute of Fiscal Studies and special adviser to the former

Chancellor Norman Lamont, describes the challenges of the social security system as follows:

> There is a commitment to pay benefits to all who meet the qualifying conditions . . . If the numbers prove greater than estimated we have (in Treasury jargon) as irresistible bid, and spending threatens to rise above target. However, total spending is subject to cash limits. So in theory, when social security spending rises other elements in the budget must be cut back . . . The inexorable growth of social security is a prime reason why the government has continually to choose between making swingeing cuts in important programmes and failing to control spending.
>
> (Robinson, 1993)

At present it is estimated that about 40 per cent of the public sector deficit can be attributed to discretionary expenditures, that is expenditures that the government committed during the 1992 election and which included additional expenditures for health, education and infrastructure. These 'discretionary' expenditure commitments have to be contrasted with the expenditures that are recession-related and which have been estimated to explain another 40 per cent of the budget deficit. The strategy of the government to reduce the deficit includes new additional taxes such as VAT on fuel, National Insurance contributions and reducing mortgage tax relief. It is estimated that the budgets of April 1993 and November 1993 have increased the tax burden by approximately £17 billion. In the meantime, the government hopes to reduce the deficit through economic growth and a decline in unemployment. The Public Spending Borrowing Requirement (PSBR) forecast of £50 billion for 1994 has now been revised downwards to £19 billion which would suggest that, with the increases in taxes, the PSBR will fall to below 3 per cent of GDP by 1997, thus allowing room for both tax reductions and lower interest rates.

However, the challenges of unemployment and the public sector deficit can no longer be discussed within the context of the UK economy; the options available to UK governments will in future years be more restricted when compared to the room that was available to governments during the post-war years. Reducing taxes to boost demand does not present a real option when the United Kingdom is faced with a large public sector and also a trade deficit. UK economic prosperity seems to depend on export-led growth which implies making the UK economy more competitive in terms of unit labour costs and increased productivity – the problem is that the major economies of Europe are also experiencing recession and lower levels of economic growth.

EXCHANGE RATE POLICY: THE UK AND THE FUTURE OF THE ERM

Market liberals and monetarist economists argued against the decision by the UK government to become a member of the ERM in 1990, emphasising that the decision represented intervention in the workings of markets dealing with currencies exchanges. However, it would be misleading to assume that the ERM debate reflected competing views of market liberals and Keynesian economists. For example, J.M. Keynes himself had in April 1930 argued that the UK depression had been influenced by depression in the international trade cycle and advocated that the currency needed to be devalued. The United Kingdom had returned to the gold standard in 1925 which had pushed up costs of the currency and made UK exports more expensive. The government devalued eventually in 1935. Likewise, in 1992, the UK government decided to leave the ERM and allowed sterling to float.

The United Kingdom joined in October 1990, a difficult policy decision for the then Chancellor John Major who decided to join against the advice of Margaret Thatcher. Thatcher was against any proposal that she saw as diminishing her government's total sovereignty over monetary and exchange rate policy. During the first Thatcher decade, sterling had been devalued by 15 per cent. Nigel Lawson in 1986 decided to abandon Geoffrey Howe's monetary strategy and replaced this with an exchange rate policy. Tim Congdon argued at the time that this was a major policy shift for the government:

> As Treasury ministers and officials meet at Chevening this weekend (9 January 1986) to discuss Budget strategy, their main problem is less economic than moral. They must decide whether, having sinned, they should enjoy it or repent. There can be no doubt that, according to the strict canon of the monetarist creed to which they were once so committed, they have sinned. In the year to December sterling M3 rose by 15 per cent, far ahead of the top end of the government's original target of 5 to 9 per cent growth. In his mansion house last October (1985) Nigel Lawson reacted to the overshoot by suspending the sterling M3 target band, claiming that this measure of the money stock gave a misleading guide to monetary condition.
>
> (Congdon 1993: 123)

In contrast, Lawson argued that the shadowing of the Deutschmark was the necessary discipline to control inflation:

> the Louvre Accord of February 1987 created a framework which for the first time made a policy of exchange rate stability credible. My decision to take advantage of this and to embark on a period of what later became known as 'shadowing the Deutschmark' arose from my desire to put a floor under sterling. Shadowing the Deutschmark (and nudging up interest rates when I had an opportunity to do so) provided both a welcome period of exchange rate calm in the run-up to the election, and a practical demonstration of sterling's ability to keep station with the Mark.
>
> (Lawson 1992: 731)

The decision to join the EMS in October 1990 reflected a bad decision made at the wrong time for the wrong reasons. The United Kingdom joined the ERM when sterling was overvalued against the Deutschmark by at least 10 to 15 per cent; this made UK exports more expensive and led to a sharp fall in exports and also high interests to maintain the value of sterling within the ERM. The United

Kingdom left the ERM on Wednesday 16 September 1992. The policy of Chancellor Kohl on German unification led to increases in public expenditure and increases in the German deficit. To control this deficit the Bundesbank had to use interest rates, which meant that there was a move away from the dollar and sterling to the Deutschmark. Inside the ERM the United Kingdom had to maintain high interest rates despite the fact that Britain was entering a recession where high interest rates were making the recession worse. However, UK inflation had fallen from 10 per cent in 1990 to 3.5 per cent in September 1992, while in the meantime GDP had also fallen by 3 per cent alongside rising unemployment. Unemployment increased from 1.8 million in 1990 to 2.9 million in October 1992. The United Kingdom then had a problem of debt overhang – where the high ratio of consumer debt meant that consumers became more averse to return to spending even when interest rates started to fall.

Inside the ERM, the high exchange rate made the United Kingdom less competitive – leaving the ERM and allowing sterling to depreciate by 15 per cent have reduced the costs of UK exports. However, the advantage of devaluation may only be of a short-term duration since devaluation also brings new risks of inflation – as the costs of imports increase, businesses and workers seek to compensate for the increase in costs through higher prices and higher wage demands. The United Kingdom was lucky in that the devaluation took place during the recession and importers felt unable to pass the costs to the consumers in higher prices. However, the decision to increase interest rates after September 1994 confirms the government's continuing fear of inflation despite the persistently high levels of unemployment and low wage settlements.

UNEMPLOYMENT: CAUSES AND CURES

The years of the Thatcher government were associated with supply-side economics and the attempt to 'reform' the supply part of the equation as related to labour markets. The government outlined a policy agenda that seemed to be consistent with market-liberal held views on the need to de-regulate the labour market and reduce labour costs. This approach suggested removing rigidities from the labour markets as a means of lowering unemployment. Such rigidities included the power of trade unions and their ability to restrict labour supply, thus increasing the wages of the trade union sector. The unemployed were described as suffering from the 'Australia factor' since they were unable to influence wage rates. The Thatcher governments, through various trade union reforms, argued that the labour market would be made more flexible and therefore more responsive to the supply and demand factors. The percentage of the workforce belonging to trade unions reached a peak of 52 per cent during the period from 1976 to 1979 when the Labour government introduced the closed shop but, since 1981 after a number of trade union reforms and also long periods of unemployment, trade union membership in the United Kingdom has fallen to below 40 per cent of the workforce.

The government also sought to transform the climate of pay bargaining by removing institutions that influenced pay in the public sector including pay review bodies and other comparability agreements. Furthermore wage councils agreements which covered some 2.5 million workers were also abolished. Wage settlements have continued to fall during the 1980s and 1990s. While in the 1980s annual settlements averaged 7.5 per cent of annual earnings, in the early 1990s they had fallen further to 3.75 per cent, the lowest figure for twenty-five years. Indeed, according to David Metcalfe:

> Pay setting institutions have certainly been transformed: fewer workers are in collective agreements, bargaining is decentralised, the century-old tradition of 'the rate for the job' has been ruptured, fair wage resolutions and comparability machinery have been withdrawn, there is greater sensitivity to the fortunes of the company and the performance of the individual. The government and their acolytes have achieved virtually all they set out to do.
>
> (Metcalf *et al.* 1992: 2)

The second labour market reform that the government introduced was related to the payments of social security. Market liberals had argued that high levels of social security payments were contributing to higher levels of frictional unemployment and unemployment duration because workers could spend more time involved in job search. Furthermore the rates of unemployment benefits were acting as a disincentive to work. Through the various reforms of social security, the government argued that the introduction of family credit provided a system of incentives for people to take up jobs that were low-paid while measures were introduced to tax unemployment benefits and tighten eligibility to benefits to those who were genuinely seeking work. The more recent introduction of a Job Seekers allowance and the reduction of entitlement to unemployment benefits from one year to six months is seen as an attempt to reduce long-term unemployment which is thought to be attributable to the UK social security system. For example, Layard has pointed to the relationships between rates of long-term unemployment and social security, arguing that countries like Japan and the United States have short periods of entitlement to social security in contrast to Britain, France and Germany:

> Above all, unemployment is profoundly affected by how people are treated. If benefits are available indefinitely, unemployment is likely to be high. In most of the European Union benefits are available for many years, whereas in the US and Japan they end after six months. So it is not surprising that in the past 10 years long-term unemployment (of more than one year) has averaged 5 per cent of the workforce in the European Union compared with 1 per cent in the US and $\frac{1}{2}$ per cent in Japan.
>
> (Layard 1993a)

In the 1990s the UK labour market has been de-regulated, it is easier to hire and fire, there is a large rise in female employment, trade union membership has fallen and the number of strikes has steadily declined. Yet even as the boom peaked in the late 1980s, unemployment remained higher than in any of the post-war decades. When the Thatcher government first took office in 1979, unemployment represented some 4.9 per cent of the workforce but was on a downward trend. After 1980 unemployment was again on the increase and had reached 3.3 million or 11.5 per cent of the workforce in 1984. Unemployment then started to fall after 1985 and continued to fall steadily to 1.7 million or 5.9 per cent in 1989. Since 1990 unemployment has again been rising and continued to rise to 1993, reaching a peak of 2.9 million.

One major consequence of de-regulating the labour market has been the widening of income inequalities between the core skilled workers and those on the periphery of the labour market, including unskilled workers. The second major difference has been that between the incomes of those in work in contrast to those who have continued to experience unemployment during the past decade.

At an international level OECD estimates indicate that nominal GDP has been growing at 3.5 per cent per annum, taking into account inflation of 3 per cent plus a real growth of 3 per cent – nominal GDP for G7 countries should therefore be growing at about 6 per cent per annum. This estimate would suggest that, at the international level, economies are suffering from a classical Keynesian demand deficiency problem. In the 1990s therefore the problem is no longer one of inflation but of demand management.

COMPETING APPROACHES TO UNEMPLOYMENT

International perspectives

Unemployment will be a serious challenge for all the major industrialised nations during the 1990s, although at the national level there are important differences in both perceptions and policy-making. Locating unemployment at the international level, it could be pointed out that within the OECD area there are now some 35 million people unemployed; the forecast for the EU points to an unemployment rate of 20 million. The issue is whether unemployment can be reduced within a framework of policy coordination at the level of G7 (now G8 with the inclusion of Russia) where a framework for monetary and fiscal policy could be outlined, or at the level of the EU, or at the national level where governments can seek to make their labour markets more flexible and more productive.

Within the context of the EU it has been pointed out that the major concerns have been the straitjacket of the ERM and the policies pursued by the Bundesbank, both of which have contributed to the sluggish recovery and increases in the levels of unemployment in France, the United Kingdom, Spain and other countries that were tied to the ERM. The move to a more flexible ERM in the summer of 1993 did ease the pressures on interest rates for individual countries but the burden of debt still remains an obstacle to a more rapid recovery. The cost of German reunification, it has been argued, has been an increase in the German public sector deficit which the Bundesbank has sought to finance through high interest rates. The consequence of this policy has been to impose high levels of interest on other EU countries which in turn have driven these countries into recession even though the economic fundamentals in France and the United Kingdom have been in better shape than those of Germany. Both France and the United Kingdom could point to lower labour costs, increased productivity, tight monetary policy and low inflation – lower than that of Germany, which is at present running at 4 per cent compared to 3 per cent in France and 1.7 per cent in the United Kingdom. Some economists have argued that the way out of European unemployment is related to the break-up of the ERM and the floating of European currencies, allowing governments to reduce interest rates and therefore reduce costs to industry. An example of this argument has been outlined in an article by six of the world's top economists including three Nobel Prize winners, which was published in the *Financial Times*:

> The result of high interest rates across Europe has been that unemployment has risen to record levels . . . It looks as if the 1930s are being re-enacted. Then, it was felt to be imperative to hang on to gold at any price: today the feeling is to hang on to the DMark. . . . In our view, the essential issue is for the EMS countries to shift priorities, putting unemployment at the top of the list and recognising that much labour can be reabsorbed through reflationary policies, beginning with a sharp cut in interest rates.
>
> (Blanchard *et al.* 1993)

In contrast to the reflationary policies outlined by Professor Modiliagni and the American economists, recent reports by the OECD and the EU seem to advocate reforms of the labour market, arguing that the problems of unemployment are much more related to issues of labour market flexibility, training, wage rate and the payment of unemployment benefits. The EC report *Community Wide Framework for Employment*, published in June 1993, has contrasted Europe, Japan and the United States and looked at how these models have fared in generating employment over the past two decades. First the report points to the low rate of employment in the EU, where 60 per cent of the total workforce is in employment, compared to 70 per cent in Japan and the United States. Second, Europe's record of job creation shows how, over the past two decades, the numbers employed in the United States have almost doubled while in Europe employment has increased by 10 per cent. During the past thirty-five years employment in North America has increased by 80 per cent while in the EU employment has risen by only 10 per cent.

Recent OECD reports on employment (OECD 1993, OECD 1994) point out that the employment record of EFTA countries was better than the EU because of the number of jobs created by EFTA countries in the public sector. The United States had created 5 million public sector jobs since 1975 while the EU had created 3.1 million. In the meantime both the United States and Canada had created 29.8 million private sector jobs compared to 5 million in the EU. From these statistics the OECD concludes that the United States had created more jobs because it had a de-regulated labour market in contrast to the EU where governments were still committed to social democratic principles. The OECD suggests that while European countries had accepted the need to create more flexible labour markets, the commitment remained more of a principle than an issue of policy.

Furthermore, the OECD also suggested that the major threat to employment in the industrialised nations was the introduction of new technologies within manufacturing. While in 1960 one in every four people had been employed in manufacturing, by 1990 this had dropped to one in six. In the United Kingdom the proportion of manual workers employed in manufacturing has declined from 56 per cent in 1971 to 50 per cent in 1990; in the United States there were 2.2 million people less employed in manufacturing. The challenge of new technology was that it needed fewer workers with low skills which made the jobs of male manual workers more vulnerable. The challenge for the industrial countries therefore was how to get the long-term unemployed back to work or, to be more specific, the challenge of how to get men with low skills back into a labour market that was more dependent on a highly skilled labour force. At present both the United States and the United Kingdom have succeeded in bringing more women into employment – about 60 per cent of UK and US women are now in work compared with 50 per cent for the rest of Europe. The problem is that most of these women have moved to jobs that are part-time, low-paid and in the service sector – jobs that men seem reluctant to move to. The question therefore is whether the government should elect a policy that persuades, through further de-regulation, the long-term male unemployed to move to these jobs or whether the government should choose a policy to offer better-quality training and create opportunities for 'good jobs' rather than just jobs at any price.

Both the OECD and the EU seem to repudiate macroeconomic policy as a strategy for dealing with unemployment. Both are agreed that unemployment in the 1990s is a structural problem that will not be resolved through policies of growth. Both are also agreed that governments need to reduce their budget deficits in order to reduce interest rates and thus allow for an expansion in private sector investment. Within a framework of lower budget deficits and lower interest rates, the role of the government should be confined to the de-regulation of the labour market by directing benefits to those who are genuinely seeking work, reducing the role of trade unions in collective bargaining, reducing the costs on employers by making the rules on hiring and firing easier and removing review bodies in determining pay.

At present it would seem that there are two models on the political agenda. The first is based on de-regulation and competition – a model embraced by the United States and the United Kingdom where the emphasis is placed on improving the supply side of the labour market through a process of market de-regulation. The second is interventionist and social democratic, founded on the European corporatist tradition based on consensus-building between governments, trade unions and employers. The success of the United States and the United Kingdom models is that both countries can be shown to have created more jobs during the 1980s when compared to France or Germany. At present the United States has an unemployment rate of 6 per cent compared to 12 per cent for the EU and 8.5 per cent for the OECD. Spain and Ireland have an unemployment rate of 20 per cent and France and Germany expect unemployment to remain stuck at 12 per cent during 1994 and 1995. The United States does not have a problem of long-term unemployment although this might be due to the social security system which provides for only the first six months of unemployment, and people therefore become very quickly defined as being economically inactive. In Europe the benefit system guarantees benefits for at least the first fifty-two weeks of unemployment and then the unemployed can start claiming social security benefits.

The second problem with the US model is that incomes from work have risen very slowly during the past decade, with workers electing to accept wage reductions and pay freezes as a trade-off for job security. So while employment has been secured for many, there has not been any significant improvement in living standards. Between 1978 and 1993 average real wages in the United States stagnated while over the same period German real wages increased by 18 per cent, in France by 26 per cent and in the United Kingdom by 31 per cent. Furthermore wage differentials have increased, reflecting the changes in demands for skilled and low-skilled workers, thus widening income inequalities even for those in work.

The concept of structural unemployment carries the implication that the solution to long-term unemployment is to price people back into work. It also suggests that people have priced themselves out of jobs, either because of high wage settlements or because of the benefit system which ensures that wages do not fall below a certain plateau. Pricing people back into jobs, according to this perspective, means reducing the levels of benefits so that wages will also fall. This policy also involves a macroeconomic environment founded on low inflation expectations so that wage bargaining takes place within a climate where workers do not have to compensate for price increases.

Making markets work also means allowing for differentials in incomes to widen so that even low wages and social security do not act as a disincentive to the labour market. The OECD report shows that in most countries there has been a widening of differentials between the top 10 per cent of earners, the median and the bottom 10 per cent. In the United States the income of the bottom 10 per cent had actually fallen by 10 per cent during the 1980s. According to Michael Prowse:

> For many Europeans, US labour markets will seem an unattractive role model. Stagnant real wages, rising inequality and limited job security will strike many as a high – perhaps unacceptable – price to pay for relatively low jobless rates. Many Americans are deeply troubled by such trends. Mr Clinton won last year's presidential election in large part by capitalising on the feelings of insecurity created by the Darwinian labour markets of the 1980s.
>
> (Prowse 1993)

It would seem that in seeking to reduce the level of unemployment, European governments will in the 1990s have to break with the social democratic and corporatist traditions which seemed to serve Europe well during the post-war years until the late 1970s. Since the 1980s Europe has been perceived as being incapable of responding to global challenges of new technology and increased competition. Euro-sclerosis implies that European economies in the 1990s are being outstripped by competition from Japan and the new industrial countries of Asia because Europe is suffering from too much regulation and inflexibility in the labour market. The consensus-building approach associated with the German economic miracle of the 1950s and 1960s is perceived to be inappropriate to deal with the unemployment of the 1990s. The process of 'concerted action' set the framework for pay bargaining, private investment and public expenditure. It has been the mainstay of stable industrial relations, economic prosperity and affluence for Germany throughout the post-war period. Some European countries, including France, Austria and the Netherlands, have sought to import parts of the German model. It is still seen as relevant to the challenge of unemployment in Europe in the 1990s.

The Social Chapter, as outlined in the Maastricht Treaty, reflects a commitment by European governments to the German model of industrial relations – a model that is seen as likely to give European employees high wages, stable employment and improved living standards. The British government, by contrast, have throughout the 1980s sought to de-regulate the labour market by reducing the burden of labour costs on employers. According to the UK government, the Social Chapter will destroy jobs rather than create them, while some EU partners argue that without the Social Chapter there will be social dumping, with each country seeking to lower labour costs by reducing benefits, reducing employee rights and making it easier for employers to hire and fire – this, it is argued, will lead to a situation of low investment in technology, low wages and falling living standards. The recent opt-outs by Employment Secretary Michael Portillo from legislating for worker directors in British companies and leave of absence for fathers, reinforces the view that the UK government will continue to move towards further de-regulation, including de-centralised wage bargaining in the public sector.

The break-up of the Soviet Empire and the emergence of the new economies of Hungary, Poland and the Czech Republic will increase the pressure on European workers to become more competitive. At present, wages in the Czech Republic are at least ten times lower than those in Germany; yet Germany shares a border with the Czechs, thus making it easier for German companies to move production to Prague, Ostrava or Liberec where there already exists a highly skilled labour force. The question for European governments is whether they are willing to invest in a programme of high-quality training so that workers can move into areas of production that have a high level of value-added, thus leaving mass production to those countries with much cheaper labour costs. The problem is that such a programme of training will not start to show any fruits for at least ten to fifteen years, while governments are judged within an electoral cycle of five years. This gap in the electoral cycle leaves governments with little political incentive to invest in the longer term.

Implications for UK employment policies

At present the interpretations of the UK economic performance during the 1980s can be located under two broad categories: one can be categorised as optimistic and seeks to associate the past twelve years with Thatcher's economic miracle, and the second can be described as pessimistic. The optimistic interpretation points to a number of long-term achievements and these include the improvements in productivity, lower wage settlements, a climate of low inflation and increased competitiveness.

The optimists point to the courageous budget of Geoffrey Howe in 1980/81 when, in the midst of recession, he decided to reduce public expenditure and increase interest rates. These sound monetary policies, it is argued, provided the framework for the rapid growth experienced after 1985 when the UK economy grew by 4 to 5 per cent per annum and when unemployment fell sharply from 3.3 million to 1.6 million between 1983 and 1987. The optimists tend to 'blame' Chancellor Nigel Lawson for engineering the 'boom' in 1987 when, after the crash of the Stock Exchange, he decided to reduce interest rates and relax UK monetary policy. Optimists would argue that the UK government in the 1990s need to revisit the policies adopted by the Conservative government in 1980. The government have to reduce the present deficit by reducing public expenditure and by regaining control over monetary policy. A macroeconomic framework founded on lowering the public sector deficit would allow for lower interest rates and increased private sector investment. In the meantime lower labour costs and a floating exchange rate would allow the United Kingdom to take advantage of its competitive edge gained in the previous decade. The optimists included economic forecasters such as Tim Congdon and Patrick Minford, both of whom are members of the panel of experts reporting to the Treasury. According to both Congdon and Minford, the United Kingdom made a mistake in entering the ERM which resulted in high interest rates and prolonged the UK recession. Both economists are agreed that UK monetary growth has been too restrictive in the 1990s and that what is therefore needed is a relaxation of monetary policy by reducing interest rates while at the same time reducing public expenditure. In contrast to this advice, the chancellor increased interest rates in September 1994. Both Congdon and Minford would argue that the economy can continue to grow at 3 per cent per annum during the next few years without any threat of inflationary pressures.

By contrast, the pessimist would suggest that during the 1980s UK unemployment continued to deteriorate. Despite the short boom of 1987, throughout the decade unemployment never fell below 2 million, in contrast to the 1950s and 1960s when unemployment peaked at 250,000 and to the 1970s when unemployment reached 1 million. In addition, despite the high levels of unemployment the UK balance of payments had widened, especially in the manufacturing sector. Pessimists would argue that during the 1980s the labour shake-out was accompanied by de-stocking and the closure of large areas of manufacturing so that any boom has resulted in increased dependence on imports. The panellist

Professor Wynne Godley has always pointed to the problem of the balance of payments constraint and has therefore argued in favour of policies that favour export-led growth. The pessimists are also described as unreconstructed Keynesians in that they still equate unemployment with demand management. Pessimists would argue that unwarranted pain was inflicted on the UK economy during the 1980s because the government had abandoned Keynesian macroeconomic tools – the unemployment of the 1980s could be attributed wholly to the government's mismanagement of the economy. The medium-term financial strategy announced by Geoffrey Howe in the 1980 budget increased interest rates, which in turn led to an appreciation of sterling. The increased costs of borrowing, together with the increased costs of exports, led to the recession of the early 1980s. It was the relaxation of monetary and fiscal policy under the chancellorship of Lawson that eventually allowed the economy to breathe again. Rather than Lawson being the villain who betrayed Thatcher's economic miracle, the policies of Lawson after 1985 allowed the economy to grow and unemployment to fall from a peak of 3.3 million in 1984 to 1.7 million by 1989.

In between there are the sceptics who do not find themselves in agreement with the monetarism of Congdon and Minford, or the commitment to the Keynesianism of the National Institute for Economic and Social Research, or the economics of Professor Wynne Godley. The sceptics would include a diversity of economic viewpoints and these would include the macroeconomics of Samuel Brittan and labour economists Richard Layard and Steve Metcalfe.

The major challenge for governments in the 1990s is how to reflate the major economies, in contrast to the 1970s and 1980s when the major concern had been the problem of inflation. Brittan has argued that governments are still fighting the problem of an earlier decade, when there is now a real problem of consumer confidence. Consumer confidence has been undermined because of the high levels of unemployment, personal debt overhang and high interest rates. A policy that aims to reduce interest rates will therefore not be sufficient to reflate the economy.

Richard Layard, Director of the Centre for Economic Performance at the London School of Economics, argues for a dual strategy to include both a social democratic and market approach to unemployment. Layard has argued that a major problem of unemployment is due to a mismatch in the labour market between the skills that people actually have and those that are required in an economy experiencing continuous technological change. Although such an adjustment could be left to the market in that wage differentials start to appear in areas where there is high demand, Layard argues that wages are not flexible enough to allow for this adjustment:

> But the pattern of skills in the European workforce has not adjusted adequately. To an extent the problem will correct itself, since the relative shortage of skilled labour has increased wage differentials and thus the incentive to acquire skills. But wages are not fully flexible and this generates an inefficient level of unemployment, requiring public intervention and public expenditure.

(Richard Layard, *Financial Times* 8 June 1993, Unemployment: a letter to Mr Delors).

(Layard 1993b)

According to Layard therefore, European governments need to pursue a twofold policy on employment: first, policy directed at high-quality training to increase the skills of the European workforce, and second, a policy of government intervention in pay bargaining. Layard argues against the de-centralised plant bargaining encouraged by the UK government. De-centralised bargains might lead to lower wage settlements when unemployment is high but as the labour market gets tighter, skilled workers in particular are likely to become involved in bargains based on leap-frogging similar to the pattern of the 1960s. Layard believes that a return to full employment can only be achieved through a process of wage restraint and consensus-building similar to Germany. Layard also accepts the market-liberal view that there is a need to increase the incentive to work by reducing the levels of unemployment benefits, but he also wants the government to be more interventionist through increases in public expenditure on training and also to intervene as the major institution that seeks to build consensus between the major social partners on wage determination.

Finally, Europe is the continent of trade unions. In this context, decentralised bargaining simply leads to wage leap-frogging as soon as unemployment is reduced. Wage restraint can only be achieved through higher unemployment or through employer solidarity and social consensus about wages.

(Layard 1993b)

Those who argue that the Thatcher governments brought a permanent transformation to the British economy point to the low wage settlements and the increases in productivity that were achieved during the 1980s. It still remains an issue, however, whether the lower settlements achieved in the 1980s did represent a cultural break in wage bargaining or whether it was the threat of unemployment that lowered settlements. It is true that trade union militancy was on the decline during the 1980s as the number of strikes and the number of days lost in work fell to the levels of the mid-1950s. One major problem has been that, despite the increases in unemployment during the 1980s, wage settlements did not fall. The unemployed were not a threat to those in work – indeed between 1983 and 1990 the real earning growth for those in work was at a record high. During the 1980s wage settlements averaged 7.5 per cent per annum, while in the early 1990s settlements have fallen to 3.5 per cent. In the meantime unemployment has expanded from 1.7 million in 1987 to 2.9 million by April 1992.

Professor Metcalfe agrees with Richard Layard that as unemployment starts to fall, there will be a resurgence of higher wage settlements, especially within the core of skilled workers. According to Professor Metcalfe (1993), 'The British pay predicament – how to get low settlements and rapid employment growth – remains intact. The pay conundrum only appears to have been solved because of the tragedy of nearly 3m unemployed.'

Another major problem on wages relates to the future behaviour of public sector workers. While governments have tried to impose wage restraint in the public sector, these have tended only to have short-term success since there has always been a process of catching up with the private sector. At present, wage settlements in the public sector are lagging behind the private sector but whether the government will be able to hold the line over the longer term is still open to question. During the recent settlements on public expenditure it seems that Chancellor Kenneth Clarke has come to the conclusion that containing public expenditure growth requires a public sector pay freeze for the foreseeable future unless wage increases can be justified through productivity increases. The recent settlements for the policy, nurses and signal workers, already point to wage drift in the public sector – despite the limit of 1.5 per cent imposed in 1993, most public sector workers settled for between 2.5 and 3.5 per cent in 1994.

THE GLOBAL ECONOMY

The most difficult challenge for the major industrial economies is the absence of one country willing to be the anchor economy and the lack of a coordinated approach to monetary and fiscal policy. The Bretton Woods Agreement served the world economy well until it had to be abandoned during the Vietnam War when the United States sought to finance the war through a large deficit and confidence in the dollar as the anchor currency eventually broke down. The break-down in international coordination from the mid-1970s meant that countries tended to deal with economic problems within the context of the nation-state without taking into consideration the effects of these policies on the international economy. One example has been the way in which countries have responded to the problems of the oil price shocks and inflation of the 1970s. As each country sought to utilise monetary policy and high interest rates to bring the money supply under control, high interest rates and tight monetary policy became the only instruments of economic policy for the 1980s and the early 1990s. Any country that sought to go it alone, like France in the early 1980s, found itself in trouble as international competitiveness on interest rates ensured that countries that broke away from this regime soon found their currencies under pressure. The long-term effect of this policy has become clearer in the 1990s: continuing high interest rates and tight monetary policy have undermined consumer confidence so that, as inflation has abated and interest rates have fallen, consumers have been reluctant to return to the market. The challenge for the 1990s is therefore whether there is likely to be a counter-counter-revolution in economic thinking and in economic policy.

The experience of the inflation of the 1970s seemed to confirm the ebb of Keynesian thinking. The economics of classical monetarism undermined by the economics of Keynes after 1945 had, by the middle of the 1970s, returned to become the conventional wisdom of most governments for the 1980s. The commitment to full employment, which had been central to macroeconomic policy-making after 1946, had been abandoned by the early 1980s as governments argued that their concern should in future be the control of inflation. The monetarist counter-revolution implied that the major concern for the 1980s was to bring inflation under control, reduce government expenditure and create more flexible markets. Furthermore monetarists also argued that issues of employment required reforms that addressed the labour market, including both the reforms of institutions such as trade unions and social security and also tax reforms. The monetarist counter-revolution also meant the break-down of international co-operation as governments sought to bring public expenditure under control and also increased interest rates as part of their monetary strategy. The overall result was that inflation was brought under control by the late 1980s but also that most countries continued to experience high levels of unemployment, certainly much higher than the levels associated with the first two decades after the war.

The question of whether the 1990s might require new thinking has been articulated by Sir Samuel Brittan a number of articles in the *Financial Times* during 1993, as follows:

> The application of monetary brakes required to deal with the much more moderate inflationary upsurge of the late 1980s has nevertheless led to a severe increase in unemployment. It is thus at least worth considering whether we may be approaching a period of secular demand deficiency – by which I mean a period when output and employment are held down by an inadequate level of private and public spending. The Keynesians who cried 'wolf' so often in the post-war decades may eventually come into their own.
>
> (Brittan 1993)

Most of the leading industrial economies continue to experience recession and high levels of unemployment. The new Conservative government of Edouard Balladur elected in April 1993 have declared that unemployment is the major priority for the French government. Through the 1980s and early 1990s the level of unemployment in France has not improved – 10 per cent of the workforce have been out of work for the past decade while in the early 1990s it has ratcheted upwards to 13 per cent. In the meantime France was able to reduce its inflation rate to less than 2 per cent and also to sustain a surplus balance of trade. The public sector borrowing requirement of 4 per cent of GDP also indicates that France has managed to bring its public finances under control. Despite the fact that France has sound economic fundamentals, it is unable to come out of recession as long as it maintains its *franc fort* policy of aligning the French franc to the Deutschmark inside the ERM and maintaining a high interest rate regime which continues to hinder recovery. The example of France applies to most countries inside the EU. The tight monetary policy adopted by the German Bundesbank to deal with the pressures of German inflation means that consumer confidence in Europe continues to be hindered by high interest rates and debt overhang.

The forecast for the United States indicates that the economy is likely to grow by 4 per cent during 1994 and 1995. The United States is a self-contained 'continental economy' – only 12 per cent of GDP is exported, which means that the United States is less likely to be hindered by the recovery of European economies. The recent budget measures of President Clinton to reduce the American deficit through a combination of tax increases and public expenditure cuts, together with the increases in interest rates announced by the Federal Reserve Bank, suggests that the United States is still not prepared to act as the locomotive for the world economy. High interest rates in the United States and the United Kingdom would suggest that both governments would prefer lower levels of growth which can be sustained without any inflationary pressures.

In bringing inflation under control, governments throughout the industrialised world have succeeded in creating a framework of comparative price stability. This in turn might result in employees adjusting their long-term wage demands to low inflation but not all workers will necessarily settle in the long term for low wage increases. If unemployment starts to fall and workers feel less threatened by unemployment, a return to the leap-frogging and wage bargaining that characterised the 1960s could be predicted. While unemployment was high, the push towards de-centralised bargains have resulted in lower wage settlements, but as unemployment falls, local bargains are likely to escalate as workers try to catch up with those setting the pace on wage settlements. In the context of low unemployment, national bargains and national settlements are more likely to achieve lower settlements. Throughout the 1980s the UK government have sought to loosen ties with institutions that it defined as being corporatist, while for the rest of Europe consensus-building remained central. In France the government have maintained the commitment to the minimum wage despite their commitment to reform the labour market. In contrast the UK government remain opposed to the Social Chapter while still arguing that intervention by government increases unemployment.

The climate of price stability is no necessary guarantee against high wage demands; even if unemployment remains at a high level, those in work, especially those with high-level skills, will make demands for wage increases that reflect their productivity and the profits of their companies. It is not sufficient that a government provides a climate of price stability. People have other aspirations and these include the steady improvement in living standards. In the meantime those with high skills might achieve higher wage settlements which will result in a widening of income differentials even for those in work. Pressures on government will increase when the majority of those in work start to feel that they see no improvement in living standards through wages despite being in work. Governments in this context could be faced with an agenda for reducing income inequality and for improving living standards through public services. For the past decade the UK government have weakened wage-bargaining institutions and have also abolished wage councils.

The UK experience confirms that there is a very tentative link between pay settlements and unemployment. Those in work, especially those with high levels of skills, have enjoyed continuing increases in real earnings while unemployment has continued to persist. The unemployed do not seem to pose a threat to those who are in work, which might suggest that a return to full employment would not increase the pressure on wages and inflation. Experience seems to confirm a trend of higher wage settlements for those in work accompanied by increased joblessness. During the present recession, wage settlements have averaged about 6.1 per cent, which is nearly double the inflation of 3.7 per cent. In contrast, during the recession of 1981 wages grew at 12.9 per cent when inflation averaged 11.9 per cent. During the 1981 recession unemployment grew by 1.5 million, while in 1991 unemployment grew by 2 million. Employment in the UK chemical industry has fallen by 25 per cent between 1981 and 1992 while wages costs increased by 160 per cent compared with 60 per cent in other countries. Since privatisation, employment at BT has fallen from 238,000 in 1984 to 165,00 now, and the forecast is that by 1997 this will fall further to 100,000. At National Grid, employment has fallen from 6,500 to 5,000, while most workers have received a pay rise of between 5 and 10 per cent. These broad trends indicate that the high levels of unemployment are not necessary and that government should resort to policies that would reduce unemployment. This argument is similar to that outlined by Professor Patrick Minford in his recent contributions to the Treasury panel of experts. Minford believes that the equilibrium rate of unemployment consistent with stable prices (Non-Accelerating Inflation Rate of Unemployment) has fallen from 3 million in the early 1980s to 1 million in the 1990s – Minford argues that the economy could take a large boost with little danger of renewed inflation.

CONCLUSIONS

The present UK recession dates back to October 1990; it has been the longest period of recession during the post-war period and certainly deeper when compared to that of the early 1980s. The duration of the present recession has been attributed to various factors including the decision to join the ERM in September 1990, the Lawson boom of 1987 and the international economic context such as the reunification of Germany, the US budget deficit and Japan's trade surpluses. Two major consequences of the present recession have been the increases in unemployment and the deterioration in public finances. Between 1990 and 1992 UK unemployment increased from 1.8 million to nearly 3 million, while public finances moved from a positive balance in 1990 to a public sector deficit of £50 billion in 1993 – an equivalent of 8 per cent of GDP. The government could claim a major success on curbing inflation, which has fallen to 1.7 per cent – the lowest for twenty-six years – but it seems to be a high price to pay in the context of high unemployment, debt overhang and a loss of consumer confidence.

While economic forecasts pointed to unemployment increasing throughout 1993, unemployment peaked at 2.9 million in February 1993 and started to fall at a quicker rate than had been forecast. One explanation for this sudden turnround has resulted in the government arguing for the success of their present policies, namely the decision to leave the ERM in September 1992, allowing interest rates to fall by 3 per cent and sterling to depreciate by 14 per cent against other ERM currencies. The Treasury view is that the government have now created a climate of sustained recovery founded on low inflation, low wage settlements, high productivity and increased competitiveness. The environment of low inflation and lower interest rates had led to lowering mortgage costs which in turn have increased disposable income and consumer confidence.

A less optimistic view suggests that the improvement in the unemployment statistics reflects the condition of the UK labour market rather than the overall economic context. According to this interpretation, the changes in industrial relations during the 1980s have reduced the costs of redundancy and made it easier for employers to hire and fire. As the United Kingdom entered the recession in 1990, employers shed more labour than was required, and as confidence seems to be returning, employers are finding that they have insufficient labour to meet the new orders. The implication of this interpretation is that the UK employment context is now more vulnerable to short-term changes in the economic cycle, with employers being able to hire employees on short-term contracts. The problem of having a large casual workforce is that living standards and disposable income will not increase even for those in work. President Clinton won the US election in November 1992 because he was able to articulate the frustrations of those employees who have not experienced any improvement in their disposable income. During his election campaign, Clinton pointed out that during the period 1973–93 real hourly wages had declined by 16 per cent, when real GDP had grown by 56 per cent. What seemed to influence popular perceptions of economic progress was not the GDP statistic but what was happening to real wages.

At present the UK government seem to have adopted the view that what is good for business must be good for the economy because it is business that creates wealth and employment. Equally the government seem to accept the argument that any intervention in labour markets must harm business confidence and also employment prospects. Responding to the EC discussion paper on employment, the UK government have pointed out that 'The Community must avoid imposing labour market regulations that increase costs, lock member states and employers unnecessary into existing rigidities or make it harder to create new jobs' (HMSO 1993).

According to the *Employment Gazette* (September 1994), 5 million workers (20 per cent of the UK workforce) now work more than forty-eight hours a week. This ranks the United Kingdom third after Ireland and Greece. Except for the United Kingdom in all EC countries the majority of those who work for more than forty-eight hours are either self-employed or employed by their families. The United Kingdom, is at present opposing the EC working time directive which proposes that those who work forty-eight hours should be entitled to a statutory paid holiday entitlement.

Despite more optimistic economic forecasts, world economic recovery is likely to be slow since most economies are hampered by large public sector deficits and cumulative private debt. Furthermore, traditional escape routes seem to be blocked. The present public sector deficit in the United States closes any option for the Clinton administration to embark on any global Keynesian economics similar to that initiated by the Reagan administration during the 1980s. The protective and regulated environment which worked well now seems inappropriate as rapid growth in Asia continues to threaten the older industries of the developed world. It is the pressure of competition both from Asia and Eastern Europe that is forcing Europe, the United States and Japan to break with intervention and welfarism. The Liberal government of Japan and the Christian Democrats in Germany have throughout the post-war period supported a liberal corporatist approach to economics and politics, each pointing out that economic success in their countries depended on creating a framework of consensus-building between employers, trade unions and government. In the 1990s both countries are producing initiatives and policy frameworks that aim to de-regulate markets, privatise large areas of public provision and remove subsidies that underpinned the consensus model.

CORE READING

Healey, N. (ed.) (1993) *Britain's Economic Miracle: Myth or Reality*, London: Routledge.

Holmlund, B. and Lofgren, K. (1990) *Unemployment and Wage Determination in Europe*, Oxford: Basil Blackwell.

Keegan, W. (1993) *The Spectre of Capitalism: The Future of the World Economy after the Fall of Communism*, London: Vintage.

Maynard, G. (1988) *The Economy under Mrs Thatcher*, Oxford: Basil Blackwell.

Mullard, M. (1992) *Understanding Economic Policy*, London: Routledge.

Smith, D. (1993) *From Boom to Bust: Trial and Error in British Economic Policy*, Harmondsworth: Penguin.

Stewart, M. (1993) *Keynes in the 1990s: A Return to Economic Sanity*, Harmondsworth: Penguin.

Symes, V. (1994) *Unemployment in Europe*, London: Routledge.

van der Wee, H. (1991) *Prosperity and Upheaval: The World Economy 1945–1980*, Harmondsworth: Penguin.

ADDITIONAL READING

Blanchard, O., Dornbusch, R., Fischer, S., Krugman, P., Modigliani, F., Samuelson, P. and Solow, R. (1993) 'Why the EMS deserves an early burial', *The Financial Times*, 29 July.

Brittan, Samuel (1993) 'Tide turns into the world economy', *Financial Times*, 25 March.

Commission of the European Communities (1989a) 'The social aspects of the internal market', *Social Europe* 11 (7/89).

Commission of the European Communities (1989b) *Community Charter of Fundamental Social Rights*, Com 89 (248) Final, Brussels.

Commission of the European Communities (1990) *Social Europe* (1/90), Brussels.

Congdon, T. (1993) *Reflections on Monetarism: Britain's Vain Search for a Successful Economic Strategy*, London: Edward Elgar.

Haskel, J. and Szymanski, S. (1993) 'Privatisation, liberalisation, wages and employment: theory and evidence for the UK', *Economica* 60(238): 161–82.

HMSO (1993) *The Growth of Social Security*, London: HMSO.

Jackman, R. and Layard, R. (1991) 'Does long-term unemployment reduce a person's chance of a job?', *Economica* 58(229): 93–106.

Keegan, W. (1989) *Mr Lawson's Gamble*, London: Hodder & Stoughton.

Lawson (1992) *The View from No. 11: Memoirs of a Tory Radical*, London: Bantam.

Layard, Richard (1993a) 'An offer the unemployed cannot refuse', *Financial Times*, 6 December.

Layard, Richard (1993b) 'Unemployment: a letter to Mr Delors', *Financial Times*, 8 June.

Manning, A. (1993) 'A dynamic model of union power, wages and employment', *Scandinavian Journal of Economics* 95(2): 175–93.

McDonnell, F. and Dearden, S. (eds) (1992) *European Economic Integration*, London: Longman.

Metcalfe, D., Wadsworth, J. and Ingram, P. (1992) *Do Strikes Pay?*, London School of Economics, Discussion Paper 92.

Metcalfe, David (1993) 'Search for solution to UK pay puzzle', *Financial Times*, 2 June.

Minford, P. (ed.) (1992) *The Cost of Europe*, Manchester: Manchester University Press.

Mitchie, J. (ed.) (1992) *The Economic Legacy 1979–1992*, London: Academic Press.

OECD (1993) *Economic Outlook, Growth and Prospects*, Paris: OECD.

OECD (1994) *Economic Outlook*, Paris: OECD.

Pillinger, J. (1993) *Feminizing the Market: Women's Pay and Employment in the EC*, Sweden: International Women's Forum.

Prowse, Michael (1993) 'No easy answers to job questions', *Financial Times*, 21 July.

Robinson, Bill (1993) 'Soft heart of our problem', *Financial Times*, 27 July.

Weiss, L. (1993) 'War, the state and the origins of the Japanese employment system', *Politics and Society* 21(3): 325–54.

Part II
Case studies

6 Public expenditure decisions

Maurice Mullard

The first 'unified' budget of November 1993 made clear that the major concern of the government is to bring public expenditure under control prior to the next election and to make room for tax reductions. Many senior members of the government are very much aware that the government needs to make the necessary tax reductions if the government are to win the next election and that there is therefore a need to reduce public expenditure and to allow the economy to grow faster than the rate of public expenditure. As for the economy, the government seem to live in the hope that there will be sustained growth in the economy which would improve the feel-good factor. Negotiations on public expenditure between the Treasury and spending ministers during the next two years are therefore likely to leave a lot of blood on the carpet as some ministers will seek to protect their expenditure priorities while the chancellor will continue to remind them of the political priority of the government which will be to reduce taxes and control spending. The chancellor will also, however, be concerned that public expenditure settlements will avoid ideological clashes between those who have urged major reforms of public provision and those who are seeking to consolidate the Welfare State and who wish the government to emphasise their commitment to the achievements of the Welfare State.

Since 1993 the chancellor has continued to suggest that he is committed to reduce public expenditure from the present level of 45 per cent of GDP to around 40 per cent of GDP by 1997 and that he seems satisfied with this boundary between public and private provision. In contrast, the messages from the prime minister reflect the tensions within the Conservative Party in that he is willing to endorse the view that the present levels of public expenditure are sustainable while also accepting the reformist zeal of the No Turning Back Group and ministers like Peter Lilley and Michael Portillo. By implication the chancellor has confirmed a widely held view that the settlements on public expenditure are going to be extremely difficult for the government between now and the next election. A debate seems to have been rekindled within the Conservative Party – a debate very reminiscent of 1983 when a number of 'believers' within the Conservative Party were pressing the government for radical reforms of public provision and to make room for tax reductions. Two recent pamphlets by David Willetts (1994) and John Gray (1994), written for the Social Market Foundation, seem to reflect the present debate within the Conservative Party about the future of the Welfare State. Willetts seems to be urging the government to continue to show their resolve on returning welfare to the market and to break with state provision, while Gray feels that the Conservatives might lose the next election because they have embraced too much the market philosophy and moved away from good Conservative pragmatism.

It seems rather paradoxical that after fourteen years of Conservative government, public expenditure at 45 per cent of GDP is 6 per cent higher than when the government first came to office. The government are spending in real terms 50 per cent more on health care, 30 per cent more on education and 25 per cent more on roads and transport. The paradox seems to be that while the government would point to the additional sums spent on the public sector, the widely held perception is that the quality of public services have deteriorated – a view held by a majority of electors. It is within this context that the No Turning Back Group of Conservative MPs is urging a review of public expenditure. Their argument is that the government cannot meet the expectations that people have of the public sector, thus leaving the government only the option of targeting welfare at those who are really in need and providing incentives for people to make private provision.

In contrast some senior Conservatives, including the Chancellor and the Foreign Secretary (Douglas Hurd), seem to be arguing in favour of having more confidence in the public sector. In his budget of November 1993 the chancellor seemed to be confirming this position when he argued that the government were not seeking to dismantle the Welfare State but to make it a better Welfare State, one that is well run and well judged and that meets the priorities of a modern society.

In his budget speeches the chancellor has made no mention that the government would seek to phase out the universal state pension; instead he seems to go out of his way to point out the government's support for the state pension and the government's commitment to retain the value of pensions – a view that contradicts the idea floated by Peter Lilley and Michael Portillo that people would be encouraged to opt out of state pensions. Furthermore it seems that the chancellor has also ensured that, between now and the election, certain Cabinet colleagues would tone down their rhetoric in their approach to the Welfare State – the emphasis from now on will be on consolidating the reform and not on running down the Welfare State.

The aim of this chapter is to ask whether a point has been reached where the arguments that favour a major review of the public sector have become more pertinent and whether the language of an inevitable crisis in public provision is justified. Are the arguments for a major review of public expenditure in the 1990s qualitatively different to those of previous decades, beginning with the Plowden recommendations of the 1960s, the setting up of the policy analysis review (PAR) and the debate on zero budgeting during the years of the Heath government, the shift to cash limits in the middle of the 1970s, and the reviews of 1983? Since the early 1960s there have been a number of panics and crises about the spiralling costs of pensions, social security and health care and the tax burden. In each cycle the questions have been asked whether taxation had reached saturation point, whether the deficit was hindering growth and whether the state could respond to the challenges of demographic pressures in terms of the numbers of elderly people and the numbers of students remaining in education. The common theme over the past three decades has been that governments need to bring public expenditure under control; that public expenditure has its own momentum towards increased growth, that it behaves like a super-tanker which is difficult and slow to turn around because of in-built inertia and the influence of many vested interests and that the best-hoped policy is for governments to keep expenditure under control.

Looking at public policy in the year 2000, the student of policy needs to ask whether it is feasible for public expenditure decisions to continue to be made within the context of the art of the possible; that is, of expenditure decisions being based on political choice, expediency and incrementalism. It is very important to ask whether a stage has been reached when electors have to make a choice about public provision and what they want the state to continue to provide and what services they would prefer to buy in the private sector. Maybe there is a point when continued incrementalism and expediency start to do more harm than good to public provision. The public sector deficit is at present a major constraint on providing additional funds to new public sector projects. The present climate makes it impossible for a minister to win additional resources for investment in railways or road transport; people who do use the public sector are spending more time travelling, faced with delays, cancellations and uncomfortable rail journeys, yet the climate in the public sector is one of restraint and retrenchment for the foreseeable future. It is, for example, within this context that the arguments for rail privatisation need to be located. Those who are against rail privatisation and would like to see new investment know that the new investment will not be forthcoming from government and that even when public finances do improve, there is no likelihood that the railways will be able to secure funding since other claims on the public sector will be in the pipeline. The railways will have to continue therefore to compete for other funds with other spending programmes. In the meantime the impartial observer would suggest that if the railway network was commercialised, this would free the railways to look to the private sector for new investment and, provided that the interests of the consumer are safeguarded, the railways could end up providing a better quality of service.

THE STUDY OF UK PUBLIC EXPENDITURE 1962–92

This section provides an outline of public expenditure changes as experienced by programmes and within programmes during the period 1962–92. The analysis represents a detailed study of ten major expenditure programmes (Mullard 1987, 1993) including health care, education, social security, defence, law and order, housing, employment, environment, roads and agriculture, which constitute about 90 per cent of total expenditure. The analysis provides an overview of expenditure changes by economic category and then economic category by programme.

The overall changes in expenditure

Between 1962 and 1975 total expenditure on these ten programmes was expanding on a year-to-year basis from 25.8 per cent of GDP to a peak of 35.8 per cent of GDP in 1975. The crisis of the Labour government in 1975 forced the government to rein back expenditure so that when Labour left office in 1979, they had managed to reduce expenditure to 32 per cent of GDP. In contrast, despite the language of rolling back the frontiers of government, total expenditure under the government of Margaret Thatcher was again on an expansionary path during the years 1979 to 1982 when expenditure again reached a peak of 35 per cent. After 1983 and up to 1987 the Thatcher government seemed to bring expenditure under control as it declined to 27 per cent of GDP in 1988, but it resumed an expansionary path during the years of John Major as prime minister. In 1992 total expenditure was again at 32 per cent of GDP which represents the same level of expenditure as when the Conservatives took office in 1979. What is significant about this study is that the ten programmes being studied here exclude expenditure on public utilities, the nationalised industries and the proceeds of privatisation; they represent the core areas of government expenditure.

Social expenditure

Social expenditure represents the total expenditure by government on education, health care, housing and social security. In 1962 this element of expenditure totalled £4 billion; in the mid-1970s it had risen to £30 billion, then to £83 billion in the mid-1980s and £138 billion in 1992. Social expenditure expanded from 14 per cent of GDP in 1962 to 22 per cent of GDP in the mid-1970s, to 23 per cent

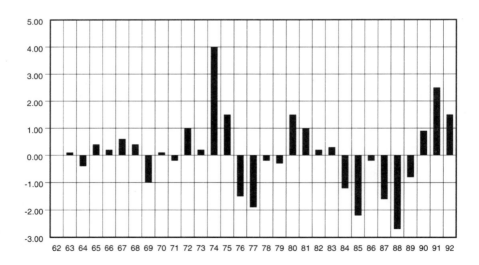

Figure 6.1 Analysis of year-on-year changes in total expenditure 1962–92 (percentage of GDP)

of GDP by 1992. In contrast, defence expenditure has declined from 6.3 per cent of GDP in 1962 to 4 per cent of GDP in 1992. Expenditure on infrastructure including roads and environment has also declined as expenditure on environment fell from 1.5 per cent of GDP in 1962 to 0.6 per cent in 1992 and on roads and transport it fell from 1.8 per cent of GDP in 1962 to 1.4 per cent of GDP in 1992. Law and order expenditure has in the meantime expanded from 0.8 per cent of GDP to 2.1 per cent of GDP in 1992.

Capital expenditure

Total expenditure on capital programmes on housing, education, health care, roads and environment represented some 3.1 per cent of GDP in 1962. This continued to expand to 4.5 per cent of GDP by 1968, declined slightly in the early 1970s but was expanded again in 1972 by the Heath government when capital expenditure reached a peak of 4.7 per cent in 1974. After 1974 capital expenditure started to decline and continued to decline sharply into the 1980s, from 3.9 per cent in 1976 to 2 per cent in 1980, to its lowest level of 0.1 per cent in 1988. Since the early 1990s there has been a slight recovery. The major reductions in capital expenditure were achieved in the housing programme which declined from a peak of 2 per cent of GDP in 1972 to 0.2 per cent by 1992.

Explaining year-on-year changes in capital expenditure

The study of the year-on-year changes expressed as a percentage of GDP confirms a trend of continued decline and reductions after 1975, with the largest reductions being experienced in 1977, 1978, 1981 and 1988. The reductions

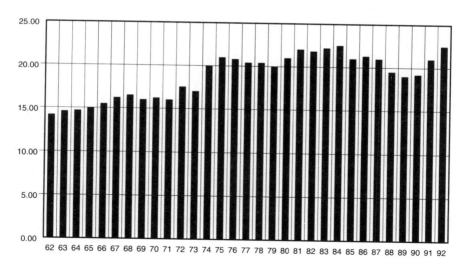

Figure 6.2 Social expenditure 1962–92 (percentage of GDP)

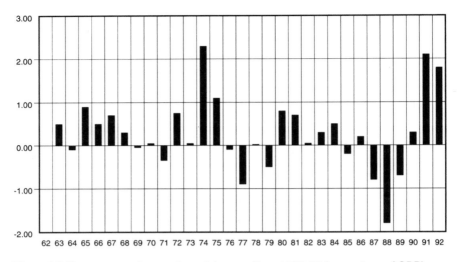

Figure 6.3 Year-on-year changes in social expenditure 1962–92 (percentage of GDP)

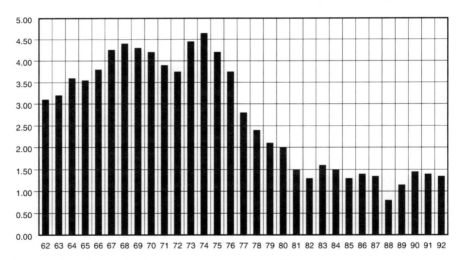

Figure 6.4 Capital expenditure 1962–92 (percentage of GDP)

reflect how the Labour government sought to achieve the 'cuts' packages announced in 1976 and also how the Conservatives continued to make further reductions from an already declining capital expenditure budget.

Current expenditure 1962–92

The study of the ten major expenditure programmes (Mullard 1987, 1992) points

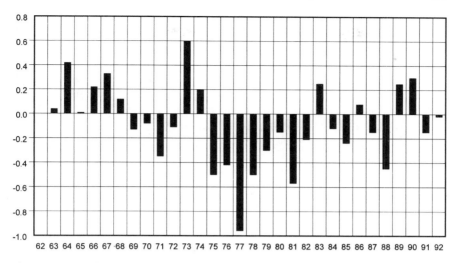

Figure 6.5 Year-on-year changes in capital expenditure 1962–92 (percentage of GDP)

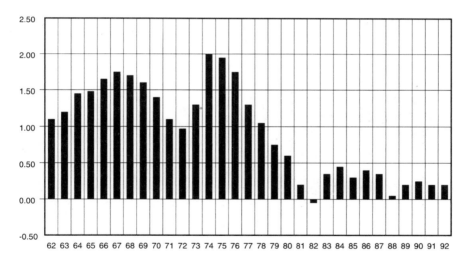

Figure 6.6 Housing capital expenditure 1962–92 (percentage of GDP)

to the robust nature of programmes with a high current component. In 1962 total current expenditure totalled 14.9 per cent of GDP; this continued to expand to the mid-1970s to 19.2 per cent of GDP. In common with the experience for capital expenditure, current expenditure was brought under relative control during the latter years of the labour government when expenditure was reined back to 17.6 per cent of GDP. This reflected the success of the government's incomes policy between 1975 and 1978. Paradoxically, during the mid-1980s current expenditure was expanding again and was brought under some control between 1987 and 1989 but this seemed to be short-lived. Between 1988 and 1992 current expenditure was again on an upward path so that by 1992 it had returned to 17.8 per cent of GDP. *

The study, by individual programme, confirms that between 1962 and 1992 defence expenditure had declined from 6.3 per cent of GDP to 4 per cent of GDP, in contrast with law and order expenditure which expanded from 0.8 per cent of GDP in 1962 to 2.1 per cent of GDP in 1992. Education expenditure expanded from 2.8 per cent of GDP in 1962 to 4.5 per cent of GDP in 1992, and health-care expenditure from 3.2 per cent of GDP to 5.6 per cent of GDP in 1992. The study of current expenditure also confirms that this component has resumed an expansionary trend since Major became prime minister. In 1989 current expenditure represented some 15.9 per cent of GDP; by 1992 this had expanded to 17.7 per cent GDP.

The expansion in health and education current expenditures confirms the long-term commitments made by the governments to two major areas of social expenditure. In 1988 current expenditure was around £74 billion; in 1992 current expenditure was £105 billion, an addition of £31 billion over four years.

Expenditure on transfers and subsidies 1962–92

This category of expenditure represents the government's expenditure on subsidies to agriculture, grants to students, and expenditure on social security, housing and roads. The biggest area of expenditure is social security. In 1962 this category represented 7.8 per cent of GDP. In 1992 this had expanded to 13.3 per cent of GDP, that is from £2.2 billion in 1962 to £79 billion in 1992. In 1962 expenditure on social security was £1.6 billion; this has now expanded to £72 billion in 1992.

The detailed study of ten core expenditure programmes confirms that expenditure has increased from 25 per cent of GDP in 1962 to 32 per cent of GDP in 1992. Social expenditure has been the major area of growth, from 14 per cent of GDP in 1962 to 23 per cent of GDP in 1992. The break-down by economic category points to the large reductions in capital expenditure during this period, especially expenditure on housing and other capital projects. The trend in current expenditure confirms the robustness of some welfare programmes, especially health care and education. Where the government were able to make large reductions in capital programmes, current expenditure has expanded, as has expenditure on social security.

This study would therefore suggest that the public sector deficit needs to be attributed to structural and cyclical factors. Between 1989 and 1992 current expenditure expanded from £80 billion to £105 billion and transfer payments from £56 billion to £79 billion; this would indicate that current expenditure increased by £25 billion during the period, in contrast to £23 billion on social security. The increases in social security do not, however, represent the total increases in unemployment; they do include increases in pensions, child benefit and other social security payments which means that about £12 billion needs to

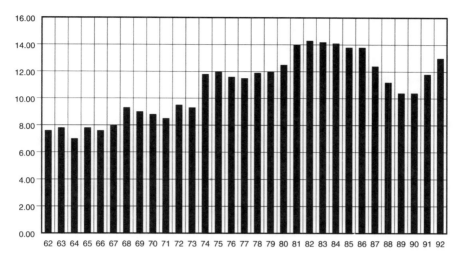

Figure 6.7 Transfer payments and subsidies 1962–92 (percentage of GDP)

be approximated to the cost of unemployment, in contrast to £25 billion worth of additions in expenditure on health care, education and other current expenditures. It is these figures that confirm therefore that the government deficit is more structural than cyclical.

CHALLENGES FOR THE 1990S

It might be argued that within the UK context there seems to be a process built in to the system which has implicitly controlled the growth of public expenditure, especially when the UK experience is compared with that of other industrial countries in Europe, the United States and Japan. Most comparisons reinforce the view that the rate of growth in social expenditure in the United Kingdom is at a lower level than any other European country. Most European countries spend around 33 per cent of GDP on social programmes, compared to the UK ratio of 23 per cent of GDP. In Sweden, social security payments to households have increased from 8 per cent of GDP in 1960 to 20 per of GDP in 1990, in contrast to the United Kingdom which also started from a point of 8 per cent of GDP in 1960, peaked at 14 per cent of GDP in the mid-1980s but has continued to decline to 12 per cent in the 1990s. The United States started from a lower level of 4 per cent of GDP in 1960 but expanded and reached a plateau of 10 per cent in the early 1980s. A study of OECD social expenditure shows that while the OECD average from 1960 to 1981 increased from 13.1 per cent of GDP to 25.6 per cent in 1981, by contrast the UK social expenditure increased from 13.9 per cent in 1960 to 23.7 per cent of GDP in 1981. So while the UK starting point was above the OECD average in 1960, social expenditure in the United Kingdom had fallen behind by 1981 (Glennerster and Midgley 1991, OECD 1993).

At present there seems to be a stalemate, with people less willing to pay tax but also unwilling to see reductions in services. While the UK government have made the reduction of personal taxation their priority, they have not really made explicit the implications of such a policy. The decision to reduce personal taxation represented a strategic choice since the government seemed to reduce the tax base and therefore the opportunity for increasing public expenditure. However, the government policy seemed to falter in that they wanted to present the argument that they had succeeded in reducing taxation while at the same time they were able to increase expenditure on social services and also to manage to reduce the public sector deficit – this represented the best indicator of success in government policy. The government did not seek to educate the electors into reducing their expectations of government, nor did they attempt to point out that there was no such thing as a free lunch – reducing taxes meant less revenue for the government and therefore more responsibility for the individual to spend the money gained from reductions in taxation on services that had previously been purchased through the government.

Studies by the Henley Centre (Lansley 1994) seem to suggest that there has been a fundamental break with the politics of collectivism and a move towards individualism, with more people being less willing to use public services but also less willing to pay for services that benefit others.

In contrast, it may be pointed out that this stalemate is due to the fact that taxes have increasingly become disconnected from the services that those taxes aim to finance (Demos 1993). People want to know where their money is going. They are not disillusioned with public services but rather with the performance of these services; they cannot see improvement in services despite the increases in expenditure and the additional increases in indirect taxes. The aim therefore has to be to create a series of referenda to reconnect taxes with services. Examples would include a referendum on health-care expenditure which asks people whether they would be willing to pay an additional tax of £34 per household to allow an increase in health-care spending of 3 per cent per annum, or to ask Londoners to pay an additional £1 in council tax to gain a world-class underground service.

The debate within the Conservative government on the need to promote a radical review of public expenditure was launched by Portillo soon after the election of April 1992. Portillo, who was promoted to chief secretary to the Treasury, made it his immediate concern to launch a debate within Cabinet on the size of the public sector and the need for the government to reduce public expenditure from 44 per cent of GDP to about 41.5 per cent before the next election. His strategy is for the government to be able to deliver further tax reductions before the next election. Portillo remarked: 'The whole point of this is to make sure our public spending goes to the people who need it most, and produces the best possible benefit' (meeting of 1922 Committee, 20 May 1993). In urging a major public spending review, Portillo has been arguing for privatisation of a major area of public provision which will move responsibility to the individual, such as pensions. Portillo hoped that more people would take out private pensions.

In contrast John Redwood, who is also a sympathiser with the No Turning Back Group agenda, has argued for a more pragmatic approach to public expenditure. At the Welsh Conservative Party conference at Llangollen in June 1993, Redwood argued that the best way of dealing with deficit was through growth in the economy rather than any major review of public expenditure: 'Recovery is the best way of stopping the deficit. We should not put tackling the deficit above the needs of the elderly, the disabled, the disadvantaged who cannot compete in the market-place.'

While John Major sought to expand expenditure on health care and education prior to the April 1992 election, the interventions after June 1992 by the chief secretary, aided by other senior ministers, seemed to indicate that the further sums added to expenditure programmes had only a 'planned' status which could be questioned now that the election was over. It is therefore in this context that the debate within the government needs to be located; between those who saw the increases in expenditure after 1990 as a confirmation of the new politics of pragmatism and those who allowed for the announced increases to be made but only as a short-term measure to win the April 1992 election.

The pre-election autumn statement of November 1991 allowed the government to provide £11 billion of additional expenditure for health care, education and roads. The estimates provided by Lamont, then chancellor of the Exchequer, indicated that expenditure was due to rise by 8.6 per cent in 1992–93, from £236 billion to £256 billion. At the time it was estimated that the PSBR would rise to £10 billion based on the chancellor's forecast that the economy was likely to grow by 2.5 per cent during 1992. Unfortunately for the chancellor the early recovery did not materialise and instead the economy entered a period of recession where the planned growth in expenditure announced in November 1991 was allowed to continue, while revenue for the government declined sharply and the budget deficit expanded from £50 billion. By July 1992 Salmon Brothers, the US investment company, was already predicting a PSBR of £40 billion which was substantially higher than the government's PSBR estimate of £18 billion.

After a series of Cabinet meetings during the period of April to July 1992 it became very clear that the government could no longer meet the commitments made in the pre-election period of allowing for planned increases in expenditure of 4 per cent in 1993/94 and beyond. The setting up of the EDX committee meant that the Treasury was again in ascendancy in the public expenditure cycle since it was now up to the EDX committee to set up the total for expenditure and for spending ministers to bargain within the agreed total:

> Blessed with the prime minister's strong support – the sine qua non of effective control over public expenditure – the Treasury gained a notable victory this week both in the changes to procedure agreed by the Cabinet and in the actual figures. The beauty – from the Treasury's point of view – of the new procedure is that it will place spending ministers, like scorpions, in a bottle of predetermined size.
>
> (*Financial Times* editorial, 25 July 1992)

Any attempt to explain the vulnerable position of Major within the ranks of the Conservative Party is partly related to the issue of whether he wishes to portray himself as one who seeks to provide leadership suitable for the 1990s or whether he is seen as the successor to Thatcher and thereby continuing with the agenda of 'Thatcherism'. The chief divide relates to the twin issues of public expenditure and taxation. Those who aim to ensure that Major continues with the agenda of Thatcherism argue that the government must reduce public expenditure in order to reduce the public sector deficit while ensuring that the government provide a policy for reducing personal taxation before the next election. It is with this aim in mind that Portillo has continued to argue that the state was doing too much and what was needed was a policy that ensured that individuals took more responsibility for their personal lives, an approach that has had the containing support of Peter Lilley, the secretary of state for social security, and Michael Howard, the home secretary. In launching his debate for a review of the social security budget, Lilley argued that his aim was to provide data and information that would allow for a debate of the social security system.

> The aim is to improve the system: to make it better focused to protect the vulnerable, to ensure that we all have the means to cope with the needs and contingencies of modern life and to make sure that the system does not outstrip the nation's ability to pay.
>
> (Lilley 1993)

The Lilley doctrine is that the United Kingdom needs to produce policies that address the pressures for inexorable growth and therefore the challenges to the social security budget – a problem that, he argues, other industrial nations are also seeking to address. According to data produced by the Department for Social Security (Lilley 1993), social security spending is likely to increase by 19 per cent by the year 2000 and that if there is no fall in unemployment, the social security budget will increase from £78 billion in 1992/93 to £93 billion by 2000 which, expressed as a proportion of GDP, would mean an increase from 12.3 per cent to 13.5 per cent. The social security budget has increased from about £10.5 billion in 1949/50 to £78 billion in 1992/93 in real terms which implies that social security has been growing at an average of 3.7 per cent per annum and that the rate of growth has been outstripping the rate of growth in the economy.

The break-down of the social security budget confirms that nearly 50 per cent is utilised to finance state pensions, while another 13 per cent is used to finance unemployment benefits. The major areas of growth in recent years have included the rate of growth in invalidity benefits and the increases in housing benefits. While pensions have increased at the rate of 1.5 per cent per annum, invalidity benefits have grown by 5.8 per cent and rent rebates by 15 per cent. Lilley argues that there is an urgent need to provide a review of social security:

> it is not possible for the system to continue indefinitely to grow more rapidly than the economy as a whole. If the underlying growth in the system remains above the growth of the economy and above the growth that can be afforded

for public expenditure as a whole, other expenditure programmes will be bound to suffer.

(Lilley 1993)

In a recent pamphlet for the Social Market Foundation, David Willetts MP (1993) has urged the Conservative Party to return to the principles of Beveridge and to target pensions to specific categories. Willetts argues that the people who really need state support during the 1990s are those who are aged 80 and over. The argument is that not all pensioners are poor and the poor are not all pensioners. There is now an expanding army of people who are benefiting from private provision and also occupational pensions. Willetts believes that there is now a problem of people living longer but giving up work too early. He has therefore suggested that the government should raise the retirement age for all to 65 and eventually to 67. In his strategy to target benefits Willetts also favours the move towards targeting child benefit to children who are under 5 years old.

There are an implicit thesis within this line of argument: – the Welfare State as presently constructed cannot be sustained without major increases in taxation. At present an argument seems to be developing that a major review of social security, including pensions, is unavoidable. The study conducted in this chapter suggests that overall during the last thirty years expenditure has remained relatively stable, although there might have been trade-off between programmes and also between capital spending projects and current expenditures. The study by Hills (1993) for the Joseph Rowntree Foundation suggests that at today's prices, expenditure is only likely to rise by 5 per cent of GDP over the next fifty years. UK social expenditure at 23 per cent of GDP is below the EU average of 33 per cent, which means that present UK arrangements are perfectly tenable but may not be compatible with a government that seeks to make tax reductions the priority.

The attempt to move towards more selective benefits and provision runs against the Conservative Party commitment to maintain the level of pensions and child benefit, but most importantly runs counter to the expectations of middle-class voters who benefit directly from the principles of universal benefits and who would therefore resist any changes to their Welfare State. It is that much easier to target the benefits that are aimed at those in need, as they are less numerous and less vocal in their protests, and therefore less important to the arithmetic of politics. The refusal by Thatcher to entertain during the early 1980s the proposal by her minister Keith Joseph to target student grants, or Chancellor Lawson's proposal to phase out mortgage tax relief, confirms the degree to which any reviews of public provision would always include a mixture of the desirable and the politically possible.

The present debate on public expenditure partly reflects the government's short-term preoccupation with the public sector deficit. While in 1989 the government could claim that they had moved into a position of debt repayment, by 1992 that position had been changed to a forecast of a PSBR of 8 per cent of GDP. This means that there has been a 9 per cent swing in the PSBR/GDP ratio during the last five years. The question for the government is whether the deficit represents a temporary fluctuation which can be attributed to the economic cycle and the recession, and the degree to which the deficit represents a structural problem in public finances. Major has argued in Cabinet that about 70 per cent of the budget deficit could be attributed to the economic cycle and the recession and that therefore, once recovery is on its way, the deficit will fall. However, there is also the argument that only 50 per cent of the deficit was due to recession while the other 50 per cent was structural and therefore had to be explained in terms of the government's additional spending commitments made prior to the 1992 election on education and health care. If the deficit is due to structural problems, the end of the recession would not cure the problem which means that the government will have to deal with the deficit through a radical review of public expenditure. If, however, the prime minister is correct, then his policy to adhere to the manifesto commitments would suggest that what is needed is adjustment at the margins. In an interview with the *Financial Times* on 26 May 1993, Major provided the following statements on public expenditure which in themselves reinforce the uncertainty that exists within the government about the future of public expenditure and the extent to which the government is living in hope that something will turn up before the next election:

> 'This is not a runaway spending spree.' Just as the huge surplus of the 1980s was 'something of a surprise' so now the pendulum has swung back dramatically. During the recession 'it was right to protect people who are hurt and to protect some of the public sector infrastructure programmes'. However, when asked to what extent the deficit was cyclical or structural and how it would respond as the economy recovered, the Prime Minister replied 'I wish I knew'.

Part of the deterioration has to be blamed on the government's policies on privatisation and taxation. While the proceeds of privatisation exceeded 2 per cent of GDP at their peak, the revenues had fallen to 1 per cent in 1990 and to zero by 1993. While privatisation brought financial proceeds in the short term, the sale of BT, for example, has meant a loss of income for the government over the longer term. Second, it would seem that changes in taxation have made consumption much more prone to changes in the economic cycle. The cycle of taxation resulted in a high feel-good factor in the late 1980s which in turn led to high spending and VAT which increased revenues to the government. By contrast, the recession slowed down revenues much further while the loss of taxes due to unemployment and recession, which have lasted longer than predicted, have also led to the deterioration in public finances. This applies also to the changes in corporation taxation in that, while during the 1980s the revenues from corporation tax continued to expand, the recession of the 1990s have led to a major turnround.

In their attempt to reduce the deficit it is estimated that the government have increased the total tax burden by £17 billion during the two budgets of 1993. The changes in National Insurance, the freezing of tax allowances and the changes in mortgage tax relief would indicate that the United Kingdom now has two tax regimes: one at 40 per cent for higher incomes, while the rest are paying a marginal tax of 35 per cent. The net effect has been that UK tax has become more regressive, with lower-income groups now financing their own Welfare State. The forecast is of low economic growth with disposable incomes rising at 1 per cent per annum in 1994 and 1995 and unemployment remaining unchanged at 2.9 million. The question is whether the government would have the resilience to meet the electors with the prospects of no discernible improvement in living standards and poorer quality public services.

Furthermore there is the question of the durability and feasibility of the present strategy. The government have, for example, announced a freeze on public sector wages for the next three years. In the previous section the study of current expenditure indicated that this category of expenditure was robust and more difficult for government to reduce. While governments have succeeded to hold down public sector pay, this has tended to be short term in that public sector pay policy has usually been followed by periods of catching up. With private sector workers settling for around 3 per cent per annum, it can be assumed that wages for private sector workers will rise by 10 per cent during the next three years. For public sector workers to achieve this form of settlement, employment in the public sector would have to decline by half a million.

CONCLUSIONS

To a limited extent the Conservative Party conferences of 1993 and 1994 confirmed the fragile nature of the present alliances within the Conservative government. On the one hand there is still a strong faction within the party which wants to push further on the frontiers of the Welfare State, and they lament the failure of the Conservative government to remove major areas of public provision to private insurance. The dilemma for the No Turning Back Group and the Group of '92 is that they are aware that many parts of the Welfare State are very popular with the electors, and public-funded education, health care, universal state pensions and child benefit are difficult areas for the government to change the present funding arrangements. Many of today's taxpayers realise that their taxes are used to pay for today's pensions and they feel therefore that it is their right to expect that future generations will finance their pensions. Today's taxpayers cannot afford to pay for the pensions of today's elderly while also trying to make private pension arrangements. In terms of pensions, therefore, it is difficult for the government to bring forward a major policy shift unless the process of private pensions is phased over a number of years.

The policy strategy of the government is to those expenditures that are at present directed at specific groups whom the government depict as less deserving. Within this context therefore, benefits directed to lone mothers are especially vulnerable as the government seek a return to the traditions of the family as defined by the government. A number of 'scroungers' are identified, including foreigners who come to England especially to draw on benefits to which they are not entitled and also those who seek to make fraudulent claims. The rising costs of invalidity and housing benefits are used as indicators to show the failures of the Welfare State and why the government need to target benefits to those who are really in need.

The squeeze on education expenditure, especially in the funding of higher education, has forced vice-chancellors and principals to argue for new funding arrangements. The attempt by the London School of Economics to introduce top-up fees of £500–£1,000 per student represented a response to pressures by government to reduce units of resources from £1,800 to £1,300 per student. While the precedent of introducing tuition fees seems to run counter to the Robbins principle of ability to take advantage, the minister of state responsible for higher education argued at the time that there was also the principle of institutional autonomy which was equally valid.

Le Grand (1993) has argued that, at best, the present Welfare State acts as a savings bank in that 60 per cent of taxes paid are returned to the individual in education, health care, child benefit and pensions:

> We estimate that over their lifetimes people pay for between two-thirds and three-quarters of the benefit they receive from social security, education and health. Hence the welfare state is acting as a 'savings bank', smoothing the flow of resources for the same individuals over the life cycle.

People pay in to the system when times are good and draw out in times of need, therefore the Welfare State represents a generation contract between the old of today and the young of today, based on an understanding that a future generation will pay for the pensions of today's young. Therefore any attempt by the government to encourage the break of this implicit contract will mean a major disruption for the present generation of taxpayers. It represents an encouragement of individual selfishness which says to those who have benefited from taxpayers who paid for education and health that they can now contract out and purchase private services for their children.

The uncertainty about the quality of public services combined with the experiences of recession and stationary living standards have produced a context that increasingly favours individual self-interest. Stewart Lansley (1994) has called this the environment of competitive individualism where taxpayers feel that they cannot pay higher taxes because they need the income to protect themselves from dependency on low-quality public services.

The study of public expenditure reinforces the view that there has been a major erosion in public confidence about the ability of governments to provide high-quality public services. The question of whether the move towards increased individualism is the result of increased affluence, where people feel that they can now provide more for themselves and their families because of increased income, or whether the public has been persuaded by the political process, remains an open one. There is, however, sufficient evidence to reinforce the argument that since the mid-1970s a number of major decisions on public expenditure have made the public sector look less attractive, with lower investment in the infrastructure and no major improvements in the quality of public provision. The policy of privatisation, the attempt to create internal markets and the drive to reduce the costs of provision, together with tight public sector budgets, have added to the erosion of quality public provision and it is this that pushes towards increased individualism – this individualism is the response to a Welfare State that behaves more as a deterrent than as a form of solidarity and increased citizenship.

CORE READING

Barnett, J. (1982) *Inside the Treasury*, London: Andre Deutsch.

Demos (1993) *Reconnecting Taxation*, London.

Glennerster, H. and Midgley, J. (eds) (1991) *The Radical Right and the Welfare State*, Hemel Hempstead: Harvester Wheatsheaf.

Gray, J. (1994) *The Undoing of Conservatism*, London: Social Market Foundation.

Heald, D. (1983) *Public Expenditure*, Oxford: Martin Robertson.

Heclo, H. and Wildavsky, A. (1983) *The Private Government of Public Money*, London: Macmillan.

Hills, J. (1993) *The Future of the Welfare State*, London: The Rowntree Foundation.

Lansley, S. (1994) *After the Gold Rush*, London: Century.

Mishra, R. (1990) *The Welfare State in Capitalist Society*, Hemel Hempstead: Harvester.

Mullard, M. (1992) *Understanding Economic Policy*, London: Routledge.

Mullard, M. (1993) *The Politics of Public Expenditure*, London: Routledge.

Willetts, D. (1993) *The Age of Entitlement*, London: Centre for Policy Studies.

Willets, D. (1994) *Civic Conservatism*, London: Social Market Foundation.

UK Treasury (1988) *Managing Public Expenditure*, London: HMSO.

ADDITIONAL READING

Friedman, R. and Gilbert, N. (eds) (1992) *Modern Welfare State*, New York: New York University Press.

Goodin, R.E. and Le Grand, J. (1987) *Not Only For the Poor*, London: Allen & Unwin.

King, D. (1987) *The New Right*, London: Macmillan.

Le Grand, J. (1993) 'Portillo Risks Targeting His Own Foot', *The Financial Times*, 25 May.

Lilley, P. (1993) *The Growth of Social Security*, London: HMSO.

Mullard, M. (1987) *The Politics of Public Expenditure*, London: Croom Helm.

OECD (1993) *Social Expenditure 1960–1990*, Paris.

Thain, C. and Wright, M. (1992a) 'Planning and controlling public expenditure in the UK: the Treasury public expenditure survey', *Public Administration* 70(1): 3–24.

Thain, C. and Wright, M. (1992b) 'Planning and controlling public expenditure in the UK: the effects and effectiveness of the survey', *Public Administration* 70(2): 193–224.

Wilkinson, M. (1993) 'British tax policy 1979–90: equity and efficiency', *Policy and Politics* 21(3): 207–17.

7 The agencification of the Civil Service

Richard Common

INTRODUCTION

> The aim of Next Steps is to improve the quality and efficiency of government services through better management.
>
> (Efficiency Unit 1991: 3)

The publication of *Improving Management in government* (Efficiency Unit 1988, and hereafter referred to as the 'Ibbs Report')[1] supposedly heralded a management revolution in the UK Civil Service by promising to deliver government services more efficiently and effectively. According to the Next Steps team, the solution to the problem of big and diverse government was to set up apparently free-standing agencies to carry out distinct activities. Also, by advocating the separation of executive functions from the policy functions of central government departments, the authors of the report promised that substantial improvements in service delivery and management performance would soon follow. Ministers would be freed to deal with the major policy questions of government, while the new heads of each agency, the chief executives, would be allowed to have financial and managerial freedom to ensure that day-to-day service delivery would be conducted smoothly and without interference from the politicians. Framework documents between ministers and chief executives would spell out the operating arrangements for each agency.

This chapter questions whether agencification is an appropriate response to the problems of government, and examines whether the separation of policy from execution is simply a return to the principles of administration propounded by Woodrow Wilson and other writers in the late nineteenth century. The 'science' of administration developed by Wilson demanded that this separation be made (the 'Wilsonian dichotomy') based on the conviction that 'there was a neutral, scientific answer to most policy problems' (Devine 1991: 90). The separation of politics from administration was, for Wilson at least, a crucial prescription for good government. If so, has agencification achieved the aims of its proponents?

THE POLITICS–ADMINISTRATION DICHOTOMY: IMPROVING THE BUSINESS OF GOVERNMENT

Hierarchical assumptions formed the backcloth to Wilsonian 'good' administration which meant a system of graded ranks subject to central political direction by heads of departments (Ostrom 1989: 24). This notion appears to be congruent with Weber's theory of bureaucracy,[2] as 'Weber concurs with Wilson's position that perfection in bureaucratic administration depends upon rigorous exclusion of politics from the routines of administration'. (Ostrom 1989: 26). But, Devine (1991: 95) notes that 'whereas Wilson had blurred the distinction betwen policy and administration . . . Weber always made this a critical distinction'. Hierarchical assumptions continued to dominate American thinking on public administration, culminating in the Brownlow Report in 1937.

Wilson's chief concerns were the promotion of efficiency and responsibility in government, and Doig (1983: 294) claimed that Wilson required administrative agencies to be organised so that 'clear-cut responsibility' is assured, which can be achieved through the '*narrowing* of discretion and close confinement at all administrative levels', ideas later advocated by Finer and Lowi. Wilson also interpreted efficiency in economic terms: 'the utmost possible efficiency and at the least possible cost of either money or of energy' (Wilson 1887: 197) and thus perfection in hierarchical ordering would increase efficiency by reducing the costs or effort needed to attain policy objectives (Ostrom 1989: 24).

As the work of Wilson and Weber and others was slowly scrutinised, rejected or simply ignored by academics and bureaucrats alike, separating politics and administration came to be viewed as unrealistic, irrelevant or dangerous. However, changing economic and political conditions in the West, especially following the oil shocks of the 1970s, apparently helped to pave the way for a return to the Wilsonian dichotomy as governments struggled to curb mounting public expenditure and to reign in their bureaucracies. Consequently, government–administration relations began to be questioned.

> Instead of being content to accept the negotiated outcomes of existing resource decision processes . . . central government politicians sought to shift the previous balance of powers within the public domain so that their requirements for reduced spending would be more clearly met.
>
> (Richards 1992: 18)

Administrators were no longer required to be negotiators but to behave like managers, and Richards sees their 'key tasks' as being to exert 'pressure on the producer domain to yield greater efficiency' and 'to deliver politician's objectives of lower spendings and increased efficiency' (Richards 1992: 18). Improving the business of government moved back up the agenda as the 'Whitehall' model of public administration began to be questioned in the late twentieth century along with political and economic demands for specialist managerial skills.

The introduction of Next Steps agencies appears to involve a re-evaluation of the relationship between politicians and civil servants. This relationship was explored by Aberbach *et al.* (1981) whose first 'image' of the relationship between politics and administration accorded with Wilsonian and Weberian ideas about bureaucracy. However, this image or Wilsonian myth that government administration is merely a technical task, to be handed over to neutral experts in the bureaucracy, has persisted to the extent that it has been charged with restricting the spread of managerialism in government as well as clouding academic thinking about public administration in general (Devine 1991: 97).

Attempts to articulate the relationship between bureaucrats and politicians tended to produce caricatures, partly due to problems of empirical testing when politicians and bureaucrats find it difficult to make a distinction between policy and administration roles. Putnam (1973) made the distinction between 'classical' and 'political' bureaucrats. The 'classical bureaucrat' corresponds to the Weberian ideal of a technical expert whereas the 'political bureaucrat' is 'more willing to treat political influences on policy making as legitimate' (Putnam 1973: 259). The political bureaucrat may share 'values and objectives' but their 'skills and immediate concerns' may be somewhat different (Putnam 1973: 259). In the UK, civil servants have always been considered to be responsive to the authority of elected politicians, and it is debatable whether or not the caricature of the 'classical bureaucrat' has ever been appropriate.

Aberbach *et al.* (1981) present an alternative image of the relationship between politics and administration that defines 'energy' as the primary quality of the politician and 'equilibrium' as the corresponding quality of the bureaucrat. This image apparently moves us closer to an acceptable model of the British civil service. Aberbach *et al.* (1981) cite Rose (1974: 418-9) who notes that: 'in practice, policy making usually develops dialectically; both politicians and civil servants review political and administrative implications of a major policy.'

The term 'Whitehall consensus', upon which Rose's observation is based, means that it is hard to tell where primary political initiatives come from. This may be true when 'the bureaucracy can become identified with a private group and, as a result, simply becomes an interest group within the bureaucratic-political process' (Suleiman 1984: 6). In the UK, a 'nominal distinction' between policy and politics is made, although the Civil Service Commission (1981) attributes a 'policy (that is, political) role to the higher Civil Service, promising would-be recruits a career of policy and planning work or the drafting of legislation or the detailed management of an executive programme' (cited in Rose 1984: 139).

The growth in the size and complexity of government tasks naturally means that both ministers and higher civil servants 'are remote from the coal face, that is, the levels of government where the actual day-to-day execution of programs is carried out. Neither higher civil servants nor ministers are meant to be executive officials or managers' (Rose 1984: 153). Ponting (1989: 62) claims that those 'at the top in Whitehall have never been much interested in executive operations' anyway. Public service is all about advising ministers, policy formulation and service delivery, but with priority given to policy. On the other hand, Caiden (1991) and Richards (1992) contend that the Whitehall model of government has been based precisely on the politics–administration dichotomy; 'the British had institutionalised the politics dichotomy at home and abroad' based on the notion of a 'generalist' higher Civil Service.

However, agencification is likely to encourage 'the subordination of the higher civil servants rather than the strengthening of the existing relationship with the politically elected executive' (Caiden, 1991: 86). Along with the invasion of business management into public services, the scene is set for the separation of policy from administration. Also, Hood (1990: 206) conjectures that the British model is losing its applicability as a consequence of the 'new machine politics' where policy is driven by pollsters and professional party strategists: 'the skills which the politicians need from the bureaucracy will lie mainly in management, not in policy formulation'. What is clear is that the debate about the relationship between politicians and bureaucrats has been brought into sharp focus by agencification.

ABANDONING THE UNIFIED BUREAUCRACY

Principal–agent theory

Agencification poses a contradiction between abandoning traditional public bureaucracies while reasserting the Wilsonian dichotomy. This contradiction is partly a result of the 'New Institutional Economics' because it too appears to offer an intellectual antecedent to the process of agencification. As part of this approach, public choice theory offers some rationales for agencification when one of its aims is to subject agencies to market-like forces wherever possible.[3] For instance, public choicers would argue that as 'non-profit behaviour declines the more competitive is the product market' (Dunsire *et al.* 1988: 365). But it is in New Zealand where public choice has probably been articulated to its greatest extent following a similar process of agencification to that in the United Kingdom. Boston (1991a: 4) posits a public choice argument that 'because departments have a vested interest in their own survival, they should not both advise their political masters **and** implement policy. Otherwise, their advice will be biased and bureaucratic capture may occur.' Such arguments have been promoted as 'theoretical underpinnings' to public sector reform in New Zealand.

Wistrich (1992: 122) also argues that in New Zealand, public choice concerns about 'rent seeking' by interest groups and the capture of policy advice has lead policy advisers to favour a government structure in which policy advice is generally separate from other functions and service delivery (see also Chapman 1989). In the United Kingdom, public choice theory would also point to 'systems and attitudes' that were 'thought to be focused more on avoiding errors which could expose officials and their Ministers to criticism than on improving results' (Goldsworthy 1991: 4). It is only a matter of conjecture whether the Efficiency Unit saw agencification as a solution to this kind of self-seeking behaviour by both politicians and bureaucrats.

Perhaps the most useful variant of economic analysis in understanding agencification has been principal–agent theory. The idea of a contractual relationship between principals (ministers) and agents (chief executives) appears to be enshrined in the framework documents. But despite the fact that the principal–agent relationship 'is fraught with the problems of cheating, limited information, and bounded rationality in general' (Perrow 1986: 224), why has it been adopted? Perrow (1986: 224) would offer that 'it appears to reflect a concern with applying the most stark assumptions of economics – maximizing utilities, where net utilities are rewards (money) minus effort – to explain contracts and thus organizations'. At first glance, framework documents appear to be a form of contract between chief executives and ministers.

Principal–agent problems have not been articulated in the UK to the same extent has they have in New Zealand where the idea of the executive agency is supported by study of the agency problem in firms. Scott and Gorringe (1989, cited in Wistrich 1992) describe the problem as 'getting agents such as managers and employees to pursue the interests of their principals in such organisations'. Framework documents may offer only a crude remedy, as in New Zealand ministers have had problems in freeing themselves from administrative responsibilities and in obtaining the quality of advice necessary to focus effectively on the larger policy questions (Tyson 1990).

In the UK, government is organised so that the minister is politically accountable for the performance of a department under his or her responsibility. If we apply a principal–agent relationship, it should follow that under the 'guidance' of the minister, civil servants 'should act as public agents in a disinterested fashion, and be efficient', as in the Wilsonian dichotomy. '*But* since civil servants are not especially recruited or trained for business life and because government departments cannot be at "arm's length" from the political process' (Dunsire *et al.* 1988: 366; my emphasis) this has necessitated the creation of alternative public sector organisations, such as agencies, in order to try to clarify a principal–agent relationship that had become difficult to define. Framework agreements between ministers and agencies, plus the introduction of fixed-term contracts for chief executives, are attempts to ensure that chief executives avoid bureaucratic capture, as well as being methods of solving principal–agent problems.

However, for instance, the framework document for the Vehicle Inspectorate states that 'existing arrangements for liaison and consultation on policy development . . . will be maintained and where appropriate, strengthened' (Department of Transport 1988). Principal–agent relations are negated by this type of ambiguity, although other framework documents are explicit about excluding chief executives from policy formulation. But 'despite the framework documents' attempts at clarification, there are potential overlaps in the responsibilities of ministers, departments' head-quarters and agencies. This obfuscation stems from the lack of a clear dividing line between policy and operational matters' (Greer 1992: 90).

Similarly, in New Zealand the relationship between ministers and departmental chief executives was highlighted as the critical link in the accountability chain (Boston 1991b). Principals (ministers) are expected to set the policy agenda, determine departmental priorities, specify outcomes (of policy) and outputs (of departments) and monitor performance. Agents (chief executives) are expected to ensure that departments satisfy ministerial requirements and take responsibility for failure. The aim was to ensure that chief executives have incentives to act in accordance with ministers and to ensure that ministers can monitor and assess the performance of their agents and hold them accountable for their departments (Boston 1992: 409–10). This is virtually identical to the UK model where Goldsworthy (1991: 7) claims that 'the aim was to establish a more contractual relationship between the chief executive and the Minister' where 'the underlying principle, of a "bargain" between the Minister and the chief executive' would provide benefits for both parties, and for the public through the political account-ability of the minister.

Principal–agent relationships can also suffer from asymmetrical information which stems from the demands placed on ministers, as well as a lack of technical knowledge in policy areas that could bias the relationship towards the agent (Boston 1992: 416–17). Therefore, information asymmetry could make ministers dependent on chief executives for advice concerning performance indicators so 'the potential for opportunistic behaviour and bureaucratic capture must not be exaggerated' (Boston 1992: 417). What Boston seems to be forgetting here is that ministers, in the United Kingdom at least, will continue to be cushioned by a layer of political administrators who are charged with monitoring and assessing agency performance, as well as preparing and maintaining framework agreements. A more realistic danger is Ponting's (1989: 73) assessment of the agency approach when he remarks that 'by invoking respect for managerial autonomy, ministers will be able to pass the buck with even greater ease than at present and will no longer be accountable for large areas of activity that they will in effect still control'.

Clarifying roles

Principal–agent theory has been used in an attempt to clarify the roles and relationships of politicians and administrators in government as part of agencifi-cation. However, scrutinising the way in which civil servants are trained, remunerated and recruited have been given added impetus by agencification. Wilson's early prescriptions of good government envisaged public administra-tion as being staffed by 'a corps of technically trained civil servants' (Wilson 1887: 216 and cited in Ostrom 1989: 24), organised 'in a hierarchically ordered and professionally trained public service' (Ostrom 1989: 24), but without the need to make principal–agent relationships explicit.

As Peters (1986: 18) notes, in the United Kingdom the relationship between civil servants and politicians is affected by the training received by civil servants, which is traditionally almost non-existent as they are expected to 'learn on the job'. Direct recruitment from Oxford and Cambridge into politics and adminis-tration tended to create a 'tightly integrated elite' which makes it difficult to distinguish senior civil servants and politicians. This 'village life' model began to be questioned, especially in the Fulton Report of 1968 which advocated the promotion of 'specialists' over 'generalists'. Putnam (1973) notes that the 'specialists' fitted the image of the 'classical bureaucrat', in other words they were less tolerant of politics or 'less comfortable in the grey area between politics and administration' (Putnam 1973: 284). It was clear that the roles of both politicians and administrators needed to be clarified and ever since the Fulton Report, critics of Civil Service management policies have stressed the need for greater specialisation and professionalism and for senior Civil Service managers to be trained in management techniques (particularly those related to financial management) (Goldsworthy 1991: 28–9).

Agencification in the United Kingdom has created the role of the chief executive to manage each executive agency, who is appointed by the minister. As a senior Civil Servant, the post of chief executive marks a break with the past. As the Ibbs Report notes, the best Civil Service talent inevitably occupies policy posts and even if 'high fliers' wanted management experience, it was assumed that they would end up in policy-making positions. The problem remains that policy jobs are more attractive. For example, Zussman and Jabes (1989) looked at the recruitment of chief executives in the Canadian federal government. They found that one factor that

> varied along hierarchical lines in the choice of employer was the index on the potential for involvement in public policy decisions. In this case, 61% of respondents one level below the DM (Deputy Minister) felt that being involved in a policy decision was important or very important.
>
> (1989: 35)

This appears to fit well with Dunleavy's (1991: 200) motives for bureau-shaping by high-ranking Civil Servants.

A further impetus to emphasising the managerial role of civil servants came in April 1980 when Sir Derek Rayner (now Lord Rayner), then head of the Efficiency Unit, urged more emphasis on managerial abilities and initiatives to eliminate waste including 'changing the education and experience of career Civil Servants to become real managers' (cited in Caiden 1991: 199). The Financial Management Initiative (FMI) was to follow in 1982 and according to Fry *et al.* (1988: 430) if Thatcher needed to keep the momentum going on civil service reform, the clash between 'the philosophies represented by the FMI and the career civil service' could only be resolved by 'a separating out of policy work and management'.

When the Ibbs Report (Efficiency Unit 1988) was published, there remained the recognition that senior Civil Servants should continue to be responsive to ministers, and ministers, 'feeling overloaded already, had told the (Efficiency) Unit that, provided no major political risk was involved, they would welcome the divesting of manager-tasks' (Fry *et al.* 1988: 432). The separation of execution from policy-making, it was hoped, would remedy this, but the Wilsonian dichotomy was not to occur at the top of the hierarchy. The real challenge for agencification is to motivate high-ranking civil servants into assuming managerial tasks, and encouraging ministers to avoid becoming involved in day-to-day matters. The Ibbs Report had identified the managerial characteristics supposedly needed by civil servants following agencification and these include vague requirements such as 'flexibility': the ability to interpret government policy and to manage so as to 'maximise results'. The report's authors also stated that 'senior management is dominated by people whose skills are in policy formulation and who have relatively little experience of managing or working where services are actually delivered' (Efficiency Unit 1988: 3). This is a consequence of the Whitehall model of government, yet agencification may reinforce this situation since policy-making cores are to be retained at departmental level (Tyson 1990).

In fact, chief executives are offered very little in the way of specialised management training, and are only expected to supplement the training provided by the Civil Service College by purchasing places on external courses on their own initiative. The Civil Service College offers no courses specifically for chief executives, and senior civil servants can choose from courses that offer a mix of management and policy skills.

Mascarenhas's (1990) prediction of a move from public servants as 'generalists' to public servants as 'integrative generalists', rather than 'specialists', with skills in both policy advice and public management appears to be well founded here. He argues that a training strategy should 'lay emphasis on developing substantive competence in one's policy area, developing interpersonal skills and an understanding of the system' (Mascarenhas 1990: 91). Presumably, although the Civil Service College offers training in the latter two of Mascarenhas's components, chief executives are not expected to have any competence in their policy area; it is not supposed to be part of their job.

Proponents of the agency initiative seem unable to understand the difficulty of excluding politics from the ingredients of public sector management. Zussman and Jabes (1989: 203) comment that 'good public sector managers must be able to demonstrate an expertise in three essential activities: subject matter knowledge, understanding of the decision-making process, and managerial skills'. They point to the tendency, already highlighted in the United Kingdom, to reward those who understand the decision-making process but pay too little attention to 'managerial skills'. Zussman and Jabes (1989: 203) go on to assert that 'good' management needs defining and 'will also require changes in the incentive and reward system. Managers are rational actors and the reward system will have to be structured so as to ensure that good management is rewarded and bad management is not.' Therefore the introduction of performance-related pay for chief executives on top of considerably higher salaries therefore comes as no surprise, especially if they are denied bureau-shaping strategies. It seems that in the absence of a coherent training strategy, chief executives are being offered crude remunerative incentives to be 'good' managers.

Furthermore, by taking this approach, Fry *et al.* (1988: 438) warn that 'there is the very real risk of hierarchical development and emulative activity in terms of salaries' which could undermine agencification by encouraging budget-maximising strategies. Ironically, in New Zealand: 'there was concern . . . that the introduction of contract employment and performance related pay, might make chief executives less willing to offer objective advice to ministers', (Boston 1992: 413) although this assumes a policy role for chief executives.

Another way to inject 'good' management into the Civil Service is to recruit chief executives with a proven commercial track record from outside the Service. The Treasury and Civil Service Committee Report (1987–8, HC 494–I) recommended that 'outsiders be recruited, that management activity should be part of the "golden route" to the top' (cited in Fry *et al.* 1988: 444). By December 1994, sixty-eight out of the 107 chief executives and chief executive designate appointments had been recruited through open competition but only thirty-seven have come from outside the Civil Service.[4] The demise of the Civil Service Department in 1981 was partly to encourage the dencentralisation of personnel recruitment, and now it is the departments that appoint chief executives on the approval of the minister. Thus the apparent 'politicisation' of these appointments may result in a bureaucracy more responsive to the government of the day, but directly opposes Woodrow Wilson's ideal of a neutral bureaucracy.

Vesting considerable power and autonomy in chief executives may be detrimental to public service delivery. Public sector managers need to establish relationships in government and government activities are often achieved through indirect means that cut across administrative boundaries, so the 'more one seeks to concentrate authority and responsibility around the chief executive (or departmental head), the more one discovers interdependence and thus the need for greater central controls through control departments' (Kaufman 1981, cited in Mascarenhas 1990: 91). Public management roles must therefore focus on 'acquiring skills of influence, coalition-building, monitoring and understanding complex institutional and interpersonal relations' (Elmore 1986, cited in Mascarenhas 1990).

There are other problems with locking chief executives into non-mobile, fixed-term appointments. The lack of transferability for chief executives may result in 'the loss of "the common culture" that facilitates policy making' (Jordan 1991: 19). It may also be dysfunctional for politicians faced with a succession of temporary chief executives, even allowing for short-termism in the political environment. Also, Jordan (1991: 23) fears that agencification will create a 'backwater administration', and I would concur if policy formulation is completely discouraged at agency level. If we add the lack of mobility for chief executives, even attractive salaries and various perquisites may fail to attract the best personnel.

Improving the management of government

Despite increasing government service provision and expenditure over the last century, Whitehall has remained as the direct purveyor of public services based on 'the nineteenth century model of a government department established primarily to make policy' (Ponting 1989: 16). Agencification needs to be placed within the broader context of government reform as the separation of politics from administration has never been formally addressed in the United Kingdom as a method of improving the management of government. Also, Chapman and Greenaway (1980: 187) note that 'the British constitution is not based on a single document and there has never been a date from which all political and administrative principles were reconsidered in relation to a framework of principles'. The close relationship between politicians and bureaucrats mitigates the appearance of purely political or managerial solutions, consequently pragmatism has been the hallmark of changes to the administrative machinery in the United Kingdom.

Although the Northcote-Trevelyan Report of 1854 was an early move towards a politically neutral Civil Service and enforced the notion of a 'generalist' Civil Service, it was not until the Fulton Report that the first serious attempt came to challenge the issue of management in government. According to Chapman and Greenaway (1980: 197), Fulton was a product of the 'growing popularity of "managerial" ideas in the 1960s' although these ideas were not couched in the language of 'efficiency' and failed to take into account the problems of managing in a political environment.

When the Efficiency Unit was established in 1979, it was conceived by the new Thatcher administration as a catalyst for managerial change. The Efficiency Unit was more than a symbolic gesture. The appointment of Sir Derek Rayner as personal adviser on efficiency to the prime minister had a cruder objective: it was the first stage to Margaret Thatcher realising her personal commitment to attacking the Civil Service as she 'believed that civil servants exercised too much influence over public policy' (Caiden 1991: 206), as well as there being too many of them. The Efficiency Unit prepared the launch of the Financial Management Initiative (FMI) which was offered by Richards (1992) as an example of the emphasis in the early 1980s on 'new public management' techniques; a means of 'promoting economy and efficiency, strengthening resource management systems and downsizing bureaucracy' (Editorial 1992: 1), but whose momentum had flagged by the mid-1980s and spurred the formulation of the Next Steps initiative.

Also, the general post-war growth in various agencies, public corporations and quangos provided a precedence for agencification: 'a view prevails that transferring functions to "non-departmental" agencies increases managerial independence and hence efficiency' (Dunsire *et al.* 1988: 367). The Fulton Report had also referred to the principle of 'hiving off', but much of what followed was done on an *ad hoc* basis (Pliatzky 1992). On the other hand, Hood (1990) put forward the view that the Next Steps initiative might be compared with the framework for managing nationalised industries expounded in a series of White Papers, and the Efficiency Unit clearly cited the nationalised industries as examples of central government functions already carried out at arm's length from ministers, with policy made at the centre (Fry *et al.* 1988: 434, Jordan 1991: 14). But Kemp, as the first project manager for Next Steps,[5] claimed that 'agencies, unlike nationalised industries remain part of their department and subject to ministerial control'

(Kemp 1988: 28 and cited in Jordan 1991: 15). Furthermore, the experience of the nationalised industries had not guaranteed Morrison's prediction that Britain would 'get the best of both worlds' with a form of organisation that combined 'business management' and 'public accountability' (Fry *et al.* 1988: 434).

Why should 'agency status' improve management and service delivery? Agencies are essentially departmental bodies, unlike quangos, and are organisational bundles of functions decentralised from their core departments. Kemp seemed to believe, almost as an 'act of faith', that agencies would be better able to perform the executive functions of government' based on the notion that 'agencies operating at arm's length from ministers will result in a "release of managerial energy"' (Fry *et al.* 1988: 440). The term 'agency' itself is vague, as the Ibbs Report admits: 'we use the term "agency" not in its technical sense but to describe any executive unit that delivers a service for government' (Efficiency Unit 1988: 9). Kemp (1990: 189) stressed that there was 'no blueprint for agencies. Each must be set up specifically to deal with a particular task or tasks.' However, with each agency structure formulated by both the proposed agency and its parent department, the problem remains about the extent to which the executive function can be separated from policy-making, especially when the proposed agency will try to defend any policy formulation role it may have. Defining 'policy' and 'executive' work is problematic, and in the case of a few agencies, this is still unresolved, as we will see later.

However, the Wilsonian dichotomy is apparently asserted when HM Treasury (1992: 2) stated that 'the Agency itself is normally only responsible for the execution of the tasks given to it, and not (except in an advisory capacity), for the underlying policies which remain the responsibility of those at the centre of the Department'. The Treasury has a strong interest in controlling the activities of the agencies and this will be drawn out later. Despite the fact that some agencies do have policy advisory roles, Kemp remarked that 'agencies were not appropriate to areas where one could *not* make a sharp distinction between policy and executive functions' (cited in Fry *et al.* 1988: 441; my emphasis).

The framework documents, which serve as the form of contract between ministers and executive agencies, are explicit about the decentralisation of functions from central departments to agencies. For example, the annexes of the framework document between the National Weights and Measures Laboratory and the Department of Trade and Industry detail financial, support services, personnel and training, and accounting 'delegations'.

If we accept decentralisation as a doctrinal component of New Public Management (NPM) (Hood 1991), then the agencification of the UK Civil Service appears to fit the 'agenda' well.[6] Similar reforms in New Zealand have also drawn upon 'the principle . . . of devolution of service delivery to agencies not closely under ministerial control. It has been described as the "decoupling" of performance from policy making' (Roberts 1987, cited in Wistrich 1992: 122).

An inherent contradiction with the moves towards decentralisation as part of the management process of agencification is that policy-making should remain centralised, but this has been compromised in some instances. For example, the

Employment Service framework document includes the chief executive as a member of the Employment Department Group which develops policy, and the chief executive is allowed to make proposals for policy changes to the minister. Furthermore, it would be interesting to know the amount of informal contact between ministers and chief executives, and what happens if there is a conflict of points of view. However, in times of crisis it is likely that the chief executive will lose his or her managerial autonomy as the minister stamps his or her authority on policy. For instance, did the chief executive of the Employment Service (Mike Fogden) have any say over the recent public clamp-down on benefit fraud, once the government saw it as a source of political capital? Mayne (cited in Jordan 1991: 16) argues that 'framework documents should explicitly allow for a temporary, emergency, crisis "takeover" by the minister'.[7] Generally, centralising tendencies are hard to escape from as 'moves towards greater delegation have to take account of areas where it may remain important to have the capacity to maintain standards across government' (Efficiency Unit 1991: 4) such as fair and open competition in recruitment and maintaining political impartiality.

It should come as little surprise that the Treasury has proved to be the greatest obstacle to decentralisation, although operational control can be decentralised within a strict financial regime. The question is how much detailed control the Treasury exercises with its rules. Decentralisation has meant there has been a nominal move from control over inputs to control over outputs with an on-line budget for chief executives but the Treasury remains reluctant to give up detailed input control. Giving managers control over the production function should improve services by moving away from a Civil Service still largely governed by a body of centrally laid-down rules. These rules prevented managers close to service delivery from being able to make decisions that would improve performance (Goldsworthy 1991: 4). It is difficult to see how the Civil Service (Management Functions) Act 1992 will improve matters. The Act allows the Treasury to delegate to agencies the responsibility for determining the terms and conditions for their staff without having to refer to their central departments, and it remains to be seen whether or not there is a genuine increase in autonomy for agencies that are staff-intensive.

However, the Treasury's reluctance over decentralisation has contributed to some contradictory tendencies, preferring privatisation or ministerial control to agency status. Continuing Treasury control over the first executive agencies forced Ponting (1989: 71) to conclude that, 'far from heralding a bold new approach to management and accountability with genuinely free-standing agencies, the move looks set to produce a real "dog's dinner"'. The chief worry for the Treasury was that 'decentralization without control would allow agencies, inadvertently, to subvert government policy, principally by raising the level of public expenditure' (Fry *et al.* 1988: 441–2). Similarly, in New Zealand the Treasury has ensured that agencification 'is a model of "top down" control' (Wistrich 1992: 123). The FMI had been similarly hamstrung by the Treasury, with the unions commenting that: 'the spark of life missing from this forlorn creature (the FMI) is, of course, the allocation of real money to managers . . . But giving them real money would, of course, mean giving them real power' (Bulletin, February 1985: 17 and cited in Fry *et al.* 1988).

One solution to the dilemma of decentralisation and the maintenance of Treasury control was to extend the 1973 Trading Funds Act to cover agencies as well as amending 'the legislation and the Treasury rules on the control of running costs to give (the new Agency) Chief Executives more meaningful financial control of their Agencies' (Goldsworthy 1991: 31). The Government Trading Act 1990 amended the 1973 Act along these lines, and that, combined with the Civil Service Act 1992, should give more freedom to the agencies. Although the trading fund notion was applicable to a wide range of agencies, especially those that deliver, or could deliver services to the private sector, as of 7 December 1994 only twelve agencies (out of 107) had trading fund status. Some agencies, such as the Civil Service College, are working towards trading fund status.

Davies and Willman (1991: 43) assert that 'the fundamental paradox of Next Steps is that it seeks to develop an enterprise culture in the public services, and to focus on outputs and the delivery of services within the input-dominated, cash limited, public expenditure system' which means that chief executives are excluded from 'financially strategic decisions and unable to influence investment levels'. I am not convinced that Next Steps was ever about developing an 'enterprise culture', privatisation and market testing are the more likely instruments for introducing market-like forces to public services. Privatisation can incentivise management and all agencies, at the three-yearly review of their framework documents, are formally considered for privatisation.[8] Also, as all agencies are departmental bodies still formally under ministerial control, private sector comparisons are inappropriate. Therefore, Goldsworthy (1991: 27) concedes that 'reconciling greater delegation of authority with maintaining firm control of public expenditure has been a major preoccupation throughout the project'. This concern has lead the Treasury to try to ensure that agencies should have adequate spending controls, as well as being able to demonstrate value for money by meeting performance targets.

As a managerial approach to public administration, decentralisation is open to public choice criticisms. Kettl (1988) remarks how 'government by proxy' makes the problem of information flow in bureaucracy even worse 'as it is hard to get useful information up the chain of command within a bureaucracy, it is even more difficult to get good, reliable information from outside an organisation'. Managers are thus encouraged to hide and disguise problems, yet agencies, as departmental bodies, retain close links with central departments; they do not stand outside the organisation. However, the pluralist forces which the New Right believed were the cause of excessive government spending could actually be rekindled as powerful lobbies grow up around the executive agencies. Also William Plowden, Director General of the Royal Institute of Public Administration, reporting to the Treasury and Civil Service Committee in July 1988 (cited in Fry *et al.* 1988: 443), warned that rational politicians and bureaucrats alike could use agencification for shuffling responsibility between them, which could blur rather than clarify the separation between policy and operational decisions. Fudge and Gustafsson (1989: 32) warned that in Sweden the demarcation of the 'organisational boundary' between government and agencies has not been found 'to guarantee the efficiency some may expect from the decentralised organisational form'. Decentralisation is no guarantee of a separation between politics and administration.

Devine (1991) also warns of the dangers of public service managers operating in relative isolation in decentralised organisations. Managers still need to be aware of the broad government picture and failure by managers to do this could result in a loss of control of policy by the political leadership with the result that policy becomes the preserve of the administration: 'since the political administrator must delegate less, he must follow up more' (Devine 1991: 174). Therefore agencification can become a policy that can atomise and decentralise the Civil Service along the lines akin to the US federal service, but without America's legal and political safeguards (Massey 1992: 84). In the United States, Reagan's government reforms were charged with resulting in a 'decentralised, polyglot collection of agencies lacking a collective identity. There is a clear reflection here of British experience with *Next Steps*' (Massey 1992: 81).

Decentralisation is potentially harmful for public administration. Not only could it damage policy coordination, Aucoin (1990: 200) notes that reforms such as agencification 'on the one hand,' will cause an even greater diffusion of power in government . . . ministers will find their capacities to manage their portfolios restricted increasingly to high policy-priority initiatives with clearly specified objectives and considered implementation strategies'. Yet surely this is one aim of agencification, to free ministers to deal with the big policy questions of government? On the other hand, Dunleavy and Francis (1990) (cited in Caiden 1991: 207) were concerned that 'greater organisational fragmentation' could lead agencies to acquire greater levels of autonomous control of their own affairs than ministers or Parliament originally intended. This is more dangerous, and it is to the question of accountability that I turn to next.

Agencification: implications for political accountability

The Next Steps initiative is supposed to enhance accountability to Parliament with the line of accountability continuing to exist along the chain from chief executives to ministers and then through to Parliament. In a lecture to the First Division Association, Sir Robin Butler (cited in Jordan 1991:12) asserted that what civil servants had in common was that 'they are all accountable through Ministers to Parliament, so that they are in the realm of politics'. On this basis, agencification would appear meaningless because it is difficult to see how separating politics from administration can actually 'improve' political accountability. Principal–agent theory implies that the advantage is that chief executives have a 'simple, straight-line accountability to just one minister, rather than being the partial agents of multiple and potentially competing principals'. The problem is that this sits 'uncomfortably with the conventions of the Westminster system under which a department's outputs, such as policy advice, are "purchased" by the government as a whole, rather than by individual ministers' (Boston 1992: 418). Sir Robin Butler appeared to be still thinking along these lines.

In practice, the permanent secretaries remain as chief policy advisers to ministers and are also responsible for advising on performance targets for each agency. Agency chief executives are accounting officers for their agencies and may be called before the Public Accounts Committee or the Departmental Select Committee to account for the use of their resource allocation. Jordan is unhappy with this arrangement; he argues that such delegation does not fit easily with the traditional system of accountability. Chief executives appear to be answering on behalf of ministers when 'we are told ministerial accountability remains. But in reality it is now accountability *to* the Minister by the Chief Executive rather than accountability *of* the Minister to the House of Commons that is now on offer: these are different' (Jordan 1991: 13–14). None of this is clear cut, and lines of accountability become confused when in some instances, the framework documents state that the chief executives act as 'agency accounting officers' (Civil Service College, HMSO) whereas another framework document (Vehicle Inspectorate) states that

> There will be no change to the practice governing the appearance of senior staff before Select Committees of the House. In the case of the Public Accounts Committee accountability will continue to lie with the Permanent Secretary as Accounting Officer. The Chief Executive may accompany him to hearings where the work of the Inspectorate is being examined.
>
> (Policy and Resources Framework, Vehicle Inspectorate 1988)

Another problem is the handling of correspondence. Prior to agencification, MPs enjoyed rights of access to ministers, but now MPs are encouraged to write directly to chief executives, and letters would only be referred to ministers where policy matters were being addressed. Framework documents are usually explicit on this aspect. However, Kaufman (1993) had problems with getting a satisfactory response from a minister with regard to a constituent's benefit claim when letters kept being sent on to the former chief executive of the Benefits Agency, Michael Bichard, by the minister, Peter Lilley. Kaufman was moved to call agencification a 'creeping abnegation of ministerial responsibility' but it also demonstrates the problem of separating policy from its execution; should it have been Lilley who replied? Furthermore, Kaufman is doubtful whether replies from chief executives, rather than ministers, to MPs' questions attract parliamentary privilege.

Chief executives are also expected to respond to parliamentary questions on behalf of ministers, but the danger is that '"policy" issues are likely to push down into "administrative" issues so as to avoid contentious questions being raised in the House and published in *Hansard*' (Greer 1992: 90). 'Whereas interested organisations could previously monitor *Hansard* for relevant answers, there was no correspondingly easy way for a group or individual to "track" answers from an agency' and the Public Information Office is claimed to be too unreliable (Jordan 1991: 11–12).

According to Fry *et al.* (1988: 443), Thatcher had thought 'agency staff would take safe options so as not to embarass ministers; ministers will intervene in the working of agencies, and, as a result, chief executives will not be as entrepreneurial as the authors of "the Next Steps" hoped. When questioned on this, Richard Luce, when Minister for the Civil Service, replied that while chief executives would be delegated as much authority as possible they would remain accountable to the minister.' Framework Documents offer little to suggest that the system of accountability will change; executive agencies are, after all, departmental bodies. However, the ambiguity that still surrounds the role of the chief executive, and what is actually delegated to him or her, and the confused boundary between policy and execution is likely to lead to poorer political accountability for service delivery.

Getting the framework document right was seen by the Efficiency Unit (1988) as a crucial method of making the chief executive accountable for getting the 'best possible results'. Framework documents effectively form a contract between minister and agency and, although they are not legally binding, each framework document has to 'reconcile several interests'. First, as the Treasury retains a strong interest in containing public expenditure, financial planning and control are a prominent feature in the documents, which usually oblige agencies to produce business plans and meet financial objectives. Second, ministers, supported by their departments, set policy objectives and performance targets for their agencies (Efficiency Unit 1991: Foreword by Angus Fraser). Annual reviews publish each agencies' performance against key targets for the coming financial year.

Monitoring the framework agreements is now a key role in the policy core of departments. Davies and Willman (1991: 33) remark how the Efficiency Unit recommended that 'a focal point must be indentified at senior level in each department to question the performance of the chief executive and helping the chief executive meet objectives and targets. To carry out such a task requires policy knowledge and management experience.' Despite this change in the job specification of permanent secretaries (the 'focal points'), it appears that the political bureaucrat remains alive and well, although the Efficiency Unit sees the function of these officials as being 'very different from the traditional Civil Service line manager: the right cut-off point between policy and service delivery' (Davies and Willman 1991: 33). Also, the departmental cores will have to make sure that operational information can be fed into the policy process. Kemp (1990: 190) confidently predicted that 'those concerned with policy and targets, and with setting resources to deliver them, will be able to concentrate on doing just that. Those actually providing services will know what is expected of them and will have the freedom to succeed in it.'

While executive agencies remain departmental bodies, it is unlikely that framework documents will be treated like commercial contracts for two reasons. First, scope for discretion for ministers and civil servants to engage in policy formulation must still be allowed. Second, the relationship between agencies and parent departments is not one of annual discussions over targets followed by an 'arm's length' relationship for the next twelve months. Price Waterhouse (1992 cited in Hogwood 1993: 13) found that about half the agencies had daily contact with officials and the rest mostly weekly. Rather than declining, this frequency of contracts had increased compared to a year earlier. This level of frequency of contacts raises the question of whether the line has clearly been drawn between policy and operational matters.

THE UK AGENCY PROGRAMME: A RADICAL DEPARTURE?

The Efficiency Unit envisaged a central Civil Service consisting of a relatively small core engaged in the function of servicing ministers and managing departments, effectively the 'sponsors' of particular government policies and services. As we have seen, agencification has left a layer of political administrators at the centre of government. Much of the work at the core 'will continue to be in supporting ministers in the preparation of policy advice, in assisting them in the implementation of agreed policy, in explaining that policy to the outside world, and in responding to interest groups' (Butler 1992: 7). Will this continue to be feasible?

The Next Steps team are currently investigating how the policy 'core' of departments sponsoring agencies should be formally structured as part of an aim to identify all potential agency candidates in the government by the end of this year. By mid-1995, it is proposed that eight categories of function will be left at departmental level:

1 Management/ownership of agencies (advising secretary of state/setting and meeting targets/performance criteria).
2 Policy.
3 Inspectorate/regulatory.
4 Other executive functions (for example, Foreign and Commonwealth Office: protocol and estate management).
5 Personnel.
6 Finance.
7 IT support.
8 Other support (for example, Foreign and Commonwealth Office: security, language training and library services).[9]

The type of service delivered by the departments will of course determine the size of the core; for example, for large delivery organisations such as the Benefits Agency, it is expected that the core will be relatively small in comparison to staff numbers, whereas in National Heritage, the size of the core is likely to be much larger in proportion to the staff. It is predicted by the Next Steps team that 25 per cent of Civil Service staff will be left in the policy cores although how much of this will be 'policy work' is debatable, and there are potential future net losses following the market testing exercises.

Boston (1991a) notes that the public choice approach in New Zealand would predict that advisory, regulatory and delivery functions should be given agency status to avoid bureaucratic capture. Has this happened in the United Kingdom? Using and modifying Dunleavy's (1991) agency typologies, I have classified the types of government services already given agency status. The breakdown is as follows:

Delivery: 16 per cent.
Regulatory: 13 per cent.
Transfer: 7 per cent.
Contracts: 5 per cent.
Taxing: 6 per cent.
Trading: 13 per cent.
Servicing: 38 per cent.
Policy: 1 per cent.

Here, I have grouped 'hybrids' with their primary roles. However, this appears to be arbitrary; for example the Driver and Vehicle Licensing Agency registers and licenses drivers and vehicles as well as collecting Vehicle Excise Duty, but I have classified it as a regulatory agency rather than a taxing agency. Registering and licensing is its primary role. Other instances include Driver and Vehicle Licensing (Northern Ireland) (regulatory and taxing); the Employment Service (delivery and transfer); Insolvency Service (regulatory and policy); National Physical Laboratory (servicing and contracting); Ordnance Survey (of Great Britain and Northern Ireland) (delivery and servicing); and the Social Security Agency (Northern Ireland) (transfer and taxing).

Clearly, the largest group is that of servicing agencies, of which 37 per cent (14 per cent of all executive agencies) provide services to the Ministry of Defence,[10] such as the Army Base Repair Organisation. However, this MoD group accounts for only 6 per cent of overall agency staff compared with the Benefits Agency, which accounts for 18 per cent of all agency staff alone. The secretary of state for defence also has the largest number of executive agencies for any minister reporting to him (sixteen in total), but his involvement in operational matters will vary greatly within that range. For instance, he is unlikely to intervene in the workings of the Defence Postal and Courier Services but is far more likely to be in close contact with the Defence Operational Analysis Centre as a prime user of their outputs.

The second largest grouping are the delivery agencies: out of the fifteen agencies in this group, seven deliver services to the Welsh, Scottish and Northern Ireland offices. Here, physical decentralisation would appear to be a rational justification for the agencification of these services and it is worth noting that Northern Ireland has the third largest number of executive agencies within its purview at nine, after the Department for Trade and Industry (ten) and the Ministry of Defence (sixteen). The Department for Trade and Industry is likely to lose some agencies as the Next Steps team were aware that the current president of the Board of Trade, Michael Heseltine, was keen to privatise all the government laboratories that are currently his responsibility at the Department of Trade and Industry, such as the National Physical Laboratory. Most of these laboratories fall into the 'contracting' category, and so privatisation would seem to be a logical next step from the government's point of view, especially as many of these agencies have private sector customers.

The other large groupings are those of regulatory and trading agencies. Regulatory agencies cover a range of activities, but motor vehicle regulation features most prominently, with small clusters in the Departments of Transport and of Trade and Industry. The classification of trading agencies (i.e. those executive agencies with trading fund status) complicates the picture as many cross the typological boundaries, for instance, the Vehicle Inspectorate is effectively a regulatory agency. It seems that exposing agencies to market-like forces was not a rationale on the available evidence. The small number of agencies that are trading appear to be potential privatisation candidates (as in the case of Companies House), but I am only aware of one other candidate for trading fund status (the Civil Service College).

Agencification of taxing services seem to be more logical in the context of Next Steps, where the organisations concerned have easily measurable outputs, so any policy change would be relatively easy to observe and predict. Delivery agencies would fall into this group too, with both groups corresponding with Wilson's (1989: 159–63) description of 'production organizations'. The separation of policy from execution may be smoother in such organisations, and the tangibility of their outputs makes it easier for the core to monitor a particular agency. The final category of policy agencies (which I have added to Dunleavy's typology) contains only one clear example, that of the Defence Operational Analysis centre whose 'primary role is to conduct OA studies to provide Defence Ministers, policy makers and Service staff with the best possible advice and analysis on which to base decisions' (Chancellor of the Duchy of Lancaster 1992: 26). Clearly, agencification in this instance could not assert the Wilsonian dichotomy, but it will be interesting to see if this example is emulated by other departments.

The general picture so far is only one of marginal agencification although some large line bureaucracies such as the Benefits Agency and the Employment Service have been given agency status. It seems that many agencies conduct operations that are peripheral to the main business of the government department, especially in defence. More radical would be the agencification of services that are politically sensitive and where the Wilsonian dichotomy is rigidly adhered to. Jordan (1991) asks the question 'why has the National Health Service Management Executive *not* been given agency status?' The response might be because it was thought that agency status removed a politically sensitive matter too far from accountability. As departmental bodies, agencies could become vulnerable to political mood swings, and agency status can be quickly reversed without the need for legislation. Are we likely to see swings of de-agencification or re-agencification depending on political priorities in the future?

CONCLUSIONS

Agencification has been an attempt to reassert the Wilsonian dichotomy, but to the advantage of politicians (who lose awkward managerial roles) and to the possible disadvantage of chief executives (who generally have no policy-making role). Those civil servants that have assisted in advising ministers and formulating policy will continue to do so in the policy cores of departments. All that appears to have happened is that the Wilsonian dichotomy has been moved to a higher level in the government hierarchy and has been made specific. Before agencification, it would have been extremely difficult to test empirically where policy-making ended and policy execution began. It is hard to see how agencification will change this in practice. Davies and Willman (1991) may be correct when they warn that service delivery is likely to be harmed if those involved in the delivery of a policy are not involved in its formulation.

MacDonald (1992: 12) is sceptical about splitting policy from administration as it implies that agencies would not be 'formally consulted about the feasibility of proposed policy changes'. This could be remedied by encouraging informal contacts with the core departments 'and the agencies should be able to press for minor legislative changes through regular consultation with the departments on the basis of the practical difficulties or limitations they experience in administration'. Although this role was envisaged for the agencies in the Ibbs Report, agencies should 'contribute to policy analysis and formulation as well as dealing with case work on operational issues'. Also, the fragmentation of public services and the lack of coordination may have some unforeseen circumstances. For instance, the framework document for the Employment Service stresses consultation between the chief executive and departmental officials but no explicit mention is made of consulting with the Benefits Agency, with whom it shares many clients.

Earlier, I discussed how NPM doctrines and principal–agent theory provided some fairly shaky theoretical justifications for agencification. Graham Mather, according to Jordan (1991: 15), attempts to develop an alternative justification for agency status when he writes about the 'end of the traditional public service'. Yet, when he looks specifically at Next Steps agencies in the light of previous attempts to control nationalised industries, he notes that it is hard to stop management developing policy objectives of their own.

> They will not, in practice, leave policy to ministers, and day-to-day administration to themselves. Nor, if the experience of the NHS Management Board is concerned, will Ministers easily renounce close involvement in the detail of service delivery, where this is politically sensitive. The weakness of the agency approach is, therefore, that is likely to lead to imprecise framework agreements between departments and agencies, which leave a significant degree of administrative discretion to departments.
>
> (Mather, 1991: 78 and cited in Jordan 1991: 15)

But surely this is the difference between running agencies that are still part of government and writing a contract to deliver services at arm's length for a private company? Perhaps allowing for discretion will be a strength of the agency approach where popularly elected politicians should be allowed to intervene in the execution of policy.

However, the introduction of private sector managerial techniques under the principle of decentralisation is more likely to weaken executive agencies for two reasons. First, as Massey (1992: 86) notes, 'managerialism is a poor substitute for proper accountability; the firm is a weak and stunted analogy for public administration; high officials are not tradesmen'. In a political environment, both politicians and bureaucrats set priorities and objectives, but often these are unclear, confused and even contradictory. The neo-Taylorism of target setting is not appropriate in many public service settings. Ponting (1989) dismissed agencification as part of the general tendency for offering 'oversimplified' managerial solutions to the problems of government, without fundamentally changing the culture of the Civil Service. It is likely that agencification is too crude an instrument to achieve such a cultural change. The Wilsonian dichotomy's reappearance is likely to be nominal because the complexities of the interaction between politicians and bureaucrats in modern government will do little to actually enforce the split.

Furthermore, during an age of public expenditure restraint, Treasury control continues to loom large; giving chief executives the spade is one thing, having no sand to shift is another. Although it appears that the dichotomy between politics and administration was reopened in 1988 with the publication of the Ibbs Report, which amounted to an attempt to resurrect Wilson's prescriptions for good government, the UK government never really saw it in those terms when their chief concern lay with controlling public expenditure and cutting back the Civil Service.

NOTES

1 Named after Sir Robin Ibbs, the then prime minister's adviser on efficiency.
2 Weber, according to Ostrom, had no influence in the United States until after the Second World War.
3 On the surface, the UK agency initiative appears to be quite straightforward. All executive agencies are, or have been, candidates for privatisation. However, 'market testing' involves investigating those functions of the Civil Service for possible contractorisation. The issue becomes more confused given the limited number of agencies with 'trading fund' status.
4 No data were available on how many appointments were from the private sector.
5 Appointed in 1987.
6 Although Sweden has had executive agencies for over twenty years.
7 None of the framework documents I surveyed referred to 'crisis takeovers' by ministers.
8 Several agencies have been identified for future privatisation, including Companies House.
9 Information obtained by author during interview.
10 These services are not always exclusive to the armed forces. For example, the Meterological Office also provides services to civilian organisations.

CORE READING

Aberbach, J. Putnam, R. and Rockman, B. (1981) *Bureaucrats and Politicians in Western Democracies*, Cambridge, Mass.: Harvard University Press.

Caiden, G. (1991) *Administrative Reform Comes of Age*, Berlin: Walter de Gruyter.

Chapman, R. and Greenaway, J. (1980) *The Dynamics of Administrative Reform*, London: Croom Helm.

Dunleavy, P. (1991) *Democracy, Bureaucracy and Public Choice*, Hemel Hempstead: Harvester Wheatsheaf.

Goldsworthy, D. (1991) *Setting Up Next Steps*, London: HMSO.

Greer, P. (1994) *Transforming Central Government*, Buckingham: Open University Press.

Hood, C. (1991) 'A public management for all seasons?', *Public Administration* 69(1): 3–19.

Metcalfe, L. and Richards, S. (1987) *Improving Public Management*, London: Sage.

Ponting, C. (1989) *Whitehall: Changing the Old Guard*, London: Unwin Hyman.

ADDITIONAL READING

Aberbach, J. and Rockman, B. (1988) 'Image IV revisited: executive and political roles', *Governance* 1(1): 1–25.

Allison, G. and Halperin, M. (1972) 'Bureaucratic politics: a paradigm and some policy implications', in Tanter, T. and Ullman, R. (eds) *Theory and Policy in International Relations*, Princeton: Princeton University Press.

Aucoin, P. (1990) 'Comment: assessing managerial reforms', *Governance* 3(2); 197–201.

Banks, T. (1990) 'Performance measurement: the needs of managers and policy makers', *Public Money and Management* 10(2): 47–9.

Boston, J. (1991a) 'The theoretical underpinnings of public sector restructuring in New Zealand', in Boston, J., Martin, J., Pallot, J. and Walsh, P. (eds) *Reshaping the State: New Zealand's Bureaucratic Revolution*, Oxford: Oxford University Press.

Boston, J. (1991b) 'Chief executives and the senior executive service', in Boston, J., Martin, J., Pallot, J. and Walsh, P. (eds) *Reshaping the State: New Zealand's Bureaucratic Revolution*, Oxford: Oxford University Press.

Boston, J. (1992) 'Assessing the performance of departmental chief executives: perspectives from New Zealand', *Public Administration* 70(3): 405–28.

Brereton, D. (1992) 'From scrutinies to market testing: the work of the Efficiency Unit', *Public Policy and Administration* 7(3): 71–9.

Butler, R. (1992) 'The future of the Civil Service', *Public Policy and Administration* 7(3): 4–14.

Chancellor of the Duchy of Lancaster (1992) *The Next Steps Agencies: Review 1992*, Cm. 2111, London: HMSO.

Chapman, R. (1989) 'Core public sector reform in New Zealand and the UK', *Public Money and Management* 9(1): 44–9.

Civil Service Commission (1981) *Appointments in Administration*, London: HMSO.

Davies, A. and Willman, J. (1991) *What Next? Agencies, Departments and the Civil Service*, London: Institute for Public Policy Research.

Department of Transport (1988) *Policy and Resources Framework*, London: HMSO.

Devine, D. (1991) *Reagan's Terrible Swift Sword*, Ottawa, Ill.: Jameson Books.

Doig, J. (1983) '"If I see a murderous fellow sharpening a knife cleverly . . .": The Wilsonian dichotomy and the public authority tradition', *Public Administration Review* 43(4): 292–304.

Dunleavy, P. and Francis, A. (1990) 'Memorandum to the Treasury and Civil Service Select Committee: the development of the Next Steps Programme, 1989–90', in *HM Treasury Eighth Report: Progress in the Next Steps Initiative*, Session 1989–90, HC 481, London: HMSO.

Dunsire, A., Hartley, K., Parker, D. and Dimitriou, B. (1988) 'Organizational status and performance: a conceptual framework for testing public choice theories', *Public Administration* 66(4): 363–88.

Editorial (1992) 'Managing the new public services: towards a new framework', *Public Policy and Administration* 7(3): 1–4.

Efficiency Unit (1988) *Improving Management in Government: The Next Steps*, London: HMSO.

Efficiency Unit (1991) *Making the Most of Next Steps: The Management of Minister's Departments and their Executive Agencies*, London: HMSO.

Elmore, R. (1986) 'Graduate education in public management: working the seams of government', *Journal of Policy Analysis and Management* 6: 69–93.

Fry, G., Flynn, A., Gray, A., Jenkins, W. and Rutherford, B. (1988) 'Symposium on improving management in government', *Public Administration* 66(4): 429–45.

Fudge, C. and Gustafsson, L. (1989) 'Administrative reform and public management in Sweden and the United Kingdom', *Public Money and Management* 9(2): 29–34.

Greer, P. (1992) 'The Next Steps initiative: an examination of the agency framework documents', *Public Administration* 70(1): 89–98.

Hartley, K., Parker, D. and Martin, S. (1991) 'Organisational status, ownership and productivity', *Fiscal Studies* 12(2): 46–60.

Heffron, F. (1989) *Organization Theory and Public Organizations: The Political Connection*, Englewood Cliffs, New Jersey: Prentice Hall.

HM Treasury (1992) *Executive Agencies: A Guide to Setting Targets and Measuring Performance*, London: HMSO.

Hogwood, B. (1993) *The Uneven Staircase: Measuring Up Next Steps*, University of Strathclyde, Strathclyde Papers on Government and Politics 92.

Hood, C. (1990) 'De-Sir Humphreyfying the Westminster model of bureaucracy: a new style of governance?', *Governance* 3(2): 205–14.

Jordan, G. (1991) *Next Steps Agencies: From Managing by Command to Managing by contract?*, University of Aberdeen, Aberdeen Papers in Accountancy, Finance and Management.

Kaufman, G. (1993) 'Privatising the ministers', *The Guardian*, 20 January.

Kaufman, H. (1981) *The Administrator Behaviour of Federal Bureau Chiefs*, Washington DC: Brookings Institution.

Kemp, P. (1988) 'Plans and progress so far', *The Next Steps: A Review of the Agency Concept*, London: RIPA/Arthur Young.

Kemp, P. (1990) 'Next Steps for the British Civil Service', *Governance* 3(2): 186–96.

Kettl, D. (1988) *Government by Proxy*, Washington DC: Congressional Quarterly Press.

MacDonald, O. (1992) *Swedish Models: The Swedish Model of Central Government*, London: Institute for Public Policy Research.

Mascarenhas, R. (1990) 'Reform of the public service in Australia and New Zealand', *Governance* 3(1): 75–95.

Massey, A. (1992) 'Due process and rectitude: US and British Civil Service reforms contrasted', *Public Policy and Administration* 7(3): 80–8.

Mather, G. (1991) 'Government by contract', in Vibert, F. (ed.) *Britain's Constitutional Future*, London: Institute for Economic Affairs.

Mayne, J. (1990) 'Whitehall watch', *The Independent*, 22 October.

Office of Public Service and Science (1993/94) *Next Steps Briefing Notes*, London: Cabinet Office.

Ostrom, V. (1989) *The Intellectual Crisis in American Public Administration*, 2nd edn, Tuscaloosa, Ala.: University of Alabama Press.

Perrow, C. (1986) *Complex Organizations: A Critical Essay*, 3rd edn, New York: Random House.

Peters, B. (1986) *The Relationship between Civil Servants and Political Executives: A*

Preliminary Comparative Examination, University of Strathclyde, Studies in Public Policy 153.

Pliatzky, L. (1992) 'QUANGOs and Agencies', *Public Administration* 70(4): 555–63.

Price Waterhouse (1992) *Executive Agencies: Facts and Trends*, London.

Putnam, R. (1973) 'The political attitudes of senior Civil Servants in Western Europe: a preliminary report', *British Journal of Political Science* 3(3): 257–90.

Richards, S. (1992) 'Changing patterns of legitimation in public management', *Public Policy and Administration* 7(3): 15–28.

Roberts, J. (1987) *Politicians, Public Servants and Public Enterprise*, Wellington: Institute of Policy Studies.

Rose, R. (1974) *The Problem of Party Government*, New York: Free Press.

Rose, R. (1984) 'The political status of higher Civil Servants in Britain', in Suleiman, E. (ed.) *Bureaucrats and Policy Making: A Comparative Overview*, London: Holmes and Meier.

Scott, G. and Gorringe, P. (1989) 'Reform of the core public sector: the New Zealand experience', *Australian Journal of Public Administration* 48: 81–92.

Suleiman, E. (1984) Introduction in Suleiman, E. (ed.) *Bureaucrats and Policy Making: A Comparative Overview*, London: Holmes and Meier.

Tyson, S. (1990) 'Turning Civil Servants into managers', *Public Money and Management* 10(1): 27–30.

Wilson, J. (1989) *Bureaucracy*, New York: Basic Books.

Wilson, W. (1887) 'The study of administration', *Political Science Quarterly* 2.

Wistrich, E. (1992) 'Restructuring government New Zealand style', *Public Administration* 70(1): 119–35.

Zussman, D. and Jabes, J. (1989) *The Vertical Solitude: Managing in the Public Sector*, Halifax, Nova Scotia: Institute for Research on Public Policy.

8   Privatisation and water

John Dickens

Of all the policies of the Thatcher years and beyond, it would seem that nothing epitomises the Conservative government's philosophy more, or is likely to endure longer, than privatisation. Since 1979 the government have privatised forty-seven major companies and altogether more than 50 per cent of state-owned sections of industry have been transferred to the private sector. Further inroads with regard to privatisation can be expected throughout the 1990s if the present government continue to remain in office. And in the event that a Labour government are elected, they will not have the resources to reinstate the public bureaucracies or embark on a programme of re-nationalisation, even if they had the will to do so. Much of what is in place will remain.

The philosophical underpinnings of privatisation provide an illuminating application of the current ideological supremacy of the principle of the market over the principle of public service. As a corollary, this clash of principles introduces moral and constitutional arguments about the nature of accountability in relation to the different forms of privatisation.

This is all the more interesting in relation to water as a public utility industry. Although the water industry was privatised in 1989, the issue of water provision and the quality of drinking water and bathing water is currently enjoying a high profile. Not only are there periodic reports and argument about Britain's non-compliance with EC law with regard to water quality, but there has also been considerable concern about the social consequences of water metering.

The government maintained that the consumer, post-privatisation, would benefit from the injection of competition between the Water Supply PLCs as private companies. Water Supply PLCs would have sufficient incentive to measure and compare each other's performance, thus instilling greater efficiency in the provision of water services and providing for the consumer the freedom of choice to use water whenever they wish and to pay only for the quantity of water that is used.

However, water provision is almost a complete monopoly even if organised on a regional basis. A potential competitor to supply water would initially have to engage in massive capital projects in order to install the infrastructure that would guarantee water from the tap. Such prohibitive expenditure suggests that competitive entry to the market is virtually impossible. Consequently, the consumer who prefers not to receive water from one Water Supply PLC for one reason or another, cannot be provided with water from a competing or neighbouring company since consumers cannot take their custom elsewhere – they are in this respect captives of the market.

In general, the government have often promoted privatisation as a common-sense policy, emphasising the importance of competition and choice. While it could be argued that there were sound economic reasons for the privatisation of strategic industries like British Steel, British Aerospace and British Telecom, it would appear that water cannot be seen in such commercial terms. Privatisation of the water industry could have far-reaching effects in terms of social policy considerations. No one individual will be left untouched if a policy allows for the provision of water on the basis of ability to pay, such that some can have the water they need whereas others can have only that which they can afford.

The privatisation of the water industry provides an interesting insight into the world of public policy. It is a useful vehicle which allows for an understanding of how the political, economic, ideological and European contexts are interrelated and impact on the determination of policy and its implementation. As part of the government's overall programme, water privatisation will have contributed to the reduction in the PSBR through the sale of public assets, and the introduction of paying for water through metered supply and the cost of compliance with EC directives undoubtedly cause concern. Not only does this raise issues in relation to cost of living but the social policy implications could be enormous. Similarly, environmental regulation of the water industry goes to the heart of issues concerning subsidiarity and member state relations in the EC. The argument about water privatisation will persist. It is justified (or opposed) by invoking a range of social and political concepts such as efficiency, justice, accountability, subsidiarity, need, market and freedom. These concepts may be overt or subterranean but they nevertheless form part of the articulation of the competing ideological paradigms.

THE PRIVATISATION CONTEXT

In order to understand the nature of privatisation, it is necessary to focus on political events since 1945 and, in particular, on what has become known as the break-down of the post-war social democratic consensus.

This consensus describes the broad measure of agreement and continuity in the policies pursued by parties when in office in the thirty years after 1945. The main thrust of that consensus consisted in the commitment by government to achieve full employment, acceptance of trade unions as an interest that the government should consult over economic policy, maintenance of the Welfare State and acceptance of the majority of public ownership measures introduced between 1945 and 1951.

Indeed, such was the consensus that Daniel Bell's (1960) analysis was an attempt to demonstrate that we had entered 'the end of ideology'. During this period there were indeed differences between the parties on levels of income tax, on the need for local authority housing programmes and with regard to selective nationalisation. For example, the iron and steel industry was nationalised in 1949, de-nationalised in 1953 and then re-nationalised in 1967. By and large, however, the commitment to higher levels of public spending and consultation with interest groups in improving the performance of the economy and determining regional economic policy were indicative of this consensus.

As Chapter 1 has already shown, the 1970s was a period of ideological resurgence, the full manifestation of which was the election to power of Margaret Thatcher in 1979. The privatisation programmes of the 1980s appear to exemplify this resurgence, for without an unswerving loyalty to market principles the programmes may not have been pursued with such vigour. This said, it is also worth recognising the expediency of the privatisation programmes. While Chapter 6 has already rehearsed the arguments in relation to public expenditure, it is worth noting that the PSBR was substantially reduced through de-nationalisation and asset sales. Table 8.1 (Hansard 1993) shows the net privatisation proceeds since 1979. These privatisation proceeds provided additional state revenue in the face of rapidly growing unemployment, decline in manufacturing output and a deepening recession and were becoming increasingly seen by government as a way of financing their tax reduction aspirations (Thompson 1990). The proceeds can be put into perspective when one considers the magnitude of the 1993 budget deficit of £50 billion.

It has been suggested that what became known as Thatcherism was 'an evolving body of policies which changed fairly radically in itself over time', and that three major tendencies can be identified, each associated with particular periods of Thatcher's government (Budge and McKay 1993: 215).

Between 1979 and 1982, Thatcher's conviction politics emphasised monetarism and non-intervention in the economy. In the attempt to reduce inflation, public expenditure was severely curbed and control of the money supply was introduced. The free market and strong state are identified as the second tendency and mark the period from 1982 to 1986. During this period, central government confronted trade unions and local government in particular. These two institutions proved to be major obstacles to the pursuit of the New Right philosophy and were dealt with through the use of police powers, coercive legislation and stringent financial controls respectively. The period from 1986 exhibits the greater tendency to privatisation and internal markets.

What, then, is privatisation? Privatisation has become a catch-all expression and one that is heavily value-laden. It is often taken to refer to a reversal of nationalisation but it is used generically to refer to policies and programmes that attempt to redress the balance in favour of private enterprise through the withdrawal of government intervention and disaggregation. Not only does privatisation relate to de-nationalisation and the sale of public sector assets to private investors, but it also involves de-regulation and liberalisation of monopolies and the development of internal markets through contracting services and competitive tendering (Marsh 1991). Essentially, each of these forms, when taken together, allows us to view the privatisation enterprise as a most significant vehicle for the promotion

Table 8.1 Net privatisation proceeds

£ billion

	1979–80	1980–81	1981–82	1982–83	1983–84	1984–85	1985–86	1986–87	1987–88	1988–89	1989–90	1990–91	1991–92	1992–93	1993–94
Amersham International			0.1												
Associated British Ports					0.1	0.1									
BAA								0.5	0.7						
British Aerospace							0.3	0.4							
British Airways								0.9							
British Gas								2.6	1.8	1.4					
British Petroleum	0.3				0.5				3.0	0.8					
British Steel									1.1	1.3					
British Telecommunications						1.4	1.3	1.3		0.1			1.8		3.7
Britoil				0.3		1.4	0.4	0.3	0.3	0.1		0.1	1.8		3.7
Cable and Wireless		0.2		0.3	0.3		0.6								
Electricity (England/Wales)												3.1	3.4		1.5
Electricity (Northern Ireland)															0.4
Electricity (Scotland)													1.1		1.0
Enterprise Oil					0.4										
GPFC															
NTL									0.1				0.1		
National Seed Dev't Org'n															
Rolls-Royce									0.2						
Rover Group										0.2					
Royal Ordnance										0.2					
Water Companies											1.5	1.5			
Miscellaneous*	0.1	0.2	0.2	0.2	0.0	0.1	0.1	0.1	-0.1	0.5	1.5	1.5	0.0	1.2	
Total	0.4	0.5	0.5	0.5	1.1	2.0	2.7	4.5	5.1	7.1	4.2	5.3	7.9	8.2	5.5**
Relative to GGR (%)	0.5	0.4	0.4	0.4	0.9	1.4	1.8	2.8	2.9	3.7	2.0	2.5	3.6	3.7	2.4**

Source: Hansard 1993.

Notes: * Includes, in any year, sales with net proceeds of less than £50 million, expenses which could not be netted off the associated sale because they arose in a financial year in which there were no proceeds from that sale and (in 1992–93) the proceeds of the Treasury's auction of privatised companies' debt.
** March FSBR forecast.

of individualist values and what has become known as public choice theory, where individuals are construed as rational actors whose sole purpose is utility maximisation.

It is interesting to note that the 1979 Conservative election manifesto made no overt references to privatisation, merely positing control of the money supply, cutting income tax and reducing public expenditure. However, as a corollary of these principles, some privatisation took place. For example, government shares in Amersham International were offered for sale in February 1982 and were substantially over-subscribed. On the other hand, 51 per cent of government shares in Britoil were offered for sale in November 1982 and were considerably under-subscribed, the loss being carried by the underwriters. Cable & Wireless and Associated British Ports were privatised in phases when the government sold their shares over the period 1981–5 and 1983–4 respectively.

In parallel with these asset sales, the government introduced legislation in 1980 to facilitate the sale of council houses. Providing tenants with the opportunity and right to buy their council homes not only offered a fillip to many tenants but also secured political advantage through the rhetoric of the enabling state. The scope for public sector housing was being considerably limited through the reduction in such provision while, at the same time, cutting back on public expenditure.

During the second Thatcher administration, privatisation developed rather modestly as an overt policy. The Telecommunications Act 1984 made provision for British Telecom to be privatised and for the setting up of the Office of Telecommunications (Oftel). Oftel was established to ensure that competition between British Telecom and private sector suppliers was conducted fairly. British Telecom's main competitor was and remains Mercury – a company set up by Cable & Wireless soon after it was itself privatised in 1981. Similarly, the Gas Act 1986 allowed for the privatisation of British Gas and the establishment of Ofgas as the regulatory authority to enforce the terms of the licence conditions under which the industry was to operate.

These two privatisations were conducted with a high-profile publicity campaign and, while British Telecom's privatisation was enormously successful in terms of subscriptions, British Gas did not enjoy comparable popularity. However, with these privatisations, the trend had been set to establish a framework for ensuring fair competition and regulating price increases as they affect the consumer.

From 1986 to 1990, the government's privatisation programme developed considerably. In 1987, British Airways and the British Airports Authority were both sold off to the private sector. In the same year, government shares in Rolls Royce, which was never nationalised by statute but rather baled out of bankruptcy by the government in 1971, were sold off.

British Steel was privatised in 1988 and attention was turned to the privatisation of the public utilities. The Electricity Act 1989 allowed for the privatisation of the supply industry, although the nuclear power stations were to be retained in the public sector. The Central Electricity Generating Board was divided into four parts: Powergen, National Power, the state-owned nuclear company and Gridco (a company to be owned jointly by the twelve distribution companies in England and Wales which succeeded the Area Boards). The water industry was privatised in 1989.

Each of these two public utility privatisations followed the earlier trend established by British Telecom and British Gas. A regulatory framework for controlling prices and economic accountability was established through the Office of Electricity Regulation (Offer) and Office of Water Services (Ofwat) respectively. The National Rivers Authority was also set up to take over responsibility, in the main for water pollution and water resource management.

THATCHER'S LEGACY

While further de-nationalisations have taken place or can be anticipated, it is vitally important to locate such developments in the wider context of privatisation. The mixture of managerialism and market philosophy which is continually being purveyed by government takes on a variety of different, yet similar manifestations. The government de-regulated the bus industry and outlawed local government contract compliance. The control of local government finance through grant reduction and penalties forced local authorities to consider the financial viability of direct service provision. Such developments, intended or otherwise, presaged future policies on privatisation.

Throughout the 1990s, the government have persisted with their policies to enforce the contracting out of those services that were ordinarily provided by staff within a given organisation. The prison service now employs Group 4 to transport prisoners (with mixed success) and privatised prisons are planned for Doncaster and Fazakerly. Local government is compelled to engage in competitive tendering with regard to the provision of services such as refuse collection and school catering. The direct labour organisations of staff in local government compete with private companies for the chance to retain their livelihoods, even if it quite often means a reduction in wages and a worsening of conditions of work if they are successful.

Local education authorities have had to contend with the policy initiative on local management of schools (LMS) which brings with it the enforced devolution of finances and responsibility from each local education authority to individual schools. Authority-wide strategies on special needs provision or on the promotion of multi-cultural education are casualties of this devolved system for they are dependent on the critical mass of local government funding. Those schools that do well out of the formula funding associated with LMS, either by accident or by design, find encouragement to hold ballots as to whether they should opt out entirely from local authority control and secure their funding direct from government as grant-maintained schools.

As Chapter 9 highlights, the internal market is nowhere as acute as in the NHS or in community care provision. The purchaser–provider split enables the health authority or local authority (for community care) to purchase cost-effective services for the health and well-being of their clients (the patients or those in need of care). The providers of such services (the hospitals) compete against each other for the health or caring contract. Equally, consideration of adequate regulation of pension rights is developed in Chapter 10, but it will be sufficient to say that the events associated with the Maxwell case have increased the anxiety of many, especially in the face of the government's latest proposal to liberalise the management of pensions. Such arrangements appear to facilitate the abdication of welfare functions to private agencies.

The two most significant de-nationalisations in the immediate future could turn out to be that of the railways and that of the coal industry. Amidst high drama right at the end of the 1992–3 parliamentary session, the House of Lords finally succumbed to the demands of the House of Commons and agreed not to press further their amendments to the Railways Bill. Rather than utilising their delaying powers, the House of Lords adopted a strategy of revision with regard to legislation originating in the House of Commons. Since the privatisation of the railways was clearly identified with a manifesto commitment, it would seem that the House of Lords chose to honour the Salisbury Agreement. This is a loose parliamentary convention which regulates relations between the two Houses, conceding legislative supremacy on manifesto issues to the House of Commons (Dickens 1993).

The plans for rail privatisation incorporate the familiar regulatory framework. There will be a government-appointed railway regulator together with regional rail users' consultative committees whose members will also be appointees. The chairmen (*sic*) of each of the regional consultative committees will be appointed by the secretary of state for transport together with the regulator and will meet in order to bring together the views of the regional committees.

Less than two weeks after the government succeeded in passing legislation to privatise the railways, the Queen's speech on 18 November 1993 (the first since John Major's electoral triumph as leader of the Conservative Party) signalled the government's plans to introduce a de-regulation bill. Such a bill will be designed to remove obstacles to contracting out by central and local government and to free small businesses from the shackles of bureaucracy.

Essentially then, the government have 'fragment[ed] public sector institutions and stimulate[ed] private and voluntary sector alternatives to create a market for service providers' (Stoker 1990: 133). Whether all this ultimately brings about efficiency and responsiveness to the consumer (as promised by the Citizen's Charters) or whether the major focus has been to damage irreparably Labour Party socialism to the extent that it will prove impossible (because of the expense) to return privatised concerns to public ownership, only time will tell. Nevertheless, intellectual credibility for these developments is provided by public choice theorists who favour small-scale enterprise in public sector provision, performance contracting rather than direct labour, multiple-provider structures of services provision and user charges rather than general tax funds (Hood 1987).

Although Budge and McKay (1993) have managed to categorise Thatcher's period of government, it is nevertheless important to recognise the existence of a unifying theme. It may be that Thatcherism was an evolving body of policies but it remains that the underlying philosophy is an emphasis on individualism and so-called free competition. This seems as true today under Major as it does in retrospect. In this regard, the argument that Thatcherism was an inappropriate label serving only to camouflage a more insidious dimension of conservatism appears to be vindicated.

The political success of implementing the different forms of privatisation might rest with the piecemeal and incremental approach that the government have, by and large, adopted. Pirie (1988) has argued that great opposition can be expected for major initiatives unless inducements are offered to those in strategic positions, thereby pursuing a policy of localised appeasement. Among the inducements for privatisation are the offer of share prices at considerably reduced levels, the availability of share options and perhaps private monopoly status as a substitute for public monopoly status. Not only will prospective investors find such proposals attractive but it is likely that the privatisation proposal will be more energetically implemented.

This micropolitics of bargaining and exchange (Pirie 1988) is commensurate with public choice theory which emphasises individuals as rational utility maximisers. However, even though the government's rhetoric is one of market dependency, it is interesting to note that government intervention preserves utility maximisation and ensures that privatised concerns operate effectively within the parameters of the competitive market. The government can retain a 'golden share' in a privatised industry, thus ensuring that the future direction of the company can be assured. Equally the government, through the secretaries of state, also appoint the director-general of regulatory agencies, like Oftel, Ofgas and Ofwat.

WATER PRIVATISATION

Improving the quality of drinking water has contributed significantly to public health standards over the last 150 years or so. Cholera has been wiped out, dysentery is rare and gastro-enteritis, where it occurs, has seldom been the product of infected water supplies. The pollution of drinking water through discharge of sewerage into rivers and by seepage from cesspools and burial grounds was the direct cause of much of the sickness and fever during the eighteenth and early nineteenth centuries. It was particularly responsible for the cholera epidemics which occurred in different parts of the country between 1832 and 1854. During the nineteenth century, there was a developing consensus for the planning and coordination of public water supply and for protection against contamination of drinking water. General powers were given to local authorities with regard to water supply, and by 1913, 80 per cent of water was supplied by local authorities and not private companies.

Such was the momentum that in 1894 Joseph Chamberlain, a leading Conservative politician, proclaimed that 'it is difficult and indeed almost impossible to reconcile the rights and interests of the public with the claims of an individual company seeking as its natural and legitimate object the largest private gain' (cited in NALGO 1988: 6). These sentiments expressed a hundred years ago epitomise the concern of many today regarding the water industry. Indeed, it is ironic that the slogan and corresponding rhetoric of the Conservative government since their party conference in 1993 should be 'back to basics'. And while the government's rhetoric throughout the 1980s reflected a nostalgic return to Victorian values, it would seem that here at least there is a profound contradiction between the reality of the present day and the social history of the nineteenth century.

In order to understand the proposals to privatise the water industry it is useful to identify how the water industry was organised prior to privatisation. The Water Act 1973 established 10 water authorities in England and Wales thus replacing 157 water undertakings, 29 river authorities and 1,393 sewage disposal authorities. The Act, which came into force in 1974, maintained local government's central role as an agent of the water authority. Surviving this grand rationalisation were 29 statutory private water companies. In supplying 20 per cent of water in England and Wales they operated within strict limits laid down by legislation. The 10 regional water authorities were responsible for Integrated River Basin Management (IRBM) – the control of water through its full cycle from rainfall to the treatment and discharge of sewage.

Privatisation in prospect

In 1984 the government were claiming that they had no intention of privatising the water industry. Thatcher was expressing concern that, while privatisation was an attraction, it would be difficult to justify on the grounds that the water industry was a natural monopoly. However, this was soon to change.

Richardson *et al.* (1992) have analysed the policy dynamics affecting the water industry and, while their emphasis relates to policy communities, their analysis would appear to serve our purpose as an example of what was earlier referred to as micropolitics. The significant impetus for privatisation came from the Thames Water Authority Chairman Roy Watts in 1985 as an objection to the repayment of £40 million of government loans and an increase in water charges of 10 per cent to cover the repayment. Essentially, the objection proved to be the vehicle for developing the argument in favour of independence from government. The Thames chairman's response was a reflection of the 'values of the (water) industry's new managers' (Richardson *et al.* 1992: 160) which promoted commercialism, managerialism and technocracy. Watts' intervention, then, stimulated the government to consider the privatisation of the water industry in earnest and overturned previous pronouncements.

From the outset there was no settled view among each of the regional water authorities as to the merits of privatisation. Some embraced it wholeheartedly, some opposed the principle, and others accepted it with reservation. However, the success of the privatisation would initially hinge on the support of those in the water industry and the prospect of independence from government control was a compelling feature. Previously, successive governments had pursued a policy of under-investment over the years and latterly had imposed borrowing limits on the industry with drastic effects – in 1975, 80 per cent of water authorities' investment was financed by borrowing. By 1988 that figure was less than 10 per cent.

Some representatives in the water industry were excited by the challenge of privatisation. They saw the release from government interference as a fillip. The water authorities had suffered public expenditure cuts and had been constrained by financial targets and performance targets imposed by government in their drive to implement 'good housekeeping' practice. These water industry chiefs had presided over a reduction in staffing levels with the consequent shortage of pollution control officers. They had witnessed deteriorating river quality standards, increasing numbers of pollution incidents and delayed compliance with EC directives on the quality of drinking water and bathing water.

It would seem that the foundations for privatisation had already been established. Privatisation was being viewed as a remedial measure in so far as public ownership of the water industry was now to give way to the market. Managerially, the market impetus had already been introduced some time earlier. The 1983 Water Act had enabled the government to appoint the board members of the water authorities directly, allowing them to meet in private. Prior to this the majority of board members were local authority appointees and the boards met in public.

However, after some consultation with the industry a White Paper was released in 1986 which spelt out the government's strategy for privatisation. What is significant about this White Paper is its celebration of the (later to be abandoned) principle of IRBM. Unfortunately for the government, this strategy was to prove the single most important difficulty facing water privatisation – how would the privatised water companies be regarded under EC law as 'competent authorities' for the control of water pollution?

The government recognised the potential for protracted legal cases in the courts and ultimately in the European Court in establishing the privatised water companies as 'competent authorities', and so, in order not to jeopardise progress, proposed a regulatory framework to comply with EC law. This regulatory framework had the effect of undermining the IRBM principle for the creation of the National Rivers Authority (NRA) would mean that the privatised water companies would have to coexist with a public regulatory authority, rather than be one and the same.

Having overcome these first-order strategic difficulties the government expediently turned their attention to courting the water industry for its support in accommodating the 'nuts and bolts' of the final stages of the privatisation. The water industry began to work in a unified fashion and extracted a number of important concessions from the government, including the write-off of £5 billion debts, a £1.6 billion Green dowry cash injection, and likely exemption from mainstream corporation tax for the next ten years (Richardson *et al.* 1992).

Water and the European Community

Despite privatisation, the government continue to struggle to accommodate the EC directives of 1975 and 1980 on bathing water and drinking water respectively. Under public ownership the standard and quality of bathing water and drinking water failed to meet EC directives. Water was a low priority in comparison to other policy areas and so the level of investment required to improve standards would be obtained by transferring ownership to the private sector. However, once transferred, any costs incurred to meet EC demands for environmental improvements must be borne either out of taxation or by increased water charges – shareholders would not be penalised. In the first five years since privatisation £13.5 billion has been spent on investment – plugging leaking mains, cutting pollution, guaranteeing standards to customers – because of years of neglect in the public sector. In the next decade, a further £25 billion will be needed to comply with EC standards.

EC directives are binding on each member state as to the result to be achieved but member states have the discretion to choose the form and method of implementation of the legislation. EC directives normally specify the period allowed to member states for implementation and require that the Commission be notified when implementation is completed. In order to become a directive, a proposal needs unanimous approval by the member states.

The directives on bathing water and drinking water should have been accommodated within five years of promulgation. Friends of the Earth have systematically monitored progress in meeting the EC directives and claim that they have been and continue to be significantly breached – in 1992 at least 14.5 million people in England and Wales were supplied with drinking water that did not comply with the drinking-water directive's standard for pesticides. In addition, 3.5 million people had supplies over the EC limit for nitrate, and as a result the government have been notified of a 'reasoned opinion' which is the last stage before the European Commission decides whether to take the matter to the European Court.

Similarly, the European Commission took legal action against the government over unhygienic bathing beaches, referring mainly to levels of bacteria in the water in 1990. The European Court of Justice in Luxembourg ruled in 1993 that Britain had not taken sufficient steps to clean up its beaches.

The government have consistently insisted over the years that the higher levels of concentrations of pesticides and nitrates do not constitute a danger to health, and that some of the directive's parameters that are breached concern the taste or appearance of water only. In challenging the defining characteristics of the parameters of the EC directives the government allow water companies to avoid their full obligation to meet standards set in EC law. Further, the director-general of Ofwat believes that the EC has set excessive and unduly expensive tap- and river-water standards and that consumers' water bills should not rise exponentially in order for water companies to comply with the directives.

This said, it remains that higher values of pollutants are nevertheless breaches of the law, whether dangerous or not. It is ironic that a government that celebrated the rule of law in its industrial disputes and in its response to inner-city problems seem disposed to overturn the principle of the rule of law in the field of environmental protection.

The notion of the rule of law draws attention to the relationship between a member state and the EC itself. It implies a settlement on the principle of subsidiarity, which caused so much constitutional consternation and anxiety in the debate about Britain's acceptance of the Maastricht Treaty throughout 1992 and 1993.

Not only will the 1990s prove to be a most interesting decade to witness the extent of compliance to EC directives, but it will be doubly interesting to observe how the principle of subsidiarity is interpreted in relation to environmental matters. Throughout the 1990s, debate has raged inside and outside the Conservative Party with regard to European Union and the Maastricht Treaty. While much of the argument has revolved around the issue of parliamentary sovereignty, it is worth recalling the controversy surrounding the government's opt-out of the Social Chapter. Adherence to the Social Chapter commits EC member states to minimum wages and minimum working relationships.

The government, while pro-Maastricht, have adamantly maintained that the Social Chapter will undermine Britain's economic development. In reality, the Social Chapter implies regulations that will inhibit the unfettered market-philosophy thrust of the government's policies. Indeed, many of the EC directives are already interventionist and perhaps the government can ill afford such dangerous liaisons implied by the Social Chapter.

It would seem that the policies and programmes of the 1980s (despite the absence of Thatcher on central stage) continue unabated in the 1990s. The key to understanding the relationship between the EC and its member states with regard to regulation rests with competing interpretations of subsidiarity. It will be of considerable interest to observe these debates over the next few years.

Water meters

The issue as to how the consumer pays for water has become very controversial and it is this feature that seems to have far-reaching social policy ramifications. Most consumers still pay their water charges on the basis of the rateable value of their property, despite the abolition of the domestic rates first with the introduction of the poll tax in 1989 and now the council tax. However, most new buildings are automatically fitted with water meters and those owning other properties can pay to have a water meter installed. Water metering can be seen as a means by which consumers are allowed to manage their own water consumption. This is an obvious manifestation of the government's individualist principles which promote the view that it is fair that individuals should only pay for services that they themselves consume. Thus, the apparent inequities of paying for water either on the basis of rateable value (akin to a property tax) or irrespective of how much water is used in comparison to that used by others are removed. It is fair, then, that an individual should pay for precisely that amount of water used and not be compelled to subsidise others' extravagance.

Indeed, the most striking parallel here is with the underpinning philosophical arguments about justice as fairness in relation to the introduction of the ill-fated poll tax. The parallel goes further, but in a less profound way. It would seem that the abolition of the old rating system undermined the notion of paying for water based on the rateable value of property. Water metering is attractive, then, since it enables the government to invoke the idea of providing more choice.

Water metering has its champions other than the government (but for different reasons). Environmental groups such as Friends of the Earth and the Council for the Protection of Rural England advocate water metering as a significant step to water conservation – consumers will be much more conscious and careful about how much water they consume because of the direct relationship of usage to costs. On the other hand, the Institution of Water and Environmental Management disagrees with the policy on water metering. While water metering might lead to a fall in consumption in the short term – 10 per cent on the Isle of Wight where meters were trialled – the costs of the reduction in consumption would be offset by meter-reading costs. Equally, such groups as the Child Poverty Action Group, National Consumers Council and Barnardos argue that water metering will have a deleterious effect on the health and well-being of many households who may not be able to afford to pay for the water they need.

In any case, water companies are compelled to find alternative methods for charging for water by the year 2000. Water metering seems to be the favoured option among water companies and Ofwat, and it is estimated that the costs of installing meters in each household will be in excess of £200. The expressed concern is that these costs will be passed on to the consumer in the form of water bills.

The Public Utilities Transfer and Water Charges Act 1988 not only allowed the regional water authorities to finance the preparations for privatisation but also to establish metering trials in advance of privatisation. However, the water metering trials which are cited as evidence to support a universal policy are not without contention.

Table 8.2 (Atkins 1992: 2.3) shows the twelve trial areas together with their ACORN (Area Classification of Residential Neighbourhoods) listing which provided the rationale for choice of area. What is immediately noticeable is that 85 per cent of all properties trialled were located on the Isle of Wight. The area with the next largest number of properties being trialled was Camberley in Surrey, and that constituted merely 2 per cent of all properties. Of all the trial areas, there are only two (South Normanton and Hutton Rudby) that are located in the north of England. Bromsgrove can be described as being in the Midlands (although well to the west of the West Midlands conurbation), while the remaining trial areas are in the south of England.

It would seem that the trial areas are not entirely representative of the country as a whole. The concentrated focus on the Isle of Wight with its high proportion of owner-occupiers and low proportion of those claiming social security benefits

Table 8.2 Trial water metering areas

	Number of properties	General location	Acorn Group
Isle of Wight	48,000	South Coast	Older housing, intermediate status/retirement area, better-off
Hotwells	839	Bristol	High-status non-family area, less well-off council estate
Bromsgrove	1,100	Worcestershire	Affluent suburban/older housing, intermediate status
Brookmans Park	1,148	Potters Bar	Affluent suburban
Camberley	1,184	Surrey	Modern family housing, high-income/affluent suburban
Hutton Rudby	797	Teesside	Affluent suburban
Chorleywood	748	Hertfordshire	Affluent suburban
Chandlers Ford	602	Winchester	Affluent suburban
Haling Park	754	Croydon	Affluent suburban/high-status non-family area
Broadstone	358	Poole	Affluent suburban/better-off retirement area
Turlin Moor	320	Poole	Better-off council estate/less well-off council estates
South Normanton	720	Wakefield	Better-off council estate/less well-off council estates
TOTAL	56,570		

Source: Atkins 1992.

clearly demonstrates the inherent bias in the metering trials survey. Even though across all the areas the trials show that 91 per cent of households reported no difficulty in paying their water bills, it needs to be borne in mind that 35 per cent of households had gross annual incomes in excess of £20,000 and only 6 per cent were receiving income support. This compares with 22 per cent and 17 per cent respectively for Britain as a whole. In South Normanton alone those with medical conditions were excluded from the trial and a special tariff operated which was 20 per cent lower than what would be the normal tariff for metered water supply. Indeed, Trevor Newton (Managing Director of Yorkshire Water) acknowledged in a recent interview that 'more than half the customers would pay more on a metered basis' (Panorama 1993).

Water metering puts into sharp relief the social consequences of a policy that is designed to promote public choice. Pre-payment systems associated with water metering (pre-payment gas cards are already available for use in gas meters) could easily disguise the number of disconnections in future as people 'choose' to consume little or no water because of their poverty (Graham 1993). Water disconnections, which trebled between 1990 and 1992 to 21,282 but dropped to 18,636 by March 1993, have been singled out by health officials in England and Wales as the main cause of a threefold rise in dysentery over the past five years. Blunkett (1993: 382) argues that 'there is a clear correlation between basic disease and basic hygiene and clean water' and that the rate for dysentery cases which was 2,709 per year in 1980 has risen (after dipping in 1990 to 2,756) to 9,935 in 1991 and 17,019 in 1992.

There is a wider perspective within which the social consequences of water metering need to be located. Household bills for water have risen by 55 per cent since privatisation, compared with a 23 per cent rise in inflation over the same period. Promised improvement in efficiency could have been expected to manifest itself in reduced charges for customers. However, with the privatised utilities, electricity and water prices have rocketed and gas charges and telecommunications have generally run ahead of inflation (although it has been announced that peak morning telephone charges are to be replaced by the standard rate which would assist businesses rather more than individual customers).

A comparison of profit performance since 1979 for companies before and after privatisation is provided in Table 8.3 (HM Treasury 1992: 29). With rare exception, profits for each company have been healthy, but it is not at all clear that there has been a universal trend for substantially greater profit maximisation post-privatisation. In a significant number of cases the profit trend exists pre-privatisation. However, of striking interest are the post-privatisation profit levels of the separate water companies.

In 1992, the profits of the ten main water companies rose to more than £1 billion – and this was after they had soared by 90 per cent in the period from 1990 to 1991. One-third of profits is being paid in dividends to shareholders, and water directors have seen their salaries rise by 80 per cent since privatisation with an average salary in 1993 of £170,000. The dash for profits in order to satisfy their shareholders has also led some water companies to diversify from their core activity of water supply. For example, Severn Trent Water paid £212 million for the Biffa waste disposal firm, and Wessex Water spent £220 million on Wimpey Waste and NFC Waste Management (Labour Research 1993). Further, a report in *The Times* (3 July 1992) stated that Thames Water had paid £50,000 to the Conservative Party to help them win the 1992 election. This was justified on the grounds that a Conservative election victory was in the best interests of the company.

This catalogue sits uncomfortably with the experience of those suffering hardship as a result of steadily rising water bills and the prospect that water metering is likely to lead to the poorest facing the greatest hardship. Metering will force people to choose between economy and personal hygiene. The claim that pricing and disconnection policy must rest with Ofwat rather than with government now seems disingenuous when so many people are potentially at great risk and a profit margin in excess of £1 billion for the water companies is of a magnitude that would not be out of place in the calculations of any Chancellor of the Exchequer.

The water companies maintain that high profits are needed to renew a neglected infrastructure but the burden systematically falls on the consumer rather than the companies borrowing and introducing new share issues. Indeed, it might be argued that to some extent the purpose of water privatisation was to make consumers pay through higher prices for essential capital spending that had not materialised while in the public sector. The justification by the water companies that increased water charges are necessary to comply with EC law needs to be viewed in this perspective. Unless the government legislate in such a way that the 'polluter pays' principle can be enforced, it would seem that the 1990s will witness the continued subsidisation by the consumer of those who pollute the environment.

WHO GUARDS THE GUARDIANS?

The Water Act 1989 established a regulatory framework comprising the government's Drinking Water Inspectorate, the NRA and the director-general of water services (Ofwat).

The director-general of water services has the duty to protect consumers from any risk of excessive charges and neglect of assets, and against poor standards of service. At the same time the director-general must ensure that the water companies can operate as viable businesses. This said, Ofwat dealt with 14,795 complaints, primarily concerning rising prices and billing matters.

The director-general (DG) of a quango like Ofwat is appointed by the secretary of state in the sponsoring government department. In turn, the DG has responsibility for operating at arm's length from the department either in an advisory capacity or an executive capacity. There is no obvious direct public scrutiny or political accountability other than that provided when the DG submits the annual reports to the secretary of state, but there is an economic accountability associated with the competitive market. It is this context that characterises the unelected and politically unaccountable custodian agencies as a new magistracy and is becoming a source of considerable concern to many.

Of further concern is the general proliferation in the number of quangos. Thatcher, on coming to power, did not significantly slash the number of quangos. While many quangos were terminated, others were established to succeed them or were the result of mergers (Hogwood 1992). Nevertheless, Thatcher's famous dislike for Civil Service bureaucracy appears to be coming to fruition in the 1990s where one form is supplanted by a new bureaucracy which is designed to operate at arm's length from ministerial control. Indeed, as Chapter 7 has shown, the Ibbs Report of 1988 heralded the coming of the Next Steps agencies. Civil Service agencies are being hived off from government departments, like the Social Security Benefits Agency. The Civil Service is charged with the responsibility to engage in market testing in order to evaluate whether the services provided by particular departments can be more efficiently provided in other ways. It remains to be seen whether market testing is a sanitised version of contracting out but the ninety-nine Next Steps agencies that the government

Table 8.3 Profit performance

£ million — Pre-tax profit (loss) – historic cost convention

Company and year of privatisation	1979	1980	1981	1982	1983	1984	1985	1986	1987	1988	1989	1990	1991	1992
PRE-PRIVATISATION (last full year in public sector)											**POST-PRIVATISATION**			
British Aerospace (1981)	50.3	52.8	70.6	84.7	82.3	120.2	150.5	182.2	161.0	236.0(7)	293.0(8)	400.0	154.0	
Cable & Wireless (1981)	59.4	61.0	64.1	89.2	156.7	190.1	245.2	287.3	340.5	356.1	420.0	527.0	609.0	644.0
Amersham International (1982)	6.0	4.0	4.8	8.5	11.7	13.7	17.1	17.6	22.1	25.3	21.4	23.9	16.5	20.7
National Freight Consortium (1982)			4.3	10.1	11.8	16.9	27.2	37.0	47.4	67.1	90.2	97.7	93.7	
Britoil (1982)		294.0	423.1(2)	486.3	550.4	650.4	730.9	134.0	403.9	(5)				
Associated British Ports (1983)	22.4	11.5	(10.3)	5.5	14.5	(7.0)(3)	17.2	26.0	38.1	46.5	57.2	60.2	31.0	
Enterprise Oil (1984)					83.2(4)	138.5	111.1	2.9	72.5	67.5	148.8	210.3	114.4	
Jaguar (1984)		(47.3)	(31.7)	9.6	50.0	91.5	121.3	120.8	97.0	47.5	(49.3)(6)			
British Telecom (1984)		424.0	570.0	936.0	1031.0	990.0	1480.0	1833.0	2067.0	2292.0	2437.0	2692.0	3075.0	3073.0
British Gas (1986)							712.0	800.0	1067.0	1018.0	1065.0	1063.0	1556(10)	
British Airways (1987)				(108)	74.0	185.0	191.0	195.0	162.0	228.0	268.0	345.0	130.0	
Rolls Royce (1987)					(115)	26.0	81.0	120.0	156.0	168.0	233.0	176.0	51.0	
BAA (1987)*					30.0	48.0	72.0	84.0	90.0	166.0	198.0	256.0	247.0	192.0
British Steel (1988)*						(229)	(378)	42.0	177.0	419.0	593.0	733.0	254.0	(55)
Anglian Water (1989)[9]							21.1	37.4	52.5	58.7	73.4	86.1	152.6	171.3
Northumbrian Water (1989)[9]							0.1	3.0	7.1	10.8	10.1	10.0	46.9	61.1
North-West Water (1989)[9]							(26.0)	(6.9)	8.9	25.3	44.3	75.3	214.5	230.0
Severn Trent (1989)[9]							(17.8)	39.0	52.0	96.6	97.5	129.9	249.0	265.0
Southern Water (1989)[9]							22.0	36.9	47.3	59.3	65.1	60.1	97.1	
South-West Water (1989)[9]							20.6	23.9	28.1	33.5	38.1	45.3	88.2	90.0

Thames Water (1989)[9]		99.4	144.1	151.1	180.7	207.2	179.2	212.3
Welsh Water (1989)[9]	(12.8)	(3.5)	11.9	16.4	24.9	39.5	128.1	138.2
Wessex Water (1989)[9]	9.9	15.0	21.5	25.0	24.1	27.0	66.0	76.9
Yorkshire Water (1989)[9]	18.4	22.2	37.0	56.7	55.7	57.7	114.1	123.9
Eastern Electricity (1990)		88.0	100.5	99.9	119.0	124.4	130.6	
East Midlands Electricity (1990)		48.2	70.9	81.9	87.0	90.9	119.1	150.0
London Electricity (1990)		84.7	95.6	96.2	112.7	126.2	141.8	
Manweb (1990)		26.9	33.1	28.5	39.5	37.7	58.9	94.7
Midlands Electricity (1990)		64.5	68.2	62.0	76.6	88.9	109.7	142.1
Northern Electricity (1990)		48.1	48.7	47.1	58.0	66.1	89.2	
Norweb (1990)		53.9	59.5	53.3	65.8	75.8	70.3	
Seebord (1990)		47.6	57.7	44.0	58.0	57.6	81.4	
Southern Electric (1990)		69.2	92.5	79.4	113.8	128.2	139.6	166.3
South Wales Electricity (1990)		24.9	31.6	21.0	30.8	26.2	58.1	
South Western Electricity (1990)		47.6	45.6	32.2	55.8	66.1	66.2	83.0
Yorkshire Electricity Group (1990)		55.3	64.5	71.8	90.2	109.5	134.6	
National Grid (1990)						428.6	385.7	497.9
National Power						178.0	479.0	
Power Gen (1991)[9]						233.6	300.7	
Scottish Hydro-Electric (1991)							60.3	
Scottish Power (1991)[9]							144.7	259.9

Source: HM Treasury 1992.

Notes: [1] Current cost convention used; [2] part of BNOC; [3] effects of coal strike; [4] nine months' figures only – trading commenced on 1 May 1983; [5] now owned by British Petroleum; [6] now owned by Ford Motor Company; [7] includes profit as a result of acquisitions of Royal Ordnance and Rover Group; [8] includes profit as a result of merger with Arlington Securities; [9] profits while in the public sector are actual, not pro-forma; [10] New year end.

have set up is set to rise by a further twenty in the short term (OPSS 1993). Further agencification of the Civil Service can be expected.

NHS Trusts, the new-style district health authorities, the Further Education Funding Council, the Higher Education Funding Council, the planned funding council for grant-maintained schools and the planned reform of police authorities are all examples of influential quangos. It has been estimated that by 1996 more than 7,700 public bodies broadly defined as quangos will be responsible for £56 billion of taxpayers' money (*Guardian*, 19 November 1993). Recently, a House of Commons report revealed gross financial and administrative mismanagement of public bodies (Public Accounts Committee 1994). Twenty-one cases were reported where public bodies are alleged to have wasted millions of pounds of taxpayers' money over the past couple of years. The worst case identified was that of Wessex Regional Health Authority which is accused of wasting £20 million on a failed computer system. The significance of the report relates rather more to the concern about standards of probity in the public service and in particular how such standards can be assured in relation to the proliferation of quangos which have become characteristic of government.

What else does the future hold? The 1993 autumn unified budget will mean a public spending clamp-down on local authorities with the allocation from central government being cut by £860 million in 1994 and over £1.5 billion the following year. As a result, local authorities will be bounced into contracting out and competitive tendering of local service provision. The prospect of motorway tolls and further extension of student loans in higher education are indicative of the inroads of privatised interests. Equally, private companies will henceforth police the abuse of sick pay in a transfer of public obligation to private duty.

While the government are committed to reducing public expenditure and encouraging indirectly through fiscal measures a greater sympathy for the application of public choice theory, individuals, as average earners, will be particularly hard hit with the cumulative (although concealed) tax rises of the 1993 budget. The accountants Cooper & Lybrand allege that such wage-earners could be more than £30 a month worse off (*Guardian*, 1 December 1993). The situation is compounded when this is coupled with VAT on fuel and a public sector wage freeze over three years which will affect several million people.

The cruel irony is that individuals are expected to exercise their new-found freedom of choice in terms of whether to avail themselves of private or public provisions when their disposable income is systematically reduced through fiscal measures. The implied consequences of such a choice appear to echo the sentiments expressed more than eighty years ago by Leonard Hobhouse who identified the shortcomings of the preoccupation with individualism when he concluded that 'liberty without equality is a word of noble sound but of squalid result' (cited in Gamble 1981: 181). The basic question, as true today as it was at the turn of the century, remains as to who has the choice and over what.

For many individuals, market fluctuations in the price and quality of the services of public utilities could have deleterious consequences for their health and well-being. This state of affairs raises a moral and a constitutional dilemma as to whether there is adequate political accountability in relation to welfare policies and with regard to the strategic rather than the operational activities of public utilities like water, gas and electricity. Control over policy matters is not within the remit of a utility's customer service committee which is intended to deal with individual complaints about charges and the quality of the service.

The challenge of the 1990s relates not only to the successful transition from government to governance brought about in part through privatisation programmes, but also to establishing new forms of accountability. Certainly, it might be claimed that parliamentary accountability has not been effective *vis-à-vis* nation- alised industries. Equally, it would appear that economic or market accountability (cornerstones of privatisation) is merely equated with managerial efficiency and ignores non-market considerations. In the face of large-scale constitutional changes being effected through privatisation policies, the challenge will be to discover new forms of accountability but in association with new forms of participation in democratic society.

CORE READING

Marsh, D. (1991) 'Privatisation under Mrs Thatcher: a review of the literature', *Public Administration* 69(4): 459–80.

National Audit Office (1992) *Department of the Environment: Sale of the Water Authorities in England and Wales*, London: HMSO.

Richardson J.J., Maloney, W.A., Rudig, W. (1992) 'The dynamics of policy change: lobbying and water privatisation', *Public Administration* 70(2): 157–75.

Riddell, P. (1989) *The Thatcher Decade: How Britain has Changed during the 1980s*, Oxford: Basil Blackwell.

Stoker, G. (1990) 'Government beyond Whitehall', in Dunleavy, P., Gamble, A. and Peele, G. (eds) *Developments in British Politics 3*, London: Macmillan.

Veljanovski, C. (1988) *Selling the State: Privatisation in Britain*, London: Weidenfeld & Nicolson.

ADDITIONAL READING

Ascher, K. (1986) *The Politics of Privatisation: Contracting-out Public Services*, London: Macmillan.

Atkins, W.S. (1992) *The Social Impact of Water Metering (First Report)*, Epsom: W.S. Atkins Management Consultants.

Barnardos (1993) *Liquid Gold: The Cost of Water in the 90s*, Ilford: Barnardos Publicity Department.

Bell, D. (1960) *The End of Ideology*, Glencoe, Ill.: Free Press.

Blunkett, D. (1993) 'Tariffs and tragedy: the geography of economics and epidemics', *Geography* 78(4): 381–7.

Budge, I. and McKay, D. (1993) 'Turning Britain around?', in *The Developing British Political System: In the 1990s*, 3rd edn, Harlow: Longman.

Dickens, J. (1993) 'War crimes: a case study in the use of the Parliament Acts', *Talking Politics* 5(2): 105–9.

Gamble, A. (1981) *Introduction to Modern Social and Political Thought*, London: Macmillan.

Gamble, A. (1990) *Britain in Decline*, 3rd edn, Basingstoke: Macmillan.

George, V. and Wilding, P. (1985) *Ideology and Social Welfare*, London: Routledge & Kegan Paul.

Graham, S. (1993) 'No phone, no water, no gas, no control', *The Guardian*, 1 November.

Greenwood, J. and Wilson, D. (1989) *Public Administration in Britain Today*, 2nd edn, London: Unwin Hyman.

Hall, S. and Jacques, M. (1983) *The Politics of Thatcherism*, London: Lawrence & Wishart.

Hansard (1993) 'Net privatisation proceeds', HC Deb., Col. 566W (table in written answer), 1 December.

Hirst, P. (1994) *Associative Democracy: New Forms of Economic and Social Governance*, Oxford: Polity.

HM Treasury (1992) *Guide to the UK Privatisation Programme*, London: HMSO.

Hobhouse, L.T. (1964) *Liberalism*, London: Oxford University Press.

Hogwood, B.W. (1992) *Trends in British Public Policy*, Buckingham: Open University Press.

Hood, C. (1987) 'British administrative trends and the public choice revolution', in Lane, J.E. (ed.) *Bureaucracy and Public Choice*, London: Sage.

Kingdom, J. (1992) *No Such Thing as Society? Individualism and Community*, Buckingham: Open University Press.

Labour Research (1993) 'Eau Water Disaster!', May: 15–16.

Mullard, M. (1993) *The Politics of Public Expenditure*, 2nd edn, London: Routledge.

NALGO (1988) *Water Down the Drain?*, London.

National Metering Trials Group (1993) *Water Metering Trials: Summary of Final Report*, Sheffield: Water Services Association Publications.

OFWAT (1993) *1992 Report of the Director General of Water Services*, London: HMSO.

OPSS (1993) *Next Steps Briefing Note*, London: Cabinet Office.

Panorama (1993) *Water: Profit or Poverty*, BBC, 8 November.

Pirie, M. (1988) *Micropolitics*, London: Wildwood House.

Public Accounts Committee (1994) *The Proper Conduct of Public Business*, HC 154 1993/4, London: HMSO.

Saunders, P. (1991) *What Difference Has Water Privatisation Made? Consumers, Shareholders and Voters*, Brighton: Centre for Urban and Regional Research, University of Sussex.

Thompson, G. (1990) *The Political Economy of the New Right*, London: Pinter.

Tomlinson, J. (1993) 'Is successful regulation possible?', in Sugden, R. (ed.) *Industrial Economic Regulation*, London: Routledge.

Waterson, M. (1991) *Regulation and Ownership of the Major Utilities*, London: Fabian Society Discussion Paper 5.

9   Health policy

Tom Burden

INTRODUCTION

For our purposes the everyday sense of the term 'health' can be employed, although in fact important debates have taken place over the meaning that should be accorded to it for policy purposes. The term 'policy' is more problematic. In one understanding of policy it is used to refer to state intervention which takes place in the pursuit of clearly defined objectives using dedicated modes of implementation. In this approach the study of policy often begins with the examination of explicit policy statements and discussions. This can cause problems. It defines policy in the terms used by the authorities. It prevents any consideration of the notion that policy might not be what it is avowed to be. It neglects the fact that policy may be claimed to have certain objectives largely because these will be seen as socially acceptable and will therefore provoke less opposition than the objectives actually being pursued. Put this way, statements of policy objectives can sometimes usefully be looked at in terms of the legitimating function they perform. This is particularly likely to occur in the case of health since good health care is something that everyone will favour.

We can also be misled by identifying policy with the work of the ministries that purport to deliver it. In this view, health policy would be seen as what the health ministry or department does. It is evident, however, that the policies of other ministries have such important implications for health that they too might be seen as involved with health policy. This problem is related to the fact that we also tend to view health policies in terms of the provision of *personal* health care. Historically, though, major advances in health have come from government intervention involving public health measures and housing improvements rather than from personal medical services (McKeown 1976). While this chapter does concentrate on personal health care, it also deals with the related issue of community care for the elderly and the disabled which is provided by local authority social service departments. Broader issues of public health policy such as health and safety at work and policy on smoking are not, however, dealt with.

Policy-making in the area of health, in common with other areas, is strongly affected by the overall economic, political and social context. For this reason, health policy-making is likely to exhibit similarities with other types of policy since these too are subject to the same influences. There are important parallels between the reforms made in the health services and those introduced in local government, for example (see Chapter 4). The political context (see Chapter 2) of health policy has been strongly influenced by the ideas of the New Right through proposals developed in its 'think-tanks'. Health has been one of the most controversial areas in which the ideas of Thatcherism have been implemented. Health forms a major item of government expenditure which has been growing due to increases in the cost and complexity of medical provision and for demographic reasons. Health has also been affected by the pressure on public expenditure plans which have been an important feature of public policy since the end of the long boom (see Chapter 3 and Chapter 6). Widely employed public expenditure control techniques such as the use of cash limits and compulsory competitive tendering have also been applied to health. The broader European context has so far been less influential in the area of health provision although occupational health and safety have figured in EU plans (see Chapter 5). It is quite likely that in the future, as EU social provision develops, common European standards for health services will be established. This broader context therefore needs to be borne in mind throughout the discussion that follows and, where necessary, reference will be made to it.

Because of the influence exercised on the implementation of the current changes by the established character of the NHS, this chapter begins by sketching its establishment and development. Throughout, a theme is the form taken by its organisational structure as it moves from a combination of bureaucratic and professional control to a more market-led structure. The main focus of the chapter concerns the reforms implemented from the 1980s, their emerging consequences and the debates surrounding them.

THE NHS AND THE WELFARE STATE

The establishment of the National Health Service

Much of the present-day organisation of medicine was established in the second half of the nineteenth century, including the existence of a range of medical specialisms, the dominant position of the medical profession in general and of hospital doctors in particular, the exclusion of GPs from hospitals and their inferior status within the profession and the practice by which patients could only obtain consultation with a hospital doctor through referral by a GP. These features have remained substantially in place despite all the changes in ownership, organisation and delivery of health care over the last century or so.

The Second World War played a major role in the creation of the conditions that led to the National Health Service (NHS). Prior to the outbreak of the war, the Ministry of Health undertook a survey of the hospital system and began planning for a huge expansion of the number of hospital beds in an Emergency Hospital Service designed to cater for the large numbers of bombing victims that the war was expected to produce. The war-time policy also involved attempts to equalise the distribution of medical staff and equipment. Popular radicalism grew during the war and a major shift in ruling-class opinion also took place. There was considerable political pressure for an improved system of personal health care. The Beveridge report of 1942 took a free and universal system of health care as one of its 'Assumptions' (i.e. preconditions) and there was clear support for a National Health Service from the war-time coalition government in a White Paper of 1944.

The NHS was the first major reform of the Labour government elected in 1945 on the tide of radicalism largely generated by the war. The NHS was established by the National Health Service Acts of 1946 and 1947 (for Scotland). It provided a universal and free system of health care covering hospital medicine and general practice. Given the absence of any threat to private firms, there was little outright opposition to the scheme from business. The organisational and administrative arrangements were strongly influenced by the top ranks of the medical profession. Although the establishment of the NHS was a quite radical measure, it is not generally appreciated that of the hospital beds that were brought under the control of the NHS over 80 per cent were already within the public sector; the rest came from the take-over of the voluntary (i.e. charitable) hospitals.

The NHS was organised in three branches. For acute hospitals, the organisational framework that had developed in the voluntary hospitals was established in the state sector. The exception involved mental hospitals, where the local authority system based on a medical superintendent was retained. Consultants kept control over 'their' beds, they were given the right to practise privately and to use NHS facilities for this purpose, and they received salaries for previously unpaid hospital work as well as the chance of substantial 'merit awards' dispensed by their representatives. The system was run centrally from the Ministry of Health through a system of appointed boards at regional and hospital level. The hospital boards had little control over the details of the provision of hospital care and their functions were mainly limited to the control of everyday administrative and domestic matters.

The second branch of the NHS encompassed general practice, along with dentistry and ophthalmic services. This was provided through local executive committees. General practitioners (GPs) remained self-employed and contracted their services. Apart from some controls over the distribution of GPs, few changes were made in the form of service provided.

The third branch of the NHS was assigned to local authorities, whose health committees became responsible for a number of services that did not involve the extensive use of doctors, such as home nursing, health visiting, ambulances, health centres, midwifery, and the care of the mentally and physically disabled.

The overall system of control in the NHS had many of the features of bureaucracy delineated by Max Weber. Authority was generally hierarchical and little discretion was left to those further down. There was to be no control of hospitals or doctors by local elected representatives. In principle policy could be determined at the centre by the government and passed down through the Ministry of Health to regional boards and then to hospital boards for implementation. Appointments were to be by merit and remuneration was to be based on salaries, again in line with Weber's conception. Funding was centrally organised and wages and conditions throughout were uniformly administered.

However, there were some interesting deviations from the Weberian model. The division of the NHS into three branches diverged from the strictly unitary Weberian model. Weber also suggested that a central feature of bureaucracy was the separation of public and private activities. However, the NHS still permitted consultants to use NHS beds for their private patients and to supplement their incomes from the fees received. Family doctors were subject to few controls since they were not salaried employees but independent self-employed professionals. In addition, the scope of central control was limited when it came to how patients were actually to be treated. This remained firmly under the control of doctors. In effect therefore, the NHS combined a largely but not wholly bureaucratic system of administration with a degree of operational control by the key professionals responsible for health care.

With the major exceptions of the new form of hospital management for former local authority hospitals and, outstandingly, the provision of free treatment, few changes had been made in the health delivery system. Hospital medicine and its senior practitioners retained their dominant status and influence. No effective system of health service planning was established. The existing pattern of priorities, which emphasised acute medicine at the expense of preventive provision and care for the chronically sick, was maintained. However, the NHS did create a substantial improvement in the access to medical care of working-class people, especially women and children.

The NHS and the post-war consensus

The NHS became part of the post-war political consensus. There was no attempt to abolish it when the Conservatives were re-elected in 1951. For the first twenty years of the NHS the main thrust of policy remained expansionary. It was widely expected at its inception that the operation of the NHS would lead to a healthier population and an eventual reduction in expenditure on health. However, medical intervention was often able to preserve the lives of patients who then required further regular and more expensive treatment. Expenditure was also increased by the rising numbers of old people. These increases in expenditure led to periodic alarms and reviews although no serious attempt to restrict the scope of the services was made. In the early 1960s, in common with other areas of policy, there was a move towards a rather more active mode of intervention including the 1962 Hospital Plan which introduced a ten-year building programme based on district general hospitals.

Costs continued to rise. A major factor in this was the advance of medical science and technology. The increased capital-intensiveness of hospital medical procedures was also associated with the growth of the paramedical professions such as radiography, physiotherapy, occupational therapy, dietetics and orthoptics, thus further increasing staff and expenditure on equipment. As a result of the increasing cost of hospital provision, the proportion of the health budget devoted to it has increased during the post-war period.

Substantial changes in the pattern of care have taken place. In physical medicine, the trend towards hospital treatment has continued. In the fields of mental illness and handicap, and social welfare generally, however, a significant move from institutionalism has taken place. The Mental Health Act 1959 encouraged an 'open door' policy based on voluntary admissions. The Act also promoted the new idea of 'community care'. Many explanations have been offered as to why the policy was adopted. New drugs increased the capacity of mental patients to live relatively independent lives. The medical profession offered little resistance to the proposed reduction in mental hospital provision, since mental hospital medicine was a very low-status specialism, largely staffed by foreign doctors. Community care also provided an answer to the critique of 'institutionalism' in mental health that developed in the 1960s. This critique arose partly as a result of revelations about the scandalous treatment of patients in some hospitals. Another source was the radical social science of the time which attacked both 'institutions' and traditional medical definitions of mental illness. Finally, community care allowed costs to be cut by shifting patients from the state to the 'community', that is, where available, the family of the patient. Former hospitals could then be sold off, thus saving more public money. In line with this policy, the number of mental hospital residents declined from a peak of 140,000 in 1954 to 96,000 by 1974. Local authorities were also designated to provide community care from 1963 but they were not given any additional finance. Critics, however, saw the danger of this policy degenerating into simply a means of saving money and providing services on the cheap.

THE NHS AND THE END OF THE 'LONG BOOM'

Changes were initiated in the public sector both as part of the 'modernisation' programme of the 1964–70 Labour government and in response to the growing crisis in the British economy. Initially reform focused on administration and involved an attempt to improve planning. Reorganisation of the NHS and the local authority welfare services was initiated by the Labour government of 1964–70 as part of the process of attempting to improve the efficiency of the Keynesian welfare state (see Chapter 1). The process was strongly influenced by the form taken by restructuring in the private sector. Reformists saw reorganisation as a means of securing social betterment without increased expenditure, while the right approved of the application of private sector management techniques to the public sector. The reorganisation proposals generally reflected the view that the existing forms of provision were satisfactory, but that problems of coordination, duplication, uneven quality and inadequate planning constituted barriers to effective services. The bureaucracy was not working efficiently.

The NHS reorganisation was not preceded by a formal inquiry. No research was undertaken to evaluate the existing pattern of provision, or to seek the views of clients. Instead, a series of proposals were published by the DHSS in the late

1960s and early 1970s under both Labour and Conservative governments. While the NHS plans were strongly influenced by explicitly managerialist ideas, the major role of medical professionalism was not questioned at this time.

The NHS (Reorganisation) Act 1973 established a new structure for health provision which was implemented in 1974. The overall structure moved closer to the bureaucratic model with the three branches of the existing service being brought within a single organisational framework. In effect, the reorganisation amounted to adding the local authority health functions to the regional hospital boards, and adding two additional tiers of control at area and district level. The local executive committees were now to be called family practitioner committees. Professional dominance over delivery was maintained. A key feature of the management structure was a system of professional consultation and management by consensus, amounting to a medical veto, which was established throughout the various levels of control. The participation of the public was to be secured by appointed community health councils with limited powers of review and investigation.

For a variety of reasons, the reorganisation failed to achieve its ostensible objectives of improving services and increasing efficiency. The process of reorganisation itself was severely disruptive, and the new administrative arrangements proved cumbersome. The internal organisational structure of hospitals and the dominance of medical professionalism was maintained. There was growing disillusionment with the results of this reorganisation. This coincided with a major ideological shift away from the largely bipartisan centrist policies of the post-war boom and the expansive period of welfare-statism.

The administrative upheaval was accompanied by two other substantive changes. There was an attempt to create a more even pattern of health provision through the work of the Resources Allocation Working Party (RAWP). This was supposed to redistribute expenditure between regions to reflect more closely their actual measured health needs rather than the costs of the existing level of provision which they had inherited from the past. There was also to be an increased focus on community care. However, as economic dislocation continued in the 1970s, and in the aftermath of the financial crisis of 1976, plans for cuts in expenditure were formulated by the Labour government. Health spending was budgeted to rise at its slowest rate since the inception of the NHS. These cuts, particularly in capital spending, were in addition to severe pressure on budgets due to the RAWP exercise.

The Labour government, with Barbara Castle as its health minister, also attempted to tackle the question of the continuation of private medicine in NHS hospitals which had been encouraged by the availability of part-time contracts for consultants, and the existence of NHS pay-beds. In 1974 the Labour government attempted to alter these arrangements. After considerable conflict, a health services board was established to phase out pay-beds. The government also attempted to introduce common waiting lists for NHS and private patients. In the meantime, and partly as a consequence, a considerable growth in the number of private hospital beds took place. Since this time, private hospital medicine has continued to increase due to dissatisfaction with NHS provision, the popularity of private medical insurance as a form of employee remuneration, the support of top doctors and substantial international demand.

The election of a Conservative government in 1979 produced a shift in policy. Labour had commissioned a report on health inequalities. The Black Report (Townsend and Davidson 1988) revealed that social class differentials in mortality and morbidity were becoming more, not less, marked. The report was not published until 1980, after the new Conservative government had taken office. The major recommendations made for improving health were to raise the material conditions of poorer groups. These recommendations were disowned by the new secretary of state for social services because of the high cost of their implementation. The attempt by Labour to separate NHS and private medicine was reversed by the Conservative government's National Health Service Act of 1980. This Act ended the phasing out of pay-beds, reduced restrictions on the development of private hospitals, and required health authorities to seek cooperation with the private sector. It allowed health authorities to undertake fund-raising activities and ended the commitment of the 1946 Act to fund all essential expenditure.

The Conservative government also initiated an element of privatisation (see Chapter 9) by encouraging the private provision of domestic services in the NHS. Since 1979 it has been government policy to subject as much of the public sector to competition as possible. In 1980 the central policy review staff identified catering, cleaning and laundry as areas of work in the NHS where contracting out could be extended. A draft circular was prepared, asking health authorities to compare external prices to in-house costs. Health authorities were required to plan a programme of competitive tendering, prepare specifications and to award contracts.

Cleaning has been the most successful area for the private sector with 89 per cent going to external contractors in 1984. For the ancillary services as a whole, the process varied throughout the country, being more successful in the south. In a study in 1986, health authorities reported an average saving of 20 per cent of previous costs. Cleaning had the greatest savings and catering the least. A fall in standards has been the main problem, with the failure rate of external contracts being much greater than for those held in-house.

In what amounted to another move away from the bureaucratic model towards a more market-based approach, the new government became concerned to introduce business methods into the running of the NHS. The administration was seen to involve considerable duplication and, from 1982, two hundred new district health authorities replaced the area health authorities. In 1983 the government announced the setting up of the NHS management inquiry known as the Griffiths Report. The strategy of the report was to seek to restrict professional power in the NHS by increasing the powers of management and by the introduction of devolved financial control procedures.

THE NHS AND THE NEW RIGHT: WORKING FOR PATIENTS?

The background to the reforms

Government health policy of the last decade has embraced New Right economic and political principles (see Chapter 2). New Right economists have long claimed that people would voluntarily pay more for health services and, in line with this, charges for eye tests, dental care and prescriptions have been introduced. The New Right view any attempts at centralised state planning with extreme suspicion. They believe that the state should keep its provision of services to a minimum in order to encourage the market mechanism to develop. Competition and market forces would then effect increases in the efficiency of the delivery of services. However, the New Right critique goes much further than simply promoting market solutions and addresses political and administrative issues. Critics hold the view that policy formulation has become too responsive to the state bureaucracies themselves and that the democratic process of consultation with pressure groups and interested parties has led to the accommodation of special interests and the over-expansion of state provision.

In the later years of the Thatcher government the practices of a number of professional groups, including teachers, lawyers and the medical profession, have been challenged. The impact of attempts to limit the autonomy and power of the medical profession through introducing private sector managers and management techniques in the NHS through the Griffiths reforms were seen to have failed to exert sufficient managerial control over the doctors. The government were therefore prepared to adopt a more radical solution.

The review of the NHS that led to the publication of *Working for Patients* was established following a series of alleged funding crises in the 1980s. Public disquiet at the plight of children in Birmingham with cardiac problems having to be placed on extended waiting lists due to cash shortfalls in the winter of 1987 is generally acknowledged as being the occasion for the review. In early 1988 Thatcher unexpectedly announced the NHS review on the BBC television programme *Panorama*. She continued to exert a personal influence over the policy-making process and chaired the *ad hoc* committee that inspired the re-organisation of the NHS. She ignored the use of Royal Commissions and the convention of consultations with interested parties and extended Cabinet discussion. Instead, an important influence on policy formulation came from 'think-tanks' such as the Adam Smith Institute, the Centre for Policy Studies and the Institute of Economic Affairs (see Chapter 2).

While the review was ostensibly established to resolve the problem of funding the NHS, what emerged was a review of management and organisation (Leathard 1990). The assertion central to the 1989 White Paper was that more funding was not the solution to the alleged crisis in health care. The government's main objective with regard to funding in the White Paper was to emphasise 'value for money' as a way of maximising the efficiency of the use of the resources available (Harrison *et al.* 1990).

The White Paper put this strategy into practice in a number of ways: by increasing the influence of local managers in relation to doctors, by altering doctors' contracts of employment and by abolishing the automatic right to medical representation on health authorities. Consequently the management changes can be seen as posing a threat to the supremacy of the medical profession by effectively reducing its influence on activity within the service (Harrison *et al.* 1990). The government's failure to include its own chief medical officer as a member of the newly created NHS policy board symbolised the displacement of the medical profession from the policy-making process. The policy also represented a shift towards greater central control and a more hierarchical health service. Locally elected and accountable district and regional health authority members have been replaced by government-nominated salaried non-executive members (Small 1989).

At the outset *Working for Patients* proved unpopular. The Department of Health (DH) spent millions of pounds promoting it with videos, 'roadshows' and booklets to households, but successive public opinion polls showed that large majorities of the general public disliked the 'reforms'. The BMA financed a major public campaign criticising the proposals, including the distribution of leaflets in doctors' surgeries. The then Secretary of State for Health, Kenneth Clarke, accused the BMA of inaccuracies and self-interest, and many critics accused the government of having produced a scheme that would fragment the NHS and encourage greater use of the private sector of health care. Bitter struggles broke out at many of the hospitals that were possible candidates for self-governing trust status.

Working for Patients marked a radical change of direction for the NHS. The changes proposed in it can also be viewed as an attempt to 'roll back the state' by opening up more of the state to competitive market forces. *Working for Patients* was also an attempt to stimulate a 'mixed economy of welfare' in health care in so much as those that can afford to do so, can exit the NHS, in favour of private health-care provision (Harrison *et al.* 1990).

Hierarchical planning was to be replaced by a 'provider market'. A provider market exists where the suppliers of a public service are subjected to market 'disciplines' by having their revenues determined by the 'demand' for their services from consumers. In theory they have to provide what the purchasers want or they will run short of funds and have to reduce the scale of their operations. Since this 'market' is established by the state rather than developing as a result of the actions of individual private consumers and producers, it is sometimes known as a 'quasi-market'. A feature of this particular quasi-market is that the consumers are not the people who actually get the service, i.e. the patients, but health authorities and GPs who act on their behalf.

The main actors in this provider market are as follows:

- *The NHS Management Executive*: This reports to an NHS policy board chaired by the secretary of state. The board determines the strategy, objectives and finances of the NHS in the light of government policy. The Executive deals with all operational matters within the strategy and objectives set by the policy board.

- *Self-governing Trusts*: NHS hospitals may apply to the DH to opt out of district health authority (DHA) control and obtain a range of powers and freedoms not available to health authorities generally in order to stimulate enterprise.
- *Fundholding practices*: Larger GP practices can apply for special practice budgets. With these they may purchase hospital services for the patients on their list.

An improved flow of information about treatments and costs is supposed to result from an extension of the resource management initiative (RMI). In addition, a process of medical audit is being introduced in every DHA to ensure that doctors monitor the quality of their work. Management access to this information will give managers some control over the effectiveness and quality of medical work which previously they did not have. Thus medical autonomy will be somewhat reduced. Managers, however, will not be in a position to interfere with a doctor's decisions to admit individual patients, diagnose this or that condition or select a course of therapy.

In the new scheme there is a clear separation between the role of the hospitals in supplying hospital services and the job of the DHA and of fundholding GPs in purchasing hospital services for the population of a defined area. A DHA, in its purchasing role, will contract to buy the services that it estimates its population will need from the hospital that offers the best bid, subject to quality standards. Significantly, DHAs will be able to purchase services from private as well as NHS hospitals. Further expansion of private provision will be encouraged by tax relief for health insurance premiums for the over-sixties.

These changes have produced a new flow of funds through the NHS. The DH allocates funds to the RHAs and they then allocate to each DHA depending on the health needs of the resident population of the district. Fundholding practices get the money direct to use to buy hospital care for patients on their lists. Non-fundholding GPs, however are financed by the family health services authorities (formerly the family practitioner committees).

CURRENT DEVELOPMENTS AND FUTURE PROSPECTS

The impact of market-based reforms

For a number of reasons it is difficult to assess the impact of the reforms. Most importantly they have only been in place for a few years and the long-term patterns of change that they may have established are not yet apparent. However, a number of indicators have been highlighted by either critics or supporters. One measure used by the government is the size of waiting lists. However, these have sometimes been massaged in the same manner as the unemployment figures, in order to reduce government embarrassment. The longest waiting times have fallen, but there has been an increase in shorter waits. The reduction has, however, been achieved through political intervention, and not through the operation of the market, since ministers have directly intervened to put pressure on health authority chairmen and general managers to meet the government's targets. According to the government, waiting lists are falling. Between April and September 1991, the number of people waiting for an operation for more than two years fell by 8,000, or 16 per cent. The controversy over waiting lists is complicated by the fact that patients not only wait to receive hospital treatment after it has been recommended for them by a hospital consultant, they may also wait long periods before their GP is able to get them an appointment to see a consultant in the first place. The government claim that nobody has to wait longer than two years for treatment; however, there is evidence that some patients have to wait longer than this just to see a consultant (*Guardian*, 2 January 1994).

Some other measures also show an improvement. The DH perceives health promotion to involve strategies such as health checks carried out by GPs under financial incentives in the new GP contracts embodied in the NHS reforms. Performance-related contracts for GPs have led to record levels of childhood immunisation. In the case of whooping cough the figure increased from 75 per cent to 90 per cent of the child population in the period 1989–91. The government have also shown some interest in promoting health more generally through establishing targets and monitoring the extent to which they are achieved. The Green Paper 'The health of the nation' (1991) continues their use with the targets being centred around individual behaviour such as smoking and specific diseases such as strokes.

There has been controversy about the politics of health authority control. Critics have pointed out that many Trust and health authority boards have been packed with Conservative supporters. For example, of the five board members of the Dartford and Gravesham Trust in Kent named in January 1994, two were Tory councillors, a third chaired a local Tory association and a fourth was the wife of the local Tory MP. Labour claims that there are four other cases where spouses of Tory MPs have been appointed to chair Trusts. More broadly, the growing number of these Trusts is seen as part of the general expansion of quangos and the increase in the role and power of non-elected appointees ('the quangocracy') over the disposition of public funds.

There are also doubts about the managerial competence of the boards managing some of the Trusts. In addition, because they have to sell their 'products' as if they were businesses, their cash flow is largely beyond their control and some are experiencing financial difficulties. A leaked report from the NHS Management Executive Committee in 1992 stated that the number of hospitals that were more than £100,000 in deficit had risen from seventy-nine to eighty-six, with 65 per cent of hospitals expecting to close beds and cut services.

Critics also point to a lack of control of public funds and to extravagance and waste. The Commons Public Accounts Committee criticised the Wessex Regional Health Authority for wasting, on their own admission, at least £20 million on buying and running a failed computer system at the expense of patient care. The West Midlands Regional Health Authority was criticised over contracts placed for a regional computer information system for patient care which cost the authority more than £43 million before it was abandoned. The manager mainly responsible was not asked to leave his job until two years after ministers had been warned by auditors about shortcomings in the contract. He was then given a severance payment of £120,000. Following these financial scandals, codes of conduct for boards of Trusts and health authorities have been drawn up by a working group headed by Sir Duncan Nichol, NHS chief executive. These are to be based on the approach of the Cadbury Committee on Corporate Governance in Industry which reported in 1992. How effective these will be remains to be seen.

There is currently a debate taking place on the impact of the reforms on the size and cost of management in the NHS. In the United Kingdom as a whole the number of NHS managers rose from 6,091 in 1989/90 to 20,478 in 1992/3. Over the same period, administrative and clerical staff rose from 144,582 to 166,363 – a 15.1 per cent increase. Taking together managers and administrative and clerical staff, the rise over the whole period was 36,168. The salary cost of managers more than trebled from £174.2 million to £532.9 million in the period 1990–3. Regional health authorities account for only 12 per cent of the increase in managers between 1989 and 1992. The real growth in NHS management has been in self-governing trusts. At the same time, the number of nursing and midwifery staff, expressed as full-time equivalents, fell by 27,235 from 1989 to 1993. Ministers argue, however, that some of the fall in nursing numbers comes from the reclassification of senior nurses as managers. In addition, more than 18,000 student nurses have been removed from nursing numbers since 1990.

A major effect of the reforms has been to put pressure on those managing the NHS to cut costs by reducing the number of acute beds. The consequent rationalisation of hospital care has involved considerable political controversy. Strategic plans for major cities including London, Birmingham, Bristol and Newcastle-upon-Tyne involve shifting resources into community and primary services and closing hospital beds and duplicated services such as casualty departments in neighbouring hospitals. Government policy for London assumes that it has too many hospital beds. An inquiry was set up under Sir Bernard Tomlinson to review the situation. This recommended a considerable degree of rationalisation involving many closures. As an interim measure, additional resources of over £100 million were allocated to the four Thames regions for 1994. It is worth noting that, as with policy on waiting lists, the market was not left to work itself out, free of interference. Instead it was augmented with hierarchical planning and transitional funding.

There was a reduction of about 28 per cent in the number of acute beds in London between 1986 and 1991 and currently further reductions are taking place. Tomlinson himself warned that this reduction had to be very carefully planned. However, it has been the occasion for disputes and campaigns about which hospitals should close and which services should be rationalised. Bed closures are likely to continue across the country because of both cost constraints and changes in the pattern of care provided, especially the use of 'keyhole' surgery which can considerably reduce the time that patients need to spend in hospital. It is likely that around a third of the acute care beds available in hospitals in 1981 will have been closed by 2001 according to recent forecasts. This will continue current trends. Between 1981 and 1991, the number of acute beds in England fell from 145,000 to 114,000. By 2001 the number may fall to between 95,000 and 100,000. The average length of stay will be 4.2 days, compared to 6.0 in 1991 and 8.6 in 1981.

Any attempt to evaluate the overall impact of the changes in the NHS at this stage is fraught with difficulty. Some critics argue that the logic of management and the market has not been allowed to operate at full strength and that the momentum of the reforms is faltering. Others argue that the reforms are a smokescreen to conceal cuts in health expenditure. It is claimed that the proportion of national output devoted to real health needs has not risen and that Britain spends less as a proportion of GDP on health than it did in the mid-1970s. The reforms have not been accompanied by any more resources except in the run-up to the 1992 general election and in real health terms resources are set to fall over the next three years.

Community care

The other major reform of health provision concerns community care. Community care has been increasing in importance over the last three decades. The increased proportion of elderly people as well as the reduction of hospital accommodation for those with mental illnesses and learning difficulties have been the main reasons for this. The gross current expenditure on community care services rose from £1,169 million in 1979/80 to £3,444 million in 1987/8, an increase of 68 per cent in real terms. Local authority personal social services spending has grown by 37 per cent in real terms, during the decade up to 1989/90. Social security support for people in independent private residential care and nursing homes rose from £10 million in 1979 to over £1,000 million in 1989. The current figure is £2.5 billion a year.

Community care as a policy goal was originally adopted some thirty years ago at a time when the policy had wide support within the post-war consensus. Community care has been based on a 'family model of care' which assumes that, as far as possible, those being cared for should be looked after by their families and in their own homes. However, feminists have pointed out that community care imposes the main burden of support on women. With the intensification of ideological differences since the advent of Thatcherism, the debate about community care has involved a conflict between these feminist concerns and the New Right social doctrine which emphasises the obligations of individuals and families. In particular the New Right wishes to reduce the state interference in the private domain, to give individuals greater 'choice' in running their own lives, to limit the power of state-employed professionals to control the lives of 'ordinary people' and to promote voluntarism (see Chapter 2). In this ideology collective state provision is replaced by 'the community' in which caring is undertaken, unpaid and generally by women, within the family.

A key document in the current resurgence of community care is the Griffiths Report *Community Care: Agenda for Action*, published in 1988. The report recommended a reorientation of the role of social services so as to ensure that individual needs are identified, care packages drawn up and care managers assigned. These ideas formed the background to the 1989 White Paper 'Caring for People', which focused on lack of coordination and cooperation between government services. The White Paper reaffirmed the government's commitment to promoting care in the community for older people, and those with mental illness, disabilities or learning difficulties, preferably in their family home. It recommended a transformation in the role of local authority social services departments from that of service providers to that of enabling agencies, concerned with assessing need, planning services and promoting consumer choice among a range of public, private and voluntary organisations (see Chapter 4). The government also wished to promote choice and to make maximum use of the independent sector. Unusually, in this case a number of pilot schemes were set up before legislation was introduced.

In 1990 the NHS and Community Care Act was passed with the new legislation to be phased in over a three-year period. In 1991 the local authorities set up complaints procedures and inspection units and by the end of 1992 they published their community care plans. The Act came into full force on 1 April 1993 with a transfer of responsibility and funds for community care to the local authority social services departments. The legislation utilised the idea of 'welfare pluralism' in which care would come from a range of public, voluntary and private sources. In particular it provided statutory stimulation for private provision. Local authorities now have to spend 85 per cent of their funds in the private sector, which mainly consists of residential and nursing homes.

One of the provisions in the legislation that came directly from the Griffiths Report was to nominate a 'care manager' to be responsible for monitoring and meeting individuals' needs. For the first time social services departments also have to provide explicit rules for who can or cannot, say, go into a home or a day centre, or have meals-on-wheels. This gives those in need more clearly defined rights. However, while the legislation appears to provide clear rights to those in need, there is some controversy about whether these will be enforceable in practice and about whether the standards established will be adequate. The majority of social services departments are producing stricter conditions for people being assessed under the new policy regime. A major problem for them is the prospect of legal challenges which may arise where need has been assessed by care managers but cannot be provided because of financial constraints. In order to avoid this, recent government guidance has warned departments that if they identify needs that cash restraints prevent them from meeting, clients could challenge them in the courts. Thus, while the success of community care depends on local authorities making full and accurate assessments of clients' needs, departments may decide not to record needs that they are unable to meet. There is also some dispute over whether local authorities have been given sufficient additional funds to provide services for all those in need. The government insist that the £565 million grant to local authorities is sufficient, although 80 per cent of directors of social services predict that it will run out. A final unresolved issue concerns the borderline between NHS and local authority community care provision. Hospitals are increasingly unwilling to cater for chronically sick patients. In January 1994 the health ombudsman required Leeds Health Authority to compensate a stroke patient whom they discharged to a nursing home which resulted in an annual bill of over £6,000 per annum, to meet the gap between his social security entitlement and the fees for the home. At the time of writing it would seem that large numbers of mainly elderly people, who were previously eligible for free NHS care, will now have to rely on means-tested community care.

CONCLUSION

The changes made in the health services since 1988 do seem to represent a qualitative shift in policy. As with the reforms made in other areas, the conventional bureaucratic structure typical of public administrative control has been replaced with a quasi-market. While central control is still important there are within the administration a mass of separate units in the form of budget centres which have a degree of autonomy. In addition, instead of operating according to clear prescriptive rules laid down by the centre they are required to adjust their own activities to the pressures of the market within which they operate. The changes taking place in the structure of the NHS (and more generally in the Civil Service) are of enormous significance. Market principles are not consonant with the mode of control traditionally exercised by the Civil Service bureaucracy which is based on conformity to legal rules rather than attempts to minimise costs. The changes being made also involve the abolition of the traditional bureaucratic role. The removal of job security, the introduction of performance-related pay and the ending of advancement based on seniority taken together mean that the NHS manager will no longer be a bureaucrat in the Weberian sense. Neither is the increased element of risk-taking which is required within the provider market consonant with the ethos of the Civil Service. There is thus a clash of cultures between the traditional approach based on rules and precedents that must be followed, and which is also sometimes associated with ideas about 'public service', and the entrepreneurial ethos in which anything legal is justified so long as it yields a reduction in costs. This is a long way from the classic form of Civil Service organisation which approximated to the Weberian model of bureaucracy.

It seems certain that the internal market will endure, whether or not the Conservative Party stays in power. In its recent health policy consultation document *Health 2000* the Labour Party accepts the separation of the purchase, or commissioning, of health care from its provision. It would allow hospitals and other health trusts to keep their self-governing status but they would be run by boards made up of local people rather than managers. Fundholding by GPs would be replaced by a system of joint commissioning, by which GPs are brought together with their local health authority to make purchasing decisions. A future

Labour government would deal with the problem of health care rationing by setting up a national panel to issue guidelines on spending and treatment priorities.

There is currently a debate taking place as to whether the steps taken through the reforms heralded by *Working for Patients* are part of a long-term strategy by the government to dismantle or privatise the NHS. Certainly there are those on the right of the Conservative Party who would view this as a desirable goal. There is no doubt that current policies are designed to stimulate private provision in both health and community care. Indeed, the expansion of the private sector in the form of nursing homes and hospices as well as acute hospitals is already taking place. It is the private acute hospitals that are the focus of the most intense political dispute. Critics claim that these undermine the approach of the NHS in which treatment is generally linked to need rather than ability to pay. Private hospitals, by contrast, provide a (growing) minority with a way of avoiding queues for services and of enjoying a higher level of amenities than are generally available in the NHS. The device of requiring local councils to purchase a proportion of their provision from the private sector will prove as effective a way of stimulating private provision as it has in other areas where it has been employed, such as in television programme production.

Even if the process of the expansion of the private sector does not accelerate, the end result may still be a two-tier system in which the private sector looks after those who can afford to pay for treatment or who have it provided for them through health insurance benefits which employers purchase on their behalf. NHS and local authority services will then deal with a residuum of the poorest people. This is certainly the pattern that is developing in public housing and, to a lesser extent, in secondary education. Even within the public sector of provision, new patterns of inequality may be developing. While standards of service have always differed between areas, it now seems as though patients whose GPs are not fundholders may be disadvantaged. Hospitals, especially trusts, are being impelled by the internal market to put fundholders' patients first. A two-tier health service is thus being created.

The factor most likely to influence the further development of policy toward the NHS is its special status in British political debate. It has been described as a 'much loved British institution' (Holliday 1992). A major reason for this is that it is clearly of benefit to everyone and, in addition, it is probably the only institution in the Welfare State in which working-class people are normally accorded something very close to the same personal treatment and benefits as members of other classes. Because of its political importance, even those who might not be seen as being naturally its strongest supporters feel obliged to offer support for it. For example, at the 1982 Conservative Party conference Thatcher declared that the principle that 'adequate health care should be provided for all, regardless of ability to pay, must be the foundation of any policy'.

The extent to which the opponents of public provision will be able to shift the current strong popular support for the NHS may depend in part on whether they can successfully promote a more individualistic ethic in relation to health. An emphasis on personal responsibility and on payment as the means of obtaining access to the best health care, and on the status of the patient as a consumer, may lead in this direction. The Patient's Charter with its emphasis on individual rights may contribute to this. Similarly, a victim-blaming approach which implies that individuals who suffer ill health or experience welfare needs do so as a result of their own deficiencies or because of their lifestyles, will tend to individualise health and welfare problems by blaming them on personal choices in consumption.

The current situation is very open and the future direction of change cannot easily be anticipated. It may well be that in the developing logic of the operation the internal market will run counter to strongly anchored features of popular ideology. Conflict both within and about health services is therefore likely to form a major element in the political agenda of the 90s.

CORE READING

Department of Health (1991) *Working for Patients*, London: HMSO.

Ham, C. (1992) *Health Policy in Britain*, 3rd edn, London: Macmillan.

Harrison, S., Hunter, D.J. and Pollit, C. (1990) *The Dynamics of British Health Policy*, London: Unwin Hyman.

Leathard, A. (1990) *Health Care Provision: Past, Present and Future*, London: Chapman & Hall.

Walby, S. and Greenwell, J. (1994) 'Managing the National Health Service', in Clarke, J., Cochrane, A. and McLoughlin, E. (eds) *Managing Social Policy*, London: Sage.

ADDITIONAL READING

Bosanquet, N. (1983) *After the New Right*, London: Heinemann.

Flynn, N. (1989) 'The New Right and social policy', *Policy and Politics*, 17(2): 97–102.

Gabe, J., Calnan, M. and Bury, M. (eds) (1991) *The Sociology of the Health Service*, London: Routledge.

Griffiths, R. (1988) *Community Care: Agenda for Action*, London: HMSO.

Holliday, I. (1992) *The NHS Transformed*, Manchester: Baseline Books.

Hugman, R. (1991) *Power in Caring Professions*, London: Macmillan.

Klein, R. (1989) *The Politics of the NHS*, 2nd edn, London: Longman.

Loney, M. (1986) *The Politics of Greed*, London: Pluto Press.

McKeown, T. (1976) *The Role of Medicine*, Oxford: Basil Blackwell.

Small, N. (1989) *Politics and Planning in the National Health Service*, Milton Keynes: Open University Press.

Townsend, P. and Davidson, N. (eds) (1988) *Inequalities in Health*, London: Penguin.

10 Pensions and politics

Kirk Mann

INTRODUCTION

Despite the apparent success of some insurance companies in the late 1980s it is not easy to persuade people, especially younger people, that they need to take pensions seriously. Often retirement is seen as a distant prospect and the transfer of resources between generations to fund pensions is given little thought. Of course, inter-generational transfer of resources, from those in work to those who have retired, has long been a feature of all pension schemes in Britain. However, a combination of demographic change, the growth of occupational and private pensions and political expediency could have profound effects for the future. The funding and control of the income that future generations of pensioners will rely upon is being decided in the 1990s. Consequently, I want to illustrate the seriousness of the current situation before setting out in this chapter to address the prospects and problems of pensions. There are two basic features that need to be highlighted: the reliability and control of pension funds, and the adequacy of the income provided to pensioners.

My first scenario has already happened. A very rich man fraudulently spends the savings of a large number of people. These people trusted the government when it told them to save for their old age, and the government trusted the rich man. When the fraud is discovered, the government initially tells the people who have been robbed of their savings that they will just have to accept being poor when they retire and that, in general, rich men can still be trusted. Simultaneously the same government proposes to sell off an industry (mining) with the savings (arguably more valuable than the industry by this stage) of the employees going with the industry. Again it assures the employees not to worry because now their savings will be protected by further regulations. Little is done to police or enforce these regulations and nothing is done to enable the employees to have a say in how their savings are used.

My second scenario is, believe it or not, the best-case scenario based on the assumption that the savings are not pilfered. It is also an example of gender inequality on a gross scale. Imagine that you are 32. You are lucky enough to have a good job and although still quite early in your career you are earning just above the average wage. Your 66-year-old mother telephones to ask if she can come and stay for a week because, for the fifth time this year, she has spent her pension and has no food in the house. While you love your mother dearly, she has very different ideas to yourself and tends to get under your feet. When you ask how she has managed to spend her pension so soon she points out that your salary, which is the same as the national average wage, is worth nine times her pension! She also wants you to help her do some repairs on her house because she cannot afford to pay anyone to do so. Although she is a fit 66-year-old you are aware that she lacks enough money to buy new clothes and has not had a holiday for a couple of years. In contrast, your partner's father has a new car, takes holidays abroad regularly, and appears to be enjoying his retirement immensely. His occupational pension, supplemented by a private scheme, gives him an income close to your own and he has never asked you to help him out. Indeed, when he got his lump sum on retirement he lent you some money to buy your car. It is not hard to see how you might come to resent your mother's requests but if, as may be the case in the next ten years, you are paying 30 per cent of your salary in taxes – which the government informs you is necessary to provide state pensions – and a further 25 per cent towards your own personal or occupational pension, you may wonder how a situation of such gross inequality could have arisen.

The answer is quite simple. Governments in the last quarter of the twentieth century refused to introduce policies that would enable future generations to provide an adequate pension for all and simultaneously refused to police occupational pension schemes adequately. A cynic might suggest that governments have in fact relied on the complacency of young people.

This chapter provides a concrete example of how political institutions can have a profound effect on the well-being of citizens. Moreover, the demographic impact of an ageing population has implications for the body politic. Successive Conservative administrations in Britain have utilised arguments about fiscal policy in a manner that has narrowed the apparent policy options. It is in this context, whereby certain interests and issues have been excluded from the political agenda in Britain, that this chapter should be read.

I shall suggest that existing pension policies are, by and large, reactionary, restrictive and regressive. In general they neglect the needs of the poorest, effectively discriminate against women, provide benefits to the better-off and are more closely tied to the interests of the finance market than of citizens. They owe more to nineteenth-century ideas of mutual self-help than to twentieth-century, let alone twenty-first-century, needs. Public pensions are under-funded and yet they are a major social expenditure. Occupational pensions are poorly regulated and yet they restrict labour mobility. Private insurance pensions are precariously making generous promises on the basis of optimistic market forecasts. In short, pensions policies are like the *Titanic*: while it is claimed by the captain of the ship that pensioners are assured of a buoyant and safe future, they are in danger of drifting toward disaster.

STATE OR MARKET?

A strange sense of *déjà-vu* surrounds current debates over pensions. A century ago many of the issues that are at the top of today's agenda were being discussed for the first time. In essence the debate has continued to be focused on the degree of responsibility that the state, the individual through the private market and employers should respectively be asked to bear. State pensions were first introduced in Germany in the 1880s, in New Zealand in 1898, in 1900 in New South Wales, Australia, and in 1908 in Britain. The motives of governments in introducing state pensions, and the pressures applied to them, at the end of the nineteenth century have been the source of much debate, but it is plain that political expediency was a major factor. In Britain it was clear, by 1900, that compelling formerly 'respectable' workers to apply to the Poor Law was unlikely to ensure their allegiance to the Liberal Party. It needs to be stressed that all these early state schemes sought to exclude the 'undeserving' and provided a bare minimum of support. In Britain it was hoped that individuals would continue to subscribe to Friendly Societies which had long been the only alternative to dependence on the Poor Law. Thus the state scheme was not originally intended to replace provisions made by the individual but to establish a safety net for those who had either exhausted their entitlements or who, through no fault of their own, had been unable to build up sufficient entitlement (Hay 1975, Castles 1985, Mann 1992).

The Friendly Societies, mutual self-help organisations which largely catered for the skilled working class, were the models for much of the insurance-based legislation of the Liberal government prior to the First World War. Of course the original state pension was not an insurance-based scheme – flat rate payments were funded directly from the Exchequer – but nevertheless the debate over the insurance principles at this time highlights the central features of subsequent debates. In the main Conservatives had argued that the individual should plan for their old age and make adequate provisions of their own. A significant section of the Conservative Party was convinced by the 1880s that it was a mistake to tar the elderly with the brush of pauperism. Others argued that the Poor Law should continue to provide a bare subsistence income which would maintain an incentive for the majority of the working class to make provisions of their own. Liberals, citing evidence from various poverty studies, took the view that this was socially unacceptable and politically short-sighted. The Conservatives may have been the first to articulate the idea but the Liberals enthusiastically adopted Balfour's approach when he said that 'Social legislation is . . . the direct opposite of Socialist legislation and its most effective antidote' (Fraser 1984: 139).

The early labour movement and the formative Labour Party was then, as now, not entirely clear what it supported, although Hay (1975) points out that state pensions had the support of most trade unions. When working-class opposition to the Liberal reforms was voiced it frequently took the form of defending existing craft, Friendly Society or sectional privileges. More vocal opposition to state welfare was expressed by syndicalists and socialists. In some cases their opposition had subsided by the time the Liberal reforms came before Parliament. Criticisms were more often centred on the cost of the insurance schemes and did not, therefore, apply to the pensions legislation which was non-contributory. In this there are similarities with their Australian counterparts, who objected to high levels of taxation – albeit in the form of National Insurance – which they felt made one group of workers pay to support another. This line of argument suggested that it was capitalism that created poverty and, therefore, capital should bear the cost from its profits, not the workers from their wage packets (Yeo 1979, Castles 1985). It is probable that these sound socialist principles found favour with many workers, and as Ginsburg (1979) makes plain, there is nothing in the insurance principle that is especially socialist. However, old age pensions were non-contributory until 1925 and, apart from the Friendly Societies, the labour movement generally supported the proposals, albeit with some groups suspicious of what they saw as 'statism' (Hay 1975, Yeo 1979, Fraser 1984, Mann 1992).

The crucial point about the history of pensions is that there have always been debates over the respective roles of the state and the market, with a corresponding discussion of individual, employer and state responsibility. Although at a very general level it is possible to point to schemes that are entirely funded and controlled by the state and those that rely on market forces, this dichotomy is difficult to sustain in practice. Nevertheless, for descriptive purposes, we can locate the market/individual and the state/taxpayers – the two modes of funding and controlling pension provisions – at either end of a continuum. In reality all pension schemes are sanctioned by the state and no state scheme could entirely neglect the market. Unemployment and labour market changes will impact on the state scheme while fiscal policy has been crucial in promoting private insurance schemes (Disney and Whitehouse 1992). For the reader who is unfamiliar with the pattern of pension provision, Table 10.1 attempts to present the state/market dichotomy as a continuum, along with some of the key features of the different types of scheme. It should be emphasised that this typology is by no means exhaustive, even in the British context, and alternatives already exist in some countries.

Nearly a hundred years after the Liberal reforms it remains the case that poverty prior to retirement continues to be followed by poverty in retirement. Access to anything other than the state's bare minimum continues to depend on previous employment. For women, part-time and temporary workers, migrant workers, the intermittently unemployed, and the disabled, any contributory system poses a problem. These groups will rarely be able to ensure a high level of contribution over a long period of time. Thus they are far more likely to have to rely on some form of non-contributory, flat-rate and/or means-tested, state pension. The income sources of pensioners provides a rough guide to the disparities that exist in the United Kingdom. In 1990–91 occupational pensions provided 22 per cent of the gross income of all pensioners, with the state providing 60 per cent of gross income. Of course these figures conceal the fact that some pensioners are entirely dependent on the state and for others the occupational pension is only worth a few pounds. Not surprisingly it tends to be

Table 10.1 A rough guide to pension schemes

The state ←   → The market

Type	Income Support	National Insurance/State Earnings Related Pension	Public sector occupational pensions	Company pension	Personal insurance
Based on	Means-tested	Income-related	Service and income-related		Market performance
Funded from	Taxation	Current NI + tax	Contributions + investment		Contributions Investment
By	State only	Tripartite: employers, state + employee	Tax subsidy		Individual + tax subsidy
Likely value in 20 years	10% AWE*	20–30% AWE	100+% AWE +30% lump sum	30–100+% AWE +30% lump sum	Unpredictable and varies
Eligibility age	65	65	50 but value declines	50 but value declines	50 but value declines
Reliability	Cuts likely	Cuts likely	Currently stable	Fairly stable, fraud possible	Unstable
Controlled by	Treasury	Govt actuary trusts + fund managers	Govt actuary + regulatory bodies company + fund managers		Securities Investment Board
Recipients 80% women Poorest 40%	40–60% of full-time employees	60% men 40–60% of full-time employees	60% men	60% men	10–20% of employed
			40% of full-time employees		
Main beneficiaries Women		Men with full-time jobs	Men in full-time secure forms of work		Insurance companies + finance market

*AWE = average weekly earnings

those with interrupted career histories (the unemployed and women who were looking after children) who are less likely to have built up their entitlements (Goode 1993: 151–3; Ginn and Arber 1993; Phillipson 1993).

Since their inception every state pension scheme has operated under a number of assumptions which reproduce social divisions. First, it is assumed that those who can afford to do so should be allowed to enhance their retirement income outside the state scheme. Insurance-based schemes operate throughout most of Europe and enable those with the higher incomes to maintain their relative privileges into old age. Second, the state has tended to operate with 'the male breadwinner' as the norm when designing state pension schemes. Given that women tend to live longer than men, and that it is now generally accepted that when discussing poverty we are frequently referring to women, there is a perverse irony in the persistent use of the male as the norm. Third, graduated schemes – where contributions and benefits increase in line with the individual's income during employment – invariably mimic the inequalities of the labour market. If women continue to have primary responsibility for childcare and domestic labour, their employment pattern and their contribution record will continue to show 'interruptions' which will, in turn, mean a smaller pension (Ginn and Arber 1992).

It should not be thought that the state has been especially mean. On the contrary, governments have made very generous commitments to their electorates which have to be paid for by subsequent generations. The SERPS (State Earnings Related Pension Scheme) is an example of how legislation passed in 1975 would develop costs that would be paid for by people born after this date. The 1986 Social Security Act goes some way to reducing the escalating costs of the scheme but it does mean a cut in benefits. Because women have interrupted employment histories and continue to have primary responsibility for childcare, not to mention care of elderly relatives and spouses, these changes will affect women more than men (Fry *et al.* 1985: 21–5; Ginn and Arber 1992).

DEPENDENCY AND POLITICS

Demographic changes since the Second World War will, for some observers, have an economic and social impact 'of vastly greater magnitude than the 1970s oil price shock or the 1980s recession' (Johnson, Conrad and Thomson 1989: 1). Certainly a combination of a falling birth rate and an increasing population of people over 65 poses some interesting social policy challenges. The social effects of a population that has a very high proportion of retirees will be sociologically fascinating. Leisure, consumption patterns and social services will all be affected, and it remains to be seen whether the political agenda will reflect these demographic changes. For example, it might be that with 25–30 per cent of the population over the retirement age, and with a high proportion of women in that category, that the female pensioner population could force their interests onto the political agenda. On the other hand, divisions among the pensioner population between those largely dependent on the state pension, others on private insurance schemes and those on occupationally related schemes might fragment the pensioner population.

Uppermost in many commentators' minds are the economic effects of demographic change, usually discussed in relation to the dependency ratio of the country. Although the term 'dependency ratio' is contentious it can be used to illustrate the debate between pessimists and optimists (Johnson and Falkingham 1992). In short the pessimists claim that demographic changes mean that the proportion of people depending on benefits will be at such a high level that the working population will be asked to carry an intolerable tax burden. While unemployment levels may fall, it will be the case that the age distribution of the population of virtually every OECD country will be skewed much more than at present to the over-65s. Since many countries, including Britain, fund their public pensions out of revenues raised from the pensioners' contemporaries who are in paid employment, it is clear that the balance between pensioners and workers is crucially important. The prophets of doom paint a picture in which different 'dependent' groups – lone parents, the sick, the retired – are competing for the scarce resources raised by an increasingly burdensome tax system (Johnson, Conrad and Thomson 1989).

On the other hand, the less pessimistic scenario emphasises the fluctuating birth rate, with the possibility of a 'baby boom' in the next few years which would increase the potential size of the paid work force. Of course there is no guarantee that there will be a surge in the birth rate, and recent trends suggest that it is unlikely, but it remains a possibility. Likewise if the retirement age is raised it could both cut the proportion of dependants and increase the paid labour force. Whether sufficient numbers would want to work after the age of 65 is debatable and it is clear that many others are attracted to early retirement.

Alternatively, policies might attempt to reverse the decline in the birth rate, thereby increasing the numbers in paid employment and reducing the pensioner to taxpayer ratio. This would necessitate improvements in maternity benefits, childcare facilities and employment rights, if women are not to jeopardise their future pension entitlements by taking time out to produce the producers. It must also be acknowledged that such proposals smack of the sort of patriarchal social engineering that produced the current situation. It would be a strange 'solution' to the inbuilt bias in the pension system against women to suggest that if they were to have more children – without any commitment to shifting the current imbalance of responsibilities for childcare – the problem would be reduced. Indeed, it would, quite literally, merely reproduce the demographic patterns of today and put off the problem until tomorrow.

The proportion of the population of working age might also be addressed by encouraging immigration. If sufficient numbers of young men and women could be attracted to countries with a high proportion of pensioners they could fund quite generous pensions. Again there are reasons that this is unlikely. Leaving aside racism within Europe (see Chapter 12) which may restrain government immigration policies, it raises the question of whether such policies would, or should, be driven by a desire to engineer, *post hoc*, a balance between workers and pensioners. Even if these issues were resolved there is a further issue of the effect that such a policy has on the countries from which the new workers came. If young people with skills and endeavour are attracted away from their country of birth, any gain for Europe has to be a loss for the country that nurtured and educated them. Is it appropriate for pension costs of richer nations to be subsidised by poorer countries who not only incur the social costs of education and training, but then see those they trained leave to contribute to the tax coffers of the richer nation?

The only reliable prediction we can make about demographic changes is that they are not entirely reliable. Based on hypothesis which can be contested and statistical models which are not always precise, demographers ultimately have to try to second-guess both social changes and responses to them. That said, demography is more accurate and sophisticated than it was in the 1940s and there is little argument over the fact that the balance between pensioners and workers will change. The crucial question is whether such a change will be so great as to promote social divisions and/or fiscal crisis. A mitigating factor might be that, although there will be a significant increase in the numbers of pensioners, the proportion seeking public pensions will decline. Michael Portillo, a Treasury minister, was suggesting in November 1993 that the state simply could not guarantee an adequate retirement income in the future and that it was the responsibility of younger workers, anyone under 40 years of age, to make their own provisions (*Guardian*, 9 November 1993).

Nevertheless optimists are quick to point out that there have been similar trends and concerns in the past which turned out to be less problematic than supposed. In 1954 the Phillips Committee had been given the task of investigating the 'ageing crisis' which it was thought would confront Britain in the 1970s. The demographers were suggesting that the labour force to pensioner ratio would reach the point where it would not be possible to fund the pension without imposing outrageously high tax rates on the working population. Titmuss was scornful of the demographic Jeremiahs, and he did not feel that there was any justification for Beveridge's earlier proposal that

> the special indulgences accorded to a privileged group in the form of tax-free lump sums, special contribution reliefs, 'back service' allowances, tax-free investment income and other pension concessions should be extended, as a matter of justice, to the self employed, controlling directors, part-time directors and employees not at present covered by any scheme arranged by their employers.
>
> (Titmuss 1958: 72–3)

Titmuss was adamant that the state had a duty to provide an adequate pension for all and that Beveridge's proposals would be both costly and socially divisive. Consequently, Titmuss proclaimed: 'If we desire more and not less equity in the social processes of adjusting to a "normal" age structure then it would seem there can be no "return to Beveridge"' (Titmuss 1958: 66). Titmuss was stoutly defending the idea of a universal public welfare system of income support for the aged which relied on progressive taxation and income redistribution between classes and, although he did not adequately address this, redistribution between generations.

In the 1980s, Conservative governments were convinced that Beveridge's idea of extending 'the special indulgences', via private insurance-based pensions, was more desirable than Titmuss's calls for social justice. By 1990, 4 million individuals had opted for personal pensions, many transferring their occupational pensions into personal pensions. As Disney and Whitehouse (1992: 4–6) point out, the government provided a powerful financial incentive while insurance sales staff made exaggerated claims for their products. The National Audit Office investigated the cost of the 'special indulgences' and, using its figures, Disney and Whitehouse concluded that the net loss was close to £6 billion between 1988 and 1993 (Disney and Whitehouse 1992: 5). Moreover, it now seems that as many as one in four people who were persuaded to take out personal pensions may have been misled by the hard sell of the insurance companies. In November and December 1993 the Securities Investment Board was asked to examine claims that exaggerated promises were made to encourage people in occupational pension schemes to transfer to a personal pension. Further promises have been made by the insurance industry that they will ensure that there are no losers and, despite the cost, the government has maintained that the policy of promoting personal pensions has been a success.

Nevertheless, and despite the growth in the numbers with an occupational or insurance pension, it is clear that the role of the public pension needs to be addressed. There is, whatever the slippage in the demographic models and irrespective of the dependency ratio, the prospect of the pensioner population being split. We can already observe a distinction between those who are relatively comfortable and can enjoy their retirement and those who are struggling to make ends meet on the public pension. In 1988 the average gross weekly income for pensioners with an occupational pension was £146.90 compared to £87.90 for those without occupational pensions. When it is remembered that the lower average of £87.90 may exaggerate the income of the poorest, because it could include better-off pensioners who have earnings, savings or private pensions, this picture of gross inequality takes on a harder edge. Indeed, between 1979 and 1991 state pensions and additional benefits rose by 17 per cent whereas occupational pensions doubled in real terms (Goode 1993: 152–3).

Most disturbing of all are the political prospects for the poorest pensioners. In 1991 there were roughly 11 million members of occupational pension schemes (Goode 1993: 2). In addition 3–4 million people are members of private/personal pension schemes and, even if some of these are in both an occupational and a personal pension scheme, it should be clear that the political constituency for improving the public pension has diminished. Although they may say that they support increased expenditure on public welfare (Taylor-Gooby 1985) the British electorate have returned governments committed to low rates of direct taxation. Politicians, who may be committed to social justice and be aware of the potential for gross inequalities among the pensioner population in the future, are consequently reluctant to spell out their plans. As Donald Dewar, the British Labour Party spokesperson on social security, acknowledged when he was asked to comment on the party's conference decision to double the value of the universal state pension, from 15 per cent to 30 per cent of average earnings:

> The labour movement, very properly, feels very strongly about the pensioners' situation. And I support it as an aspiration. It looks, I mean, broadly speaking, as though that, if you tried to implement that resolution now, you're looking at about £25 billion of additional spending. And, of course, I have to say that that's not a commitment that we can carry into an election and have any chance of being taken realistically.
>
> (BBC Radio 4, 'Analysis', 22 October 1992)

In other words this fairly modest proposal to raise the income of British pensioners was seen as an electoral liability, despite the fact that the British state pension is currently only worth around 15 per cent of average weekly earnings (AWE), compared to 30 per cent in Germany, 25 per cent in France and 25 per cent in Australia (OECD 1988, Ginn and Arber 1992, Mann 1993).

There is a very real danger that the public pension will be effectively 'reserved for the poor' (Deacon and Bradshaw 1983). If the value of the public pension declines it is only to be expected if those who are able to do so increasingly look to their employer or an insurance company for income support in old age. Once the proportion of the population who rely on a previously universal service drops below 50 per cent the political constituency for improving that service is also likely to fall. Thus a service that is used in the main by poorer people increasingly becomes a poor service. A downward spiral develops quite rapidly in these circumstances as everyone who is able to do so makes alternative arrangements while those who are unable to escape are left in a trench of acute dependency. Lump-sum payments on retirement and a pension worth 30–40 per cent of former earnings may be the carrot that has attracted people to occupational and private pension arrangements but the inadequacy of the public pension is the stick that will drive others. A similar process has occurred in housing tenure patterns over the last thirty years and this has led some to suggest that public housing is now a 'residualised' form of tenure (Forrest and Murie 1989). If public pensioners become as politically marginalised as tenants in public housing, they face a bleak and uncertain future.

DEPENDABILITY AND PROFITS

All state-funded and controlled pension schemes are unreliable. Virtually every government in Europe has been tempted, or compelled, to alter entitlements, funding, qualifying ages, or benefit levels (OECD 1988). The idea that it is only the market that is unreliable is simply not the case. In fact it might be argued that it is the predictability, due to their economic conservatism in the money markets, of occupational pensions that is one of their biggest failings. Supporters of the state schemes have to acknowledge that, despite the volatility of the market, occupational pension schemes (although this is clearly not the case for personal pensions) have thus far proved to be more reliable, as well as providing a higher income, than state schemes. Compared to occupational pension schemes for public sector workers – for example the schemes for teachers, university lecturers and the police – the state pension not only fails to provide an adequate income but neither does it provide any security in terms of planning. For example, whereas an academic might be able to plan his or her retirement on the basis of promises made by their pension scheme to provide a pension equivalent to a proportion of their earnings, anyone who tried to make similar long-term plans on the basis of the state schemes would find that the rules kept changing.

Dependability and reliability are vital for anyone approaching retirement age so that they can plan. Maxwell may have highlighted the vulnerability of some company pension schemes but New Zealand, one of the first countries to intro-duce a state pension, provides evidence that the state cannot be relied on either. The introduction of means testing by the New Zealand government in 1993 has taken away from thousands the right to a state pension. These pensioners point out that they have contributed for the whole of their working lives and often regard the state pension not as some beneficial act of government but as an entitlement for which they have previously paid. In February 1993 it was reported in the press that the British government were also planning 'to axe state pensions for the better-off' (*Sunday Times*, 7 February 1993), plans that some observers believe were only temporarily shelved following a humiliating by-election defeat shortly afterwards at Christchurch, a constituency with a large pensioner population.

The crucial point here is that security in retirement depends on both an adequate income and the dependability of the provider. If governments are looking for public expenditure savings, the state pension is likely to offer possi-bilities. If such savings can be justified to the broader electorate, for example on the grounds that the state pension represents a small proportion of the pensioners' total income, the temptation to tinker will be strong. However, governments have generally been much more cautious, and arguably much more generous, in their treatment of occupational and private pensions.

In Chapter 5 Maurice Mullard highlighted some of the central issues surrounding the UK economy. Not least among these has been the pattern of investment that leading institutional investors have pursued. It is in this context, along with the social and political framework, that occupational and private personal pensions have to be considered. Occupationally related superannuation pensions are not just a means of providing income support in old age but also a massive source of investment capital. Any government that neglected this feature of superannuation could jeopardise the financial markets and thereby the actuarial assumptions that underpin pension provision. In Britain the growth in pension fund assets has been remarkable. Schuller has estimated that from a 7 per cent share of UK equities in 1963, pension funds increased their holdings to 29 per cent by 1983. What is more, pension funds have increased their holdings in property, farmland and overseas equities at a time of underinvestment in the British economy (Schuller 1986: 12–15). In Australia in 1991 superannuation assets were approximately 5 per cent of Australian gross domestic product and worth Aus. $140 billion. It has been suggested that these figures could rise to 7.5 per cent of GDP and Aus. $1,400 billion by the year 2010, although more conservative estimates use a figure of Aus. $600 billion, irrespective of legislative changes in 1992 (SSCS 1992: 20–1; Mann 1993). The Goode Committee estimated that the combined assets of British pension funds in 1992 was £500 billion and that this had profound 'implications for economic policies designed to encourage the growth of the UK economy' (Goode 1993: 157). The widespread view is that pension funds are distorting the British economy by their 'short-termism'. As the Goode Committee made plain:

> Those who identified this as a problem saw it as making long term investment decisions in research and development or capital projects impossible for company managements to pursue. Any short term disappointment in profit performance was thought to invite the attention of corporate predators, who found pension fund managers anxious to realise short-term gains on the take-over of under-performing companies in their portfolios.
>
> (1993: 159)

Consequently, although pensioners can be seen as a political lobby, it has to be acknowledged that they are not the only lobbyists. Finance capital in the City of London appears to regard pension funds as an asset that should be part of the money market. With a number of industries being privatised, the pension funds could be seen as attractive adjuncts. Where an industry is not regarded as attractive in itself it may be that the pension fund is the only thing of interest to a prospective purchaser. There is a perverse irony of having, on the one hand, industries with huge funds with overseas assets and, on the other hand, closure and redundancies confronting the membership of these funds. This was high-lighted in October 1992 when the British government announced the closure of thirty-one coal mines. The Mineworkers Pension Scheme had enormous assets of £8 billion and the government were proposing to cream off some of the surplus. Likewise these assets, some of them undoubtedly invested in overseas mining interests, made the future of the fund far more significant for city financiers than the future of the miners or the industry that had accrued the funds (*Financial Times*, 19 October 1992).

Occupational pension funds were never intended to be a central plank in the investment markets (Schuller 1986: 151). Their roots lie in the soil of industrial relations with employers offering, and employees demanding, improvements in their wages and conditions. In some cases funds were set up by paternalistic employers, while more recently other schemes developed as a consequence of 'harmonisation' strategies whereby manual workers accept staff working conditions and benefits. For some employees it has been a major objective to extend and improve pension rights or to promote the pension during a period of wage restraint. Not surprisingly the trade unions tend to regard pension contributions as deferred wages. Employers are inclined to treat their responsibilities as either an obligation they have undertaken or as a generous gesture of goodwill towards their employees. However, it is important to stress that even where employers have offered pension rights to their employees it has usually been with the expectation that there will be some kind of 'return' on this cost. Thus they may have introduced or extended a pension fund at the same time as they sought to introduce new working practices, or to retain skilled labour, or to create an image with consumers that the company is a good employer, or as Titmuss observed, 'to buy good industrial relations' (Titmuss 1958, Hannah 1986, Mann and Anstee 1989).

The important point is that employees are encouraged to think of the contributions to the pension fund as theirs. Indeed contributions to the fund will usually have been deducted from the employees' wages, in some cases irrespective of the individual's wishes. In this context it is perhaps surprising that there has not been more widespread interest in who controls and regulates pension funds. Unfortunately we know virtually nothing about the views of pension fund members but it seems unlikely that very many of them take an ongoing interest in the investment decisions, membership of the board of trustees and the security of their fund. Most people probably take the investment side of the superannuation package for granted. Events in the UK have highlighted the dangers of this rather complacent approach but it is doubtful whether piecemeal reform can 'plug a few gaps in the ramshackle structure of pension law. To do so would be like trying to stop a leak from a colander' (Davies 1992: 1).

The two most well-publicised cases that have illustrated the problem of control over pension funds have been the Mirror Group Newspapers pension fund and the National Union of Miners High Court challenge to British Coal's pension fund management. In the Maxwell case, it is alleged that huge sums were taken from the pension fund and, via a circuitous route, used to prop up other investments in the Maxwell empire. Clearly the regulatory framework which should have protected fund members' interests was not very effective, to say the least. However, fraud is not the only problem for pension fund members and their representatives. In 1985 the NUM were concerned about the possibility that the miners' pension funds were being invested in pits in competitor countries and especially in South Africa at the time of the international boycott. The NUM action through the courts proved unsuccessful, with the court deciding that pension fund managers had a duty to ensure prudently the maximum return on investments, not whether these investments conformed to any social or political objectives that fund members, individually or collectively, might have. This case effectively defined the trustees' role as a supervisory one, with the key decisions resting with fund managers and the money market. Only if trustees could find investment opportunities that were as, or more, advantageous is it deemed appropriate for them to direct investment on social, political or ethical grounds. In effect this means that the pension fund might be invested in a competitor company or industry.

Thus the law favours the interests of prospective pensioners over current employee contributors. There are sound actuarial principles underpinning this approach but it highlights a peculiar and paradoxical situation. The perverse but very real possibility is that astute trustees and fund managers can ensure both the success of the fund, in terms of a return on investments, and the demise of the company/industry that initially established the fund. Indeed, if the management of the company or industry is less astute than competitors, or is relying on a longer-term model of success than that being used by the trustees, investment in the competitor is almost obligatory. Thus sound investment decisions by trustees and fund managers may hasten unemployment for members who work for bad company managers or in industries that are unable to guarantee high returns on investment. However, the Goode Committee recommended that the law was quite adequate and saw no reason to change the existing obligations of trustees (Goode 1993: 349–50). In Britain the prospect of a shift in the idea of members' interests, or of some kind of directed investment in which employees have a genuinely greater say in how their funds are used, is therefore unlikely. So despite the rather tepid proposals for more involvement by, and greater accountability to, employee members, it was the narrowly defined interests of investment capital that appear to have held sway over the Goode Committee.

It is clear that the Goode Committee were more concerned with 'self-investment' and the opportunities that this afforded for fraud than with the problem of investment in competitors. Unfortunately it is not even the case that the Goode proposals will monitor and prevent fraud. As the Maxwell case demonstrated, trustees can be put under tremendous pressure from their employer. Without some form of legal protection, for example against discrimination by their employer, trustees are liable to be pressurised by the unscrupulous employer into approving decisions that may, at best, be unethical and, at worst, illegal. If the most a trustee can do is ask questions of the fund managers it is always possible for an employer to browbeat the employee representative into silence or compliance. Had the NUM High Court action been successful it may have enhanced the power of union trustees and prevented the Maxwell scandal. In contrast, the Australian labour movement has had considerably more success in promoting the interests of both workers and pensioners.

CAPITAL FOR LABOUR

Deaton in 1989, before the Maxwell scandal had promoted pension reform up the political agenda, observed:

> Reforming the pension system is a potentially volatile political issue because it affects the structurally determined interests of all major groups and institutions in a capitalist political economy: workers, unions, the finance and industrial sectors, the state, and the increasing proportion of the elderly.
>
> (1989: 342)

Earlier it was claimed that the crucial issues affecting the operation, principles and funding of retirement pensions in the twenty-first century were similar to those discussed at the end of the nineteenth century. Moreover, the same countries provided the new models. Thus it is the German, Australian and New Zealand models of the 1990s that are attracting most interest as they did in the

1890s. The focus here is on the Australian system because it provides both a radical model and an example of how that radicalism was modified once the labour movement had to engage seriously with the finance markets.

The introduction in 1992 of compulsory superannuation contributions, by all employers for all employees, is an example of government extending occupational welfare as Beveridge desired. The Australian Council of Trade Unions (ACTU) was a leading light in the reform process and it seems that Australian pensioners, by and large, will be considerably better off than their British counterparts in the next century (Mann 1993). Moreover, the Australian labour movement seems to have been more attuned to the questions of fraud and control in the 1980s. The ACTU has, for over ten years, taken a keen interest in the management of superannuation funds. In 1979 the ACTU launched a campaign for a superannuation scheme which would provide for a fund managed by an ACTU-controlled trustee company, with minority employer representation on the board (Plowman and Weaven 1988: 6). At the 1985 Congress resolutions were passed which called for the administrators of funds to be fully accountable to the members and for employees to have a say in how funds were invested (ACTU 1985; Plowman and Weaven 1988: 7).

There have even been proposals that would have given the labour movement a considerable say in the finance markets. Thus in 1987 the ACTU/TDC 'Mission to Western Europe' advocated the establishment of a National Development Fund that would have access to 20 per cent of superannuation funds. It was proposed that this National Development Fund be used in a counter-cyclical fashion to stimulate the economy. When investment was low, the fund would be active and it would taper off its activities when investment picked up. A further proposal to limit overseas investments for superannuation funds to 15 per cent by the year 1992 illustrates the ACTU/TDC view, in 1987, that superannuation could be seen as a legitimate source of national investment revenue. Nor did the ACTU appear to have a problem with the idea of interfering in the finance market. Supporters of this interventionist approach argue that superannuation has a privileged tax status, a decision that government makes to encourage social objectives, and consequently government can legitimately have some say over what happens to those privileged funds (ACTU/TDC 1987: 16–23).

Had the 'Australia Reconstructed' proposals been accepted, 35 per cent of the monies held by funds would have been directed, to a degree. However, since 1987 there has been a significant shift in ACTU policy. With the recession deepening in 1992 there were no proposals for massive investments, drawn from superannuation funds, to pump-prime the economy. The 1991 Congress resolution

> calls on the Federal Government to facilitate the provision of funds for socially and economically desirable infrastructure expenditure including through the following initiatives:
>
> (i) . . . allocation of a significant proportion of Government revenue generated by the 15 per cent superannuation tax on fund contributions and earnings;

(ii) reduced taxation rates to apply to funds invested . . . in socially and economically desirable investment.

(ACTU 1991: 168)

These proposals are little more than tinkering with the tax revenue raised on superannuation investment funds by Treasury. The vagueness of these objectives contrast markedly with the radicalism and detail of the ACTU's position in 1987 (ACTU/TDC 1987). Some back-bench Labour MPs have continued to call for super funds to be restricted in their overseas investments to 20 per cent of all investment (*Sydney Morning Herald*, 6 May 1992) but this has not been adopted, to date, by the Federal Labour government.

The reasons for the change are set out in a document produced in May 1992, 'Superannuation Directed Investment in Development Capital'. The emphasis in this document is completely at odds with the interventionist proposals of 1987. Thus a statement of the ACTU position is that 'We believe the key to promoting investment in these areas [is] the promotion of a climate which encourages, rather than compels, superannuation funds to invest.'

The document goes on to explain why compulsion is no longer thought to be appropriate. Limited expertise is the first factor mentioned. There was genuine fear that the market would be flooded with investment funds. Fund managers are often criticised for their conservative investment decisions. The ACTU now appears to accept that, conservative or not, it is necessary to have a balanced investment portfolio. Striking a balance between the high-risk/high-return investments and the low-risk/low-returns is a skilled task which requires an expertise that the ACTU now acknowledges it does not have. A point not directly addressed by the ACTU in this context, but deserving mention, is the assumption made by the left that finance capital will not invest in long-term, high-risk developmental projects. In reality it may be that such ventures are more attractive than many short-term investments, according to the ACTU. In general, however, decision-making by fund managers is endorsed by the ACTU who have backed away from interfering in the market.

Second, the need for additional funds to be compulsorily invested in development, infrastructure or speculative ventures, is no longer an issue for the ACTU. Indeed, they now take the view that there is more than enough capital in Australia. Rather, the problem is what to do with the money that fund managers are sitting on. The ACTU accept that the amount of uninvested capital held by fund managers is evidence of a shortage of suitable investment projects. The introduction of the Superannuation Guarantee Bill in 1992 will have increased further the uninvested reserves held by the funds. Of course it is wise for any fund to hold reserves against the possibility of a major market failure, something that may also have modified the ACTU's enthusiasm for directed investment.

However, a third, and possibly the most important, factor in explaining the ACTU's shift, is the performance of investments in areas that were previously seen as desirable. Quite simply, development and venture capital investments in Australia have a poor rate of return. The bitter irony is that the success of the

ACTU, in pressing for widespread superannuation membership, has witnessed both a growth in fund membership and a corresponding growth in economic conservatism. The intention of boosting the economy with investments from superannuation funds has been overturned by the desire to maximise members' retirement incomes. Whereas it was thought that funds could be used to support the economy, it is now thought that if the finance market is reluctant to invest in specific developments, perhaps it is too risky to do so. If a particular project is not considered by the finance markets as a viable project, they can no longer see why superannuation funds should jeopardise members' money. Market forces in this case provided a more potent argument than political principle. Simultaneously the ACTU has argued that some form of national interest investment fund could be a logical part of balanced investment portfolios. However, 'trustees should look at each investment on their merits' (*Superfunds* May 1991: 10–12). In fact it appears that there is now a widespread feeling, despite the radical statements of the mid-1980s, that the finance markets have to be the arbitrators of what is, and what is not, a sound investment prospect. Fund managers in both the United Kingdom and Australia will surely feel that their conservatism has been vindicated by some of the most radical pension reforms in the English-speaking world.

CONCLUSION

There are lessons here for British commentators and reformers. First, it is worth noting that the pension fund managers in Australia were not opposed to the 1992 reforms, although they had specific points of disagreement. Despite the pessimism engendered by fifteen years of Conservative rule, British reformers can take heart from the fact that, in the right circumstances, it is possible to construct alliances that undermine the hegemony of vested interests.

In contrast to the United Kingdom, where personal pensions have been favoured, the reform process in Australia sought to improve occupational pensions. In neither Britain nor Australia is there any real commitment to the idea that state pensions are, of themselves, likely to provide an adequate income. However, in Australia the trade union and labour movement has confronted the problem head-on and pushed for occupational welfare, while in Britain ideological dogma failed to secure any meaningful reforms when Labour were in power or any prospect of radical reform if ever they are able to win an election. It is a sorry tale of a trade union and labour movement giving a relatively low priority to pension fund management during the 1960s and 1970s when they had some influence (Schuller 1986: 154–5). In the much harsher environment since the 1980s it has been finance capital that has called the tune. Narrowly defined actuarial principles and the dictates of the financial markets have taken precedence over income support for the elderly. Trying to find some idea of social justice, never mind equity, in the debate in Britain is not easy. In contrast the Australian labour movement, particularly the ACTU, has in its own pragmatic fashion thrashed out a position that seems, from a British perspective, remarkable. Nevertheless, the position that has been established is a long way from the more radical ideas of the early 1980s. The industry funds do provide a greater measure of regulation and the tax privileges on certain types of investment could be seen as an interference in the market. The support of the fund managers and the fact that Labour has been in power for eleven years has clearly been significant.

Pension provisions will be one of the central social policy issues confronting most industrial countries in the next twenty to thirty years. The funding of state schemes will continue to be a major social expenditure for governments despite attempts at shifting responsibility onto the market, employers and the individual. Pension funds are major players in the finance markets which, in turn, makes them a powerful political lobby able to resist certain changes. However, the Australian example suggests that they do not always and necessarily favour the anarchy of the market. It is possible to 'encroach' (Deaton 1989) on the power of capital.

For all but a few the key question is whether they are guaranteed an adequate income in their retirement. Fraudsters are quite rare but, in Britain, employers are still able to 'dip into' the company pension fund legitimately to support 'restructuring' and redundancy plans which may benefit them but have nothing to do with retirement incomes. State schemes make outrageous promises to future generations and then renege on their commitments. Insurance companies are selling products that are heavily subsidised by the taxpayer and yet they simply cannot guarantee to be able to fulfil the promises they make. Certainly there is no realistic possibility of personal pensions providing a retirement income for everyone. Governments have tended to talk of the need for actuarial soundness and long-term planning while simultaneously seeking short-term popularity and minimal expenditure. Perhaps the most remarkable feature of pension provisions is not that there is currently so much discussion of 'crisis' but that it has taken so long for this to be acknowledged. If women are not to be condemned to poverty in old age, if the poor are not to be even poorer when they are forced out of the labour market and if equity, social justice and security are to be asserted, pension reforms will have to be much more radical. Perhaps more than any other feature of social policy, pensions raise the need for: control over capital; redistribution within generations and between men and women, and classes; strict regulation and enforcement policies in the market; and long-term planning. The prospect that these objectives might be met seems slim and the most likely scenario is that social divisions within the pensioner population will continue to widen.

CORE READINGS

Davies, B. (1992) *Locking the Stable Door: The Ownership and Control of Occupational Pension Funds*, London: IPPR.

Davies, B. and Ward, S. (1992) *Women and Personal Pensions*, London: EOC/HMSO.

Deaton, R.L. (1989) *The Political Economy of Pensions*, Vancouver: University of British Columbia Press.

Disney, R. and Whitehouse, E. (1992) *The Personal Pensions Stampede*, London: Institute for Fiscal Studies.

Fitzgerald, R. (1988) *British Labour Management and Industrial Welfare 1864–1939*, London: Croom Helm.

Ginn, J. and Arber, S. (1993) 'Pension Penalties: The Gendered Division of Occupational Welfare', *Work, Employment and Society*, 7(1), March 1993.

Goode, R. (1993) *Pension Law Reform: The Report of the Pension Law Review Committee*, vol. 1, CM2342-1, London: HMSO.

Hannah, L. (1986) *Inventing Retirement: The Development of Occupational Pensions in Britain*, Cambridge: Cambridge University Press.

Johnson, P., Conrad, C. and Thomson, D. (eds) (1989) *Workers Versus Pensioners: Intergenerational Justice in an Ageing World*, Manchester: Manchester University Press.

Johnson, P. and Falkingham, J. (1992) *Ageing and Economic Welfare*, London: Sage.

Schuller, T. (1986) *Age Capital and Democracy*, London: Gower.

Titmuss, R. (1958) *Essays on the Welfare State*, London: Allen & Unwin.

ADDITIONAL READING

ACTU (1985) *Congress Resolutions*.

ACTU (1991) *Congress Resolutions*.

ACTU (1992) 'Superannuation Directed Investment in Development Capital', May, Melbourne.

ACTU/TDC (1987) *Australia Reconstructed: Report of the 1986 ACTU/TDC Mission to Western Europe*, Canberra: AGPS.

Castles, F.G. (1985) *The Working Class and Welfare*, Hemel Hempstead: George Allen & Unwin.

Deacon, A. and Bradshaw, J. (1983) *Reserved for the Poor*, Oxford: Basil Blackwell.

Fitzgerald, R. (1988) *British Labour Management and Industrial Welfare 1864–1939*, London: Croom Helm.

Forrest, M. and Murie, A. (1989) 'Fiscal Reorientation, Centralization and the Privatization of Council Housing', in McDowell, L., Sarre, P. and Hamnett, C. (eds) *Divided Nation: Social and Cultural Change in Britain*, London: Hodder & Stoughton.

Fraser, D. (1984) *The Evolution of the British Welfare State*, London: MacMillan.

Fry, V.C., Hammond, E.M. and Kay, J.A. (1985) *Taxing Pensions: The Taxation of Occupational Pension Schemes in the UK*, London: Institute of Fiscal Studies.

Gilbert, B.B. (1966) *The Evolution of National Insurance in Great Britain: The Origins of the Welfare State*, London: Michael Joseph.

Ginn, J. and Arber, S. (1992) 'Towards Women's Independence: Pension Systems in Three Contrasting European Welfare States', *Journal of European Social Policy* 2(4).

Ginsburg, N. (1979) *Class, Capital and Social Policy*, London: Macmillan.

Hay, J.R. (1975) *Origins of the Liberal Welfare Reforms 1906–1914*, London and Basingstoke: Macmillan.

Mann, K. (1991) 'Occupational Welfare: A Class Struggle Perspective on the Social Division of Welfare', in Manning, N. (ed.) *Social Policy Review 1990*, Harlow: Longman.

Mann, K. (1992) *The Making of an English 'Underclass'? Social Divisions of Welfare and Labour*, Milton Keynes: Open University Press.

Mann, K. (1993) 'Supermen, Women and Pensioners: The Politics of Superannuation Reform', *International Journal of Sociology and Social Policy*, 13(7): 29–62.

Mann, K. and Anstee, J. (1989) *Growing Fringes: Hypothesis on the Development of Occupational Welfare*, Leeds: Armley Publications.

OECD (1988) *Reforming Public Pensions*, Paris.

Phillips, T. (1954) *Report of the Committee on the Economic and Financial Problems of the Provision for Old Age*, (Cmnd 9333) London: HMSO.

Phillipson, C. (1993) 'Poverty and Affluence in Old Age: Resolving Issues of Economic and Social Justice', in Sinfield, A. (ed.) *Poverty, Inequality and Justice*, New Waverly Papers Social Policy Series No. 6, Edinburgh: University of Edinburgh.

Plowman, D. and Weaven, G. (1988) *Superannuation: A Union Perspective*, Sydney: University of New South Wales.

SSCS (1992) *Safeguarding Super: The Regulation of Superannuation*, first report of the Senate Select Committee on Superannuation, June, Canberra: Commonwealth of Australia.

Taylor-Gooby, P. (1985) *Public Opinion, Ideology and State Welfare*, London: Routledge & Kegan Paul.

Yeo, S. (1979) 'Working Class Associations, Private Capital Welfare and the State in the Late Nineteenth and Twentieth Centuries', in Parry, N., Rustin, M. and Satyamurti, C. (eds) *Social Work, Welfare and the State*, London: Arnold.

11 The politics of training

John Konrad

THE ORIGINS OF THESE CHANGES

The great debate and its consequences 1976–88

It is necessary to locate this debate within the developments from the critique of the British educational system, the 'great debate', launched by the then prime minister, James Callaghan, in his Ruskin College speech of 1976. A widespread belief gained ground from 1976 to 1979 that the systems of education and training were 'failing the nation'. Much of the evidence for this view was provided by the surveys of the school curriculum carried out by Her Majesty's Inspectorate (HMI). Although much of the debate of the time focused on falling standards of basic skills, the issues raised went much deeper.

The late 1970s saw the end of the consensus, established by the 1944 Education Act, that educational provision should be based on 'a national system locally administered through a partnership between central government, local education authorities and teachers. In specific terms, the important policy issues identified (National Commission on Education 1993: 27–8) were as follows:

- education as a preparation for work, rather than for a particular set of philo-sophical aims of 'general education';
- teaching methods and the curriculum, especially the need to establish nation-ally agreed content and process around a 'core curriculum';
- teachers and their professionalism;
- a more interventionist role for central government through the Department of Education and Science and HMI;
- more lay influence (parents and 'community representatives' as opposed to that of local politicians) on school governing bodies;
- a new deal for 16–19-year-olds, in terms of improvements in the quality of vocational education and preparation for work.

This debate was adapted by the Thatcher government in the early 1980s in the context of 'supply-side economics'. This policy sought to improve UK economic performance by improving the supply of factors of production (especially labour) by weakening the power of organised labour through changes in the law and reducing costs by the introduction of competitive tendering. The public expenditure background is discussed in Chapter 6, and provides an important context to this debate. The key aspect of this context was the goal of reducing the total spend and the unit cost of vocational education and training by, crucially, transferring the burdens of this aspect of provision to those who benefited – principally the students and employers. This was achieved by the following:

- privatisation of statutory bodies such as the industrial training boards;
- rationalisation of training schemes for the non-employed (principally the Youth Training Scheme) and the unemployed (Employment Training);
- transferring the administration of provision from the Manpower Services Commission of the Employment Department to employer-led Training and Enterprise Councils (TECs) in England and Wales, with similar bodies being established in Scotland (Local Enterprise Companies – LECs);
- introducing new funding mechanisms for further and higher education through administrative changes and, in the 1992 Further and Higher Education Act, a network of incorporated institutions managed by two funding councils, one for higher and one for further education.

The main policy goals were set out by the Manpower Services Commission (1981) which put forward a 'New Training Initiative'; this sought to introduce a new kind of national standard in education based on competence in employment.

> The NVQ statements of competence are derived from an analysis of employment requirements, i.e. an analysis of the functions employees carry out, paying particular attention to purpose and outcome. In addition, the analysis is carried out by, or on behalf of, employers and employees in the relevant sector and is endorsed by them. Thus the term 'employment-led standards'.
>
> (Bees and Swords 1990: 22)

This analysis by Gilbert Jessup, the director of research and development of the National Council for Vocational Qualifications (NCVQ), is highly significant. From the centre of one of the most powerful quangos in education, the structure of vocational qualifications developed over more than a century is being overturned within a decade. The debate on the issues raised by this change have often been marked more by ideological polemic than rationality as indicated by such studies as Gleeson (1991).

These changes were originally designed to broaden the existing base provided by traditional apprenticeship training which was largely restricted to heavy industries such as engineering, construction and mining. Ashton *et al.* (1989) point out that it was virtually impossible to gain admission to this system except immediately after leaving compulsory secondary education. In addition, entries to such apprenticeships were heavily biased towards males. In part, this bias reflects the gender bias of the school curriculum, where girls traditionally underachieved in such subjects as mathematics, science and computing. However, stereotypes of occupations also played a significant part.

This radical reform preceded and created a precedent for the fundamental changes originated by the Education Reform Act of 1988. This Act and its successors over the next five years changed the landscape of the public education system by:

- introducing a national curriculum for schools linked to a national assessment and testing programme;
- weakening the role of local education authorities (LEAs) from the 1944 Education Act system of 'a national system locally administered', by restricting their powers and forcing the delegation of powers and finance to school and college governing bodies which were to have a majority of non-LEA appointees;
- establishing a regulating framework of the Funding Agency for Schools designed to replace the functions formerly carried out by the LEAs;
- setting up new types of school (City Technology Colleges and Grant-Maintained Schools) which were not under the control of LEAs;
- removing higher and further education (including sixth-form colleges) from the control of LEAs and establishing the colleges as independent legal corporations under the direction of funding councils appointed by the secretary of state – the Higher Education Funding Council (HEFC) and the Further Education Funding Council (FEFC).

The stated aim of these changes was to shift the balance of control from the state to a market mechanism where customers (parents and students) would have sufficient information and freedom to choose appropriate provision. One of the lesser goals of the incorporation of the further education colleges was to end the network of arcane labour practices maintained by strong teacher unions for the previous twenty years – part of the common theme of government policies in the 1980s. As with the privatisation of major public utilities such as telephones, electricity, gas and water, central government retained control through quangos charged with the control of this aspect of the public sector in a manner removed from direct public accountability. This issue is explored more fully in Chapter 7.

The reform of vocational education and training

In 1989 both the Trades Union Congress (TUC) and, far more influentially, the Confederation of British Industry (CBI) demanded major changes. In 'Towards a Skills Revolution' (CBI 1989) a clarion call was issued for a radical change in policy and provision to ensure that the UK economy developed a labour force that attained 'world-class standards'. The response of the government was to dismantle their key agency for vocational education, the Manpower Services Commission (MSC), and establish in 1990/91 eighty-two TECs in England and Wales and LECs in Scotland. These bodies were to be controlled by a board of directors with a majority of senior executives of large local employers and staffed initially by ex-MSC civil servants seconded from the Employment Department.

The strategy of the government was set out in their 1991 White Paper 'Education and Training in the 21st Century'. The prime function of these

TECs/LECs was to mobilise local business involvement to regenerate the local economy, primarily through training and education. In short, these reforms were designed to create a market in vocational education and training that will be flexible to the changing needs of the economy in a much shorter time and with a higher level of quality than ever thought possible. The Japanese model of 'just in time' production, based on the efforts of a core labour force without outward hierarchies (supported by a network of subcontractors on short-term contracts), has considerable influence here.

As a case study, the 1994/95 Summary Business Plan of Greater Nottingham TEC (GNTEC 1994) lists its sixteen Board members:

- eight managing directors, one area manager and one chairman (eight male, two female);
- one union regional secretary (one male);
- two local government senior politicians (two male);
- a university vice-chancellor (one male);
- the local Anglican bishop (one male);
- the chief executive of the TEC (one male).

The aim (or mission statement) of GNTEC is

> to enhance the economy of Greater Nottingham by working in partnership with local organisations and ensuring that the training, education and enterprise resources are directed towards the agreed priorities with high quality and value for money.
>
> The priorities of the Board are expressed through its key objectives:
>
> 1 Partnerships for economic growth between private and public sector organisations.
> 2 Achieving the agreed 'Local' Targets for Education and Training in Greater Nottingham by working in Partnership to raise the awareness of, and participation in NVQ/GNVQ. The Careers Service Partnership will ensure high quality provision of guidance for schools and the community.
> 3 Ensuring additional support for any sector of the community which is put at an educational or training disadvantage through disability, gender or ethnic origin.
> 4 Substantial GNTEC income generation from outside Government funding.
> 5 Improving the market for vocational education and training to ensure an effective response to the changing needs of employers and individuals.
>
> (GNTEC 1994:3)

GNTEC's budget for 1994/95 is £24 million, of which £14.4 million (60 per cent) is provided for operating the main central government training programmes for young people (Youth Training) and the adult unemployed (Training for Work). The majority of the other programme funding comes from the regional government office, established in April 1994, to ensure that there is a subtle blend between national requirements and local priorities.

On the economic growth side, there are references to 'helping wealth creating companies become more competitive' (through targeting six industrial sectors), 'business start-ups for the unemployed' (445 planned, with 421 to survive fifty-two weeks and 286 to survive seventy-eight weeks).

The training side includes the following:

- targets for Youth Training (where the allowance is raised to £40 per week for each trainee, with a minimum of 35 per cent of all trainees being employed while training);
- a plan to introduce Youth Training Credits on a pilot basis – these are vouchers designed to 'give a young person a real say in the direction of their training and will ensure that our young people gain information that will enable them to make a properly informed decision based on real choice';
- Training for Work, covering people who have been unemployed for six months or more, with targets for numbers of qualifications achieved and that 25 per cent of trainees will be in employment by the end of the year;
- a longer-term strategic aim to consider how the Modern Apprenticeship Scheme may be developed through Training for Work aimed specifically towards individuals aged 18–24. (GNTEC 1994: 6, 7)

The Education Business Partnership covers the following:

- projects developed to drive forward competitiveness at local level;
- placements for teachers in industry and employers in education;
- raising the aspirations and achievements of 14–16-year-olds through Compacts (schemes for involving local employers in improving the attendance and performance for children in years 10 and 11);
- Work-Related Further Education;
- the market for vocational education and training. (GNTEC 1994: 10, 11)

The vision and framework for these operations is provided by the government's national targets for training and education. These targets, based on a structure of NVQs developed during the 1980s, called for the following achievements:

Foundation learning
1 By 1997, 80 per cent of young people to reach NVQ II (or equivalent).
2 Training and education to NVQ III (or equivalent) available to all young people who can benefit.
3 By 2000, 50 per cent of young people to reach NVQ III (or equivalent).
4 Education and training provision to develop self-reliance, flexibility and breadth.

Lifetime learning
1 By 1996, all employees should take part in training or development activities.
2 By 1996, 50 per cent of the workforce aiming for NVQs or units towards them.
3 By 2000, 50 per cent of the workforce qualified to NVQ III (or equivalent).
4 By 1996, 50 per cent of medium to larger organisations to be 'investors in people'.

The whole issue of the status and validity of NVQs is a matter of continuing debate. The case for NVQs is perhaps best advanced in a collection of papers edited by Bees and Swords (1990). The report of the National Commission on Education (1993: 287) comments:

> We are convinced of the desirability of adopting a target whereby at least 90 per cent of young people will by AD 2000 be working for nationally recognised educational qualifications at least until they are 18 years old . . . those who stand to gain most are the young people themselves. It is the most practical way of ensuring that the vast majority of them will in future start a lifetime of work properly prepared and with a foundation of knowledge and understanding on which they can build as time goes on. Nothing less will be good enough.

Paradoxically, however, the initial result of the establishment of the TECs/LECs was that the national, regional and local mechanisms were all staffed by the same civil servants who had operated the previous system! A rearguard action was fought by the Employment Department to ensure that the real power remained in their hands, particularly as the TECs/LECs had, by the end of 1993, returned most of their seconded staff back to an increasingly over-staffed Department. Despite this close link between the clients and the contractors, the issue of methodology in measuring the achievement of the above national targets is extremely complex. The funding of the TECs/LECs in 1994/95 onwards will be based on the achievement of the constituent parts of these targets.

The political support given to this initiative was such that, in the context of the long-running tension between the Departments of Education and Employment, the Department for Education pressed the Employment Department to launch a broader NVQ – the General National Vocational Qualification through NCVQ. This programme of one-year and two-year courses was designed to replace a range of post-16 vocational qualifications, principally BTEC First and National Diplomas. Despite problems in the 1992/93 pilot year, this development was generally welcomed by ministers and the TECs as being likely to contribute to the achievement of national targets. Indeed, as a summer 1993 leaflet from the Employment Department claimed (ED 1993a):

> From June next year young people will be applying for jobs with:
>
> - GNVQs at Foundation level or Intermediate level or Advanced level – the new 'Vocational A level' in Art and Design; Business; Health and Social Care; Leisure and Tourism.

The immediate source of competency-based assessment in the 16+ (and increasingly 14+) population derives from the work of the National Council for Vocational Qualifications (NCVQ) for England and Wales, and its Scottish counterpart SCOTVEC. The National Vocational Qualifications (NVQs or in Scotland SVQs) and the new General NVQs (GNVQs) are the basis of the reform of UK vocational qualifications into a system of five levels. NVQs attest to competence to do a particular job or range of jobs (together with the necessary 'underpinning knowledge and understanding') based on clear standards set by employers through industry-led bodies.

> Although GNVQs are primarily aimed at the 16–19 age group, they are available to adults and credit towards them may be gained by the 14–16 age group. One of the main objectives of GNVQs is to provide a genuine alternative for the increasing numbers of students staying on in full-time education beyond the age of 16. In particular GNVQ at Level 3 (now Advanced) is designed to be of comparable standard to A Levels. GNVQs provide a broad-based vocational education. In addition to acquiring the basic skills and knowledge underpinning a vocational area, all students will have to achieve a range of core skills. This combination of vocational attainment plus core skills will provide a foundation from which students can progress either to further and higher education or into employment and further training.
>
> (Young 1993)

To date, despite adverse criticism of the early pilot GNVQs, take-up and achievements of GNVQ are encouraging. Of the first cohort of 3,800 students, 50 per cent did not complete the two-year programme leading to GNVQ Advanced, 700 (18 per cent) were still working to complete units and 900 (23 per cent) applied to university with 85 per cent being successful (*Times Higher Education Supplement*, 9 September 1994, part 2: 9). For a new programme these results are encouraging, bearing in mind that many students came in with low-grade GCSEs. By comparison, failures at GCE A-Level are about 40 per cent and 75 per cent of A-Level candidates are offered places at university. This approach to vocational education represents another stage in the long-running history of attempts to establish a 'parity of esteem' between academic and vocational education.

The CBI continued to support this approach. For example, in its report *Making it in Britain II*, published in January 1994, the CBI pointed out that one of the government's key roles in improving British manufacturing competitiveness was ensuring achievement of these national targets.

Work-Related Further Education (WRFE): a case study in central government management of vocational education and training

The aims and objectives of the Employment Department's £100 million WRFE programme are set out below (ED 1993b: paras 3.1–3.3):

> The aims of the WRFE Programme are to improve the responsiveness of the FE sector to the needs of employers and individuals, and to increase the cost effectiveness of WRFE provision. The LEAs, and after 1992 the TECs were required to ensure the achievement of strategic objectives that fitted the needs of the local labour market, as well as striking a balance between local and national relevance, and short and longer term interests.
>
> The 1994 National Objectives focus on the promotion of the National Targets for Education and Training, the continuing spread of National Voca-

tional Qualifications (NVQs) and the introduction and implementation of the new General National Vocational Qualifications (GNVQs). Participation rates post-16 are to be increased by improving flexibility of access to programmes.

Additional issues which TECs might take up include availability of high cost provision (e.g. engineering, construction, printing etc.) in the light of labour market need, provision for identified disadvantage groups, meeting the adult training needs of employers, and facilitating progression to higher level skills.

This case is interesting because the 'creative tension' that existed in 1985 between the Departments of Education and Employment has now been reproduced for their agents – respectively the FEFC and the TECs. Thus the FEFC strategic planning document is the vehicle that brings together both sets of pressures on a FE College.

In both sections, the wording appears to have changed little in style or content from the equivalent documents issued to LEAs before the incorporation of FE Colleges in 1993. The Further and Higher Education Act of 1992 transferred most LEA functions to the new FEFC. Many of these functions overlap with those of the Employment Department and the TECs. One is left with the inescapable conclusion that the administrative reforms of 1991/92 have had little effect on the FE Colleges apart from increasing the volume of paper and requests for returns to parallel agencies of central government. Little wonder that some FE Colleges looked back to the days of a relaxed relationship with LEA officers that left them relatively free of this sort of bureaucratic pressure. Clearly the creation of a market in vocational education and training is a long way from the results of this 'reform'. Serious doubt exists as to whether the aims of industrial regeneration embodied by the New Training Initiative of 1981, and commanding wide support across industry and political life, have not been put in serious jeopardy by the unthinking application of the standard ideology of 1980s privatisation.

Vocational and training policy for the 1990s: the key issues

Ashton *et al.* (1993) point out that a broad consensus exists within industrial nations that a well-educated labour force is vital for economic prosperity. This view has shifted the nature of the debate on the UK economy from the Thatcher–Reagan monetarism of the 1980s to a development of the human capital approach to the economics of education which had formed part of the consensus of the 1960s and 1970s. Economic globalisation through such developments as the European Union and the North American Free Trade Area (NAFTA) is reshaping economies. Finegold and Soskice (1988) and Ashton *et al.* (1989) have documented the widespread recognition of the inhibiting impact of long-standing skill deficiencies in the British workforce on competitiveness in many industries.

A more penetrating analysis of these issues has been developed by Reich (1991). This study raises a number of key issues for the twenty-first century, including the following:

- the impact of the global market in factors of production on the idea of a national economy;
- the rise of new regional trading groups or blocs such as the European Community and European Economic Area, the North Atlantic Free Trade Area, and the more informal linking of the economies of Japan, South Korea and the other countries of the Pacific Basin.

The shift from mercantilist autocracy to liberal democracy from the late seventeenth century was associated with the growth of nationalism in the nineteenth century, even among those groups such as the Irish, Poles, Czechs, Slovaks, Hungarians and Greeks who lacked their own national state. The national revivals of such areas as Latin America and Central Europe were as much concerned with economic as with political self-determination. Hence the idea that the citizens of a nation shared responsibility for their economic well-being developed hand-in-hand with this nationalism. Adam Smith (in 1776) identified two key factors: the level of gainful employment and the level of training and education.

The impact of the industrial revolution of the nineteenth century created a dramatic expansion of national economies which then competed with each other across the world in the years between 1870 and 1914. 'The size and influence of a national economy came to signify the nation's strength and determination. . . . On the battlefield of national economic ambition, the production worker was the new foot soldier' (Reich 1991: 30–3). After the Depression of the 1930s, itself extended by the decline in world trade caused by the multiplicity of new states with closed economies, the post-Second World War period saw attempts to liberalise world trade and the growth of large multinational corporations. These multinationals, whose turnover was larger than the gross domestic product of many smaller nations, extended the hierarchical structure of the mass-production company across national boundaries. Thus for a great corporation like IBM, the old ideal of nationality (such as the *civis brittanicus sum* of mid-nineteenth-century Britain) was replaced by the corporate conformity and enforced personal mobility of the professional and managerial employees of companies like IBM. Attempts during the New Deal of the 1930s to make the corporations more socially responsible and introduce planning strategies by the government had been abandoned soon after the end of the Second World War.

The US government's responsibility for education and training was limited to ensuring that an adequate supply of children were prepared for their places in gainful employment.

Not even the Soviets' successful launch of *Sputnik* in 1957, which caused the nation momentarily to question the quality of America's education, challenged this vision . . . [the] response was . . . to appropriate additional funds for training teachers to be more efficient at mass production – particularly in mathematics and the sciences.

(Reich 1991: 60–1)

By the 1980s, however, much of the necessity for manufacturing production to be located on a national base had disappeared. Not only was much of the production for US and British manufactured products imported, but increasingly what national production existed was foreign-owned.

Reich's analysis suggests that much of the local employment in advanced economies will be located in the low-skill/low-wage areas of routine production and personal services (45 per cent in 1990) with the former in rapid decline and the latter growing rapidly. This feature was also noted in the British economy during the 1980s. The major growth in employment has taken place in the problem-solving and brokering activities of the globalised economy where the key trading processes are the manipulation of symbols – data, words, oral and visual representations. This last group are described as *symbolic analysts* whose key contribution is to use knowledge to solve problems. This sector of the US labour force has grown rapidly in the 1970s and 1980s, in terms of both average earnings and proportion of the labour force.

The education of this growing part of the population has tended to be drawn from schools, whether privately or publicly funded, that emphasise such processes as abstraction, system thinking, experimentation and collaboration. The curriculum is fluid and interactive, with the main focus on judgement and interpretation with a concern for the development of sceptical, curious and creative adults.

If this pattern is relevant to the development of the British economy and its labour force, then the current debate about vocational education and training takes on a new dimension. Professor Charles Handy, in a BBC Radio 4 interview (1994) predicted that in the next decade, 70 per cent of jobs will need one or two A-Levels or equivalent. This suggests that the National Target 3 for Lifetime Learning which calls for 50 per cent of the workforce qualified to NVQ III is likely to have a partial success in meeting future needs. It is certainly not, in demand terms, an over-ambitious target. This chapter now addresses some of the supply-side issues.

EDUCATIONAL PARTICIPATION AND ATTAINMENT

International comparisons

This aspect involves an examination of the distribution of participation and achievement of qualifications, in the context of a labour force that has grown by over 10 per cent in the last twenty-five years. The UK unemployment rate at the beginning of 1994 had dropped to just under 10 per cent, masking a higher than average rate among males of 13.5 per cent.

One of the effects of the recession of 1990–93 has been to reduce the proportion of young people who left formal education at the age of 16. This improvement in post-16 participation leaves untouched the effects of historically low post-16 participation which has been a major problem in the education and training system. Figure 11.1 indicates some of the effects of this problem.

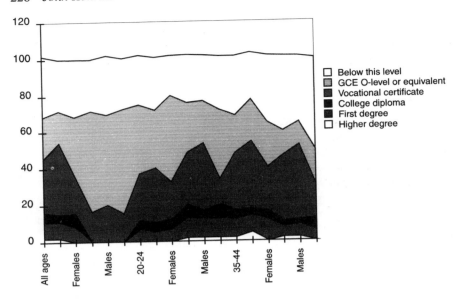

Figure 11.1 Distribution of qualifications by age and gender

Source: Ashton *et al.* 1989

Some 12 per cent of males have a university degree compared with 10 per cent of females, largely gained between 18 and 25. The recent growth in adult degree course enrolments will not have a great effect in the short term and the success rates for these adults is still an important question of quality. At the next level down, the college diploma (such as Higher National) is relatively less important than the vocational certificate (such as BTEC National). The largest group is the male 35+ age group who are likely to have gained these qualifications through the traditional three-year apprenticeships formerly found in manufacturing industry. This traditional route to work-based skills has been in decline during the 1980s, partly through deliberate government policy and partly through the decline in UK manufacturing industry during the recessions of the 1980s. In all age groups the proportion with qualifications below GCE O-Level or its GCSE equivalent is greater than 30 per cent. The levels of participation in the 16–18-year-old age group tends to drop much more quickly than in similar countries.

It is widely agreed that the central weakness of the educational system in England and Wales is the narrowness and exclusivity of its post-compulsory (i.e. post-16 years) phase. In 1990 only 23 per cent of UK 18-year-olds were in full-time education, compared with 80 per cent in Germany, 70 per cent in France and 51 per cent in Spain. In 1990, 19 per cent of UK 16–18 year olds were in full-time education, of which only 30 per cent took the academic route, mainly taking two or three subjects at GCE A level. By 1992, 22 per cent of 19-year-olds had two or more A-Level passes, compared with 17 per cent in 1988 (ED 1993c).

In addition, about 10 per cent gained vocational qualifications at NVQ 3 level. The government hope that the introduction of GNVQs will accelerate the progress towards the 50 per cent national target of 2000.

In response to this situation, IPPR (Finegold *et al.* 1990) proposed a curriculum based on the following principles:

the British Baccalauréate . . . of:

- breadth and flexibility;
- connections between core and specialist studies, and general (academic) and applied (vocational) studies;
- opportunities for progression and credit transfer;
- a clear sense of the purpose of the curriculum as a whole.

(Finegold *et al.* 1990)

Currently, the vocational alternatives (e.g. BTEC First and National) are much less available (25 per cent of the places provided for A-Levels). More crucially, the vocational routes are perceived as being of poorer quality (in academic terms) and therefore lacking in esteem. The IPPR report argued that these weaknesses are the outcome of having separate academic and vocational tracks leading to separate qualifications, hence the recommendation for *a unified system of qualifications*, which will have important implications for the delivery of the curriculum, including its modes of assessment.

The failure to tackle the issue of a divided system post-16, where the academic track is assessed on a *norm-referenced* basis, has also serious implications for compulsory education, especially Key Stage 4 of the National Curriculum (Years 10 and 11). Hence recent developments where the review of the National Curriculum by Sir Ron Dearing proposes vocational and occupational as well as academic routes post-14, and the removal of controls over recruitment of 14–16-year-olds into post-16 colleges, are increasingly significant. It is not too difficult to imagine that a future system will see a break in provision at 14 rather than 16. Whether this is simply a question of starting separate tracks earlier, or possibly beginning the move towards a curriculum for the future based on a non-divisive, flexible system of work organisation is in some doubt. In February 1994 the government promised that they would make available 'a wider range of vocational options . . . designed to facilitate progression to vocational courses post-16' (DfE 1994). This was followed by the reform of compulsory education through the introduction of a National Curriculum, accompanied by an increase of employers' influence over schools and colleges in the Education Reform Act of 1988 and the subsequent legislation which aimed to reduce the power of LEAs. The original vision of this National Curriculum, as pointed out by Finegold *et al.* (1990) in the IPPR paper on the British Baccalauréate, was that

In the 21st century, education will be the foundation of material as well as intellectual progress. The challenge is to develop an education system adequate to the economic and social demands of the next century . . . (and) that innovative capabilities be spread throughout the whole population.

This view, supported by the finding of the National Commission quoted earlier, could well provide a means for achieving the major improvement necessary to enable the national provision of vocational education and training to support the goal of achieving world-class standards in the British economy.

CONCLUSIONS

The educational and industrial history of England and Wales over the last century and a half has been marked by a consistent failure to develop a system of vocational education and training that meets the long-term needs of the economy. Whatever the political contradictions inherent in the current situation, there would appear to be a greater consensus on a remedial strategy between government, large corporate organisations and organised labour than at any time since the end of the nineteenth century. Despite the confused rhetoric of the descriptions and the debates, much of the structure created by the changes of the period 1988–94 appear to be increasing participation and raising quality of provision. As with the schools sector, the pace of change is frenetic and there is a similar need for a period of stability to allow for consolidation of the changes, not least in terms of funding patterns and institutional structures. It may well be that the structure of TECs/LECs and incorporated colleges will prove one of the more successful products of the changes in policy of the 1980s.

The framework provided by the national targets initiative and the proposed reform of Key Stage 4 of the National Curriculum could well lead to a historic improvement in provision. The real issue could well be whether the high level of rhetoric is matched by the reality of delivery. As with the National Curriculum, the real danger is that rhetoric proves a substitute for significant improvements in organisation, management and levels of resourcing. There is also a serious danger that these changes, advocated by educational interests and bringing the United Kingdom closer to the rest of the European Community, could be limited or destroyed by the unreconstructed right wing of the Conservative Party.

CORE READING

Bees, M. and Swords, M. (eds) (1990) *National Vocational Qualifications and Further Education*, London: Kogan Page in association with the National Council for Vocational Qualifications.

Employment Department (1991) *Education and Training in the 21st Century*, Sheffield: Employment Department.

Finegold, D. and Soskice, D. (1988) 'The Failure of Training in Britain', in Esland, G. (ed.) *Education, Training and Employment*, Milton Keynes: Open University Press.

Finegold, D., Keep, E., Miliband, D., Raffe, D., Spours, K. and Young, M. (1990) *A British Baccalauréate: Ending the Divisions between Education and Training*, London: Institute for Public Policy Research.

Gleeson, D. (ed.) (1991) *Training and its Alternatives*, Milton Keynes: Open University Press.

National Commission on Education (1993) *Learning to Succeed: A Radical Look at Education Today and a Strategy for the Future*, London: Heinemann.

Reich, R. (1991) *The World of Work*, London: Simon & Schuster.

Young, M. (1993) 'A Curriculum for the 21st Century? Towards a New Basis for Overcoming Academic/Vocational Divisions', *British Journal of Educational Studies*, XXXXI (3), September: 203.

ADDITIONAL READING

Ashton, D. *et al.* (1989) 'The Linkages between Education and Employment in Canada and the United Kingdom: A Comparative Analysis', *Comparative Education*, 29(2): 125–43.

CBI (1989) *Towards a Skills Revolution*, London: CBI Publications.

CBI (1994) *Making it in Britain II*, London: CBI Publications.

DfE (1993) 'International Statistical Comparisons of the participation in Education and Training of 16 to 18 year olds', *Department for Education Statistical Bulletin 1993*, August.

DfE (1994) *Final Report on the National Curriculum and its Assessment: The Government's Response*, London: HMSO.

Employment Department (1993a) *General National Vocational Qualifications: A Guide for Employers*, Sheffield: Employment Department, Summer.

Employment Department (1993b) *Work Related Further Education 1994-95: A Handbook of Guidance for TECs and Colleges*, Sheffield: Employment Department, December.

Employment Department (1993c) *Skills for Success: A Challenge for Training and Education*, Sheffield: Employment Department, November.

GNTEC (1994) *Summary Business Plan 1994/95*, Nottingham.

Manpower Services Commission (1981) *A New Training Initiative: An Agenda*, London: HMSO.

NCVQ (1993) NCVQ Information Note, General National Vocational Qualifications, April, page 3, London: NCVQ.

12 Immigration and the politics of ethnic diversity

Ian Law

INTRODUCTION

The challenge that issues of migration pose to modern territorial states, which have attempted to construct particular and different forms of citizenship and nationalism within their geographical borders, is one of the most pressing and difficult problems facing governments and their people across the globe. The growth of international economic inequalities, increasing ethnic conflict and the growth of free trade areas are all factors that have contributed to the acceleration, globalisation and feminisation of migration. For these reasons Castles and Miller (1993) have predicted that the last decade of the twentieth century and the first decade of the twenty-first century will be the 'age of migration'. This chapter is concerned with the migrants who have come to constitute permanently resident ethnic minorities and those who are likely to migrate in the 1990s. The focus will be on politics and policies in Britain, and this will be placed firmly in the European context.

This chapter follows most directly from the discussion of political ideas in Chapter 1 and the discussion of the European context in Chapter 3. It assesses Tory and Labour discourse on 'race' and immigration and the impact of the EC on these debates and on the shape of future policy.

The prospects for 'civilised' (Elias 1982) progress towards the triple goals of anti-racism, racial equality and multi-culturalism in Europe, rather than decline into increasing levels of racism, racial inequality and cultural exclusion, seem poor. The ambivalence in both individual moral restraint and state regulation of such racialised behaviour and violence, combined with the shifting contextualisation of racist discourse indicates that direct political and policy challenges to these practices are likely to be weak and to have a marginal impact. Securing progress towards these goals is, nevertheless, of fundamental importance for the stable future of this region. The failure of governments to respond adequately to the challenges of migration and ethnic diversity, or indeed to debate and establish what such an adequate response might constitute, can lead to societal insecurity, political conflict and war. This is often also accompanied by the retreat to defensive and exclusive notions of ethnicity which can form the basis for the renewal of racism. The future for racist politics, policies and ideologies through the 1980s and 1990s has often been perceived as one of reconstruction, expansion and institutionalisation given the experience of Thatcherism in Britain, the emergence of the Front National in France and the emergence of political racism in many other European countries. The 'resurgence of ethnicity' (Bauman 1990) as a defensive reaction to processes of globalisation, and the 'de-centring of the West' (Hall 1992) which has been linked to shifting economic and power relations, are processes that can lead to the undermining and fracturing of national identities. The renewed debates over nationalism in the face of Europeanisation are seen as highlighting the criteria for citizenship and belonging, and providing political and cultural space for the re-articulation of racist discourse (Miles 1993). The questions of identity and immigration are central to the discourse of the extreme right and concern over their activities and the emergence of more widespread racist and fascist activity has been increasingly evident. Barker (1981) attempted to identify a 'new racism' emerging in the political discourse of the right in Britain, and Hobsbawn (1980) asked 'Are We Now Entering a New Era of Anti-Semitism?' following a series of attacks on Jews in France. A recent report by the Board of Deputies of British Jews (1994) noted an 85 per cent rise in anti-Semitic incidents in Britain between 1984 and 1992 and increasing fears among Jews about the rise of the far right. The report echoed the comment of the Irish Cabinet Minister Conor Cruise O'Brien that anti-Semitism was a 'very light sleeper' and called for legislation against religious hatred in mainland Britain, vigilance in media stereotyping and moves to ensure teaching about Judaism and the holocaust in schools. The rise of 'European' (Balibar 1991) or 'Eurocentric' (Sivanandan 1989) racism has been identified, and warnings of a 'Fortress Europe' based on racially exclusive immigration policies have become common particularly on the left in Britain.

There are four themes evident in the contemporary debates in this field which relate to the politics of immigration, anti-racism, the extreme right and cultural identity. First, the nature of Margaret Thatcher's 'racecraft' (Layton-Henry 1992) and the post-Thatcherite legacy in terms of government policy on race relations and immigration are the subject of debate and review. This will be examined in this chapter together with discussion of Labour Party and European Community policy. Second, the proposed 'end of anti-racism' (Gilroy 1990) and the critique of 1980s municipal anti-racism from both the left, for its cultural essentialism in representing the 'black' constituency, and from the right, for its failure to acknowledge an essentialist 'white British' ethnicity, indicate weaknesses in anti-racist discourse and practice (see Chapter 1 for general background on the New Right and anti-racism). The re-emergence of anti-racism as a political force in the 1990s with, for example, the reformation of the Anti-Nazi League and the establishment of the Anti-Racist Alliance as well as indications of the professional institutionalisation of anti-racism (CCETSW 1991) indicate that the strength of such social movements have been underestimated, although the flaws may still remain. Third, political racism and the rise of the extreme right is of great concern. There is clearly a more significant extreme right movement in Europe and the question of the rise in electoral support for racist policies in

Britain in the coming decade is one of the most worrying scenarios to be contemplated. Fourth, much of the debates about Europe, immigration and racism has to do with perceptions of cultural and ethnic identity. The critiques of 1980s anti-racism, the impact of post-modernist debates on the conceptualisation of ethnicity and debates over substantive policy issues, e.g. trans-racial family placement and representation in the media, have all led to an increasing focus on what may be called the cultural politics of difference and the nature of cultural identity. The attempts to construct, represent and articulate these new ideas about ethnicity may provide some of the conceptual bases for a bold new political agenda that emphasises the importance of ethnic diversity, in building both the European Union and nation-states, and the positive benefits of immigration. The likelihood of such an agenda emerging are addressed through a focus on the British context.

IMMIGRATION POLICY: ELECTORAL POPULISM OR 'STATECRAFT'?

Britain is traditionally a net exporter of people, the majority of immigrants are white and immigrants represent a declining proportion of the minority ethnic population, and yet indications from opinion surveys indicate that about half the people in this country feel that immigration of minority ethnic groups has led to a decline in their quality of life (Skellington and Morris 1992). This strong base of social attitudes has both led to and been nurtured by racist immigration controls from the Aliens Act 1905 to the Asylum and Immigration Appeals Act 1993. Explanation of the development of racist immigration legislation has often been made by reference to a direct political response to the pressure of public opinion against black immigration e.g. Labour 'pinching the Tories' white trousers' in 1965 when they introduced the White Paper on Immigration from the Commonwealth (Foot 1965, Smith 1989). The collapse of idealistic elements in the ideologies of Conservative imperialism, liberalism and labourist socialism in the face of anti-immigrant agitation has also been noted by Rex and Tomlinson (1979). But the way in which the politics of race relations and immigration has been handled by successive governments and by political parties in opposition cannot simply be read off from public attitudes or legislation outcomes. An alternative way of interpreting this process has been through an emphasis upon the centre's 'race' statecraft (Bulpitt 1986, Saggar 1992). This approach down-plays the simple explanation of electoral populism combined with a determining cultural reservoir of racist ideologies and emphasises instead three concerns: first, an attempt to preserve the autonomy of the political centre from race-specific demands of white and black voters; second, pursuance of strategies to marginalise or push to the periphery management of 'race relations' through the Commission for Racial Equality (CRE) and local authorities. Third, a desire to maintain continuity in protecting the centre from the difficulties of race politics and so help to ensure the relative freedom of the centre to pursue policies it sees as having greater importance. The extent to which this form of statecraft has characterised the approach of the Tory government and the Labour opposition and may determine policies in the future is an issue that will now be explored.

TORY DISCOURSE: 'NEW RACISM' OR CONTINUITY?

Barker (1981), Gordon and Klug (1986) and other writers have attempted to identify the emergence of a revised core element of Conservative Party ideology, a 'new' political discourse on the themes of immigration, racism and nation. This has been described as 'a theory of human nature . . . all of us form exclusive communities on the basis of shared sentiments shutting out outsiders' (Barker 1981: 21–2).

Some of the key elements of this discourse include reference to an essential white culture which finds its most important expression as a nation, the socio-biological or 'naturalised' explanation of racial hostility to others who may be inside or outside the nation-state, the absence of any overt reference to 'race' or hierarchy and a related denial that such a perspective is racist. These notions can be found in the statements of Enoch Powell, editorials and articles in the popular press, comments from the New Right and among sections of the Conservative Party. This discourse is therefore differentiated from conceptions of racism that emphasise the division of the world's population into a racial hierarchy with different capacities for civilisation and related explicit forms of scientific racism. But the claim that this is a 'new' form of racism can be criticised in that many earlier racist ideologies have used coded language, not asserted notions of racial hierarchy, looked to 'natural' explanations of racial conflict and combined with ideologies of nationalism (Miles 1989). Also the extent to which such statements 'serve merely as a self-consciously erected smoke-screen behind which lurk older forms of determinism' (Mason 1992: 13) should be recognised. Moreover the extent to which they are articulated and represent wider forms of racist discourse among the Tory Party is questionable. The language of 'inferior races' has tended to disappear from parliamentary debates but the persistence of the political construction of problematic notions of migration, integration and race relations continues, as does the expression of explicit racism among the grassroots of the Tory Party. In these senses a continuity can be traced in racist ideologies.

It may be appealing but far too simple to see such racist ideologies as the driving force for Tory policies. For example, the sanctioning of major pro-grammes of housing investment in black-led housing associations through the Housing Corporation from the mid-1980s onwards cannot be explained by refer-ence to hostility and racism. The establishment of Channel 4 with an explicit commitment to respond to the excluded voices of black minorities was an initiative that was not 'killed at birth' by Thatcher, unlike many others (BBC 1992). This indicates a concern more for facilitating inclusion than maintaining white English notions of cultural identity. Equally, in the field of immigration, both authoritarian populism and liberal pragmatism are evident in policy decisions, although unlike social policy the former set of values is more in evidence. Statements on swamping, the 1981 Nationality Act and the claim to 'end New Commonwealth immigration' highlight the former approach and, rather than breaking with tradition as Layton-Henry (1992) argues, they seem to have achieved the aim of previous governments in de-politicising the issue of immigration. This can be substantiated in that during the general elections of 1983 and 1987 immigration was not seen as an important political issue facing the country for much of the electorate. Further evidence of 'statecraft' is indicated in the pragmatic approach to certain decisions, for example demands for entry by citizens of Hong Kong.

The perceived 're-politicisation' of race by the Tories in the 1980s, or the 'risky lurch to the right' in such policies as some commentators have called it, was accompanied by fears over the persistent influence of the New Right and the extension of government policy beyond tight immigration control to repatriation. The 1981 Act aimed to cut further the ties of Empire and took away the right of abode for British passport holders who obtained citizenship by their connection to a British colony. It also aimed to prevent a Tory government being faced with the entry of groups of black British citizens from abroad due to unforeseen events, such as the entry of Ugandan Asians during the Heath government in the early 1970s. The actual scale of primary immigration of black ethnic minorities and the entry of their dependants declined sharply and the Tory government continued to implement restrictive legislation including the Immigrant (Carriers Liability) Act 1987 and a further Immigration Act in 1988. The persistent message was given that it was 'necessary to keep immigration control in good repair' and to exclude New Commonwealth immigrants as far as possible. Policy implementation of this message involved both the Immigration Service contravening the Race Relations Act 1976 (Commission for Racial Equality 1985) through its racialised practice, a classic example of the tension in government policy, and instances of illegality according to rulings of the European Court of Human Rights. But the fears of a more proactive approach to repatriation policy were unfounded and the influence of the New Right in this arena was overestimated.

The decline of immigration as a domestic political issue can be explained by reference to a variety of factors. The effectiveness of regular legislation in stopping fresh immigration, the increasing precedence of urban unrest and domestic 'race relations' and the strength of 'one-nation' Toryism are all elements that have shifted the terms and focus of the debate. Reference to simple, rational and systematic racist discourse cannot, also, adequately explain the set of 'statecraft' concerns related to winning the vote in the inner cities, building the Tory vote among black minority ethnic voters, retaining indirect responsibility for managing 'race relations', as seen in continued support for the CRE, and liberal pragmatism in response to Vietnamese refugees' and Hong Kong citizens' demands for the right of abode in Britain. This last issue was a reversal of government strategy on immigration and their handling of the issue was clearly driven by 'statecraft' rather than New Right racist discourse. The 1981 Act had made most people in Hong Kong British Dependent Territories' Citizens (BDTCs). This category of citizenship was constructed to exclude such citizens from migrating and settling permanently in the United Kingdom. The arguments for change were based on a number of factors: fear of Chinese repression of democracy in the wake of events in Tiananmen Square in 1989, an emphasis on the moral and political duty of Britain towards its subjects and racially signified contradictions in citizenship where some BDTCs had full rights, e.g. those in Gibraltar and the Falklands, and some did not. The government announced in December 1989 that full rights would be restored to 50,000 key personnel and their families. Thatcher defended this U-turn against the open hostility of Norman Tebbit and eighty Tory MPs on the grounds that it was needed to preserve stability and prosperity in Britain's last colony until handover to the Chinese in 1997. In this instance the government showed themselves more willing to compromise than the Labour front bench who refused to state how many people they would 'let in' and opposed the action due to its elitist nature. Exactly the opposite position on immigration policy is taken by the Labour Party in Australia, who have opened up the country to 'Asianisation' but retain elitist control through rigorous checks on skills and resources of migrants.

The perception of Thatcherism as being a period when the political consensus around policy in this field was broken, followed by consistent onslaught upon the rights of black ethnic minorities, has been a pervasive feature of comment on the left. This is now being called into question, particularly in the light of the rise of racism and fascism in Europe and the related search for an explanation of the weakness of overt political racism in Britain. One important legacy of this period is seen to be the emphasis on inclusion of black people through assimilation into the British nation using the traditional discourse of nationalism, i.e. 'Labour say he's black, Tories say he's British', combined with the emphasis on strict racialised immigration controls and represention of this as being in the nation's interests. These twin elements are seen to have silenced the extreme right by restricting the political space available to them.

The concern with Tory leadership in the post-Thatcherite era is that a 'softer' approach may create political space for rising electoral support for the extreme right in Britain. This possibility or threat has also been used by the government themselves to argue for the need to persist in restrictive policy on asylum-seekers. This argument is, of course, a familiar one to those working in the field. The threat of a 'white backlash' has been used to obstruct and argue against most of the initiatives taken to counter racism and discrimination at various times and such threats need to be addressed directly rather than discounted or appeased. Also the review of Thatcher's 'racecraft' indicates that a simple distinction between a 'hard' Thatcher and a 'soft' Major may not stand up to close scrutiny. In fact, despite Major's early statements expressing his determination to bring about a 'classless' society free from discrimination, his approach has been in many ways a continuation of that of his predecessor. The debate in the House of Commons in June 1992 was one of the first on race equality issues for some years and in it clear statements were given by the Home Secretary Kenneth Clarke on Tory policy. The government's aim was said to be one of establishing a fair and integrated society. The notion of integration has been criticised many times but a recent critique by Miles (1993) has extended this through a comparative analysis of OECD, Dutch and French policy. The key problematic identified here is that the notion that integration policy is needed is premised on a denial of the actual integration of minorities, e.g. in the economy, since their arrival. It 'exteriorises' these groups, problematises differences of language and culture and prescribes that minorities are required to belong to some imagined notion of national culture. In fact it could be argued that in certain institutional areas minorities suffer from problems of excessive integration: 'It would seem that the Dutch reserve army of labour and Dutch prisons are very open to "these people"' (Miles 1993: 179).

Black migrants in Britain tend therefore to be seen by the government as a 'disintegrative' force requiring integration and immigration control, and such policies are presented to the British people as being the state acting in their interests. The support for the CRE, for ethnic monitoring and positive equal opportunity policies in employment and for the commitment to stamp out 'the most obvious and obnoxious barrier . . . racial discrimination' given by the Home Secretary are therefore set within a discourse that at the same time repudiates racist actions and articulates racist ideas.

The introduction of the Asylum Bill in 1991 showed a continuity in immigration policies in the post-Thatcher period, but also showed that such policies were now resulting from and contributing to high-level debate between European governments. Major in 1991 spoke of the potential 'wave' of illegal immigrants if Europe was not able to establish a strong 'perimeter fence'. When the Bill was published, the Home Secretary claimed that it was a 'fair and proper' response, and also that 'if we are too generous it is the population of our inner cities, our urban poor and our homeless who will be the main sufferers from our misguided liberalism' (Hansard, 2 November 1991).

Therefore, in the interests of the disadvantaged, or more particularly in the interests of the black citizens of the United Kingdom it was necessary to appease racist sentiment by portraying 'others' as unwelcome intruders. This was further articulated by statements from various ministers that asylum was being used to 'bypass' existing immigration controls, that it was necessary to distinguish between 'deserving, genuine' political refugees and 'undeserving, bogus' economic refugees and also that all this would help to prevent the rise of racism and facism in Britain. The development of a systematic media campaign to support the 'playing of the race card' immediately prior to the 1992 general election was clearly evident. Major, Hurd and Baker all emphasised the 'flood' of asylum-seekers in the final weeks of the campaign and highlighted Liberal Democrat proposals to let in 'thousands of Hong Kong Chinese'. The debate over the Asylum Bill showed the glaring inconsistencies in the government's position. The exaggeration of Britain's civilised tradition of being a safe haven for refugees was a recurring theme and ignored the century of racially signified restrictive measures taken by successive governments. The Bill contradicts the UN Convention on refugees in its new criteria for determination of claims for asylum. No reference was made to the European Convention on Human Rights and in particular to victims of torture and organised state violence referred to in

Article 3 of the Convention. Failure to recognise adequately such victims in the definition of a refugee creates a danger that some may be denied refuge (Medical Foundation 1992). The disproportionate impact of removing the rights to appeal from visitors and students will fall on black minority ethnic migrants, as is evident from racially differentiated rates of refusal of entry. The implications of this began to be felt in Christmas 1993 when 323 passengers of the Jamaican charter flight 767 were detained at Gatwick. This has been called the 'worst case of official racism for nearly a decade' (*Sunday Times*, 30 January 1994). The motive was the sustained intention to cut down on entry from the Caribbean, a policy that led to a sharp rise in refusals for Jamaicans from 1:430 in 1986 to 1:40 in 1989. The opportunity was the Asylum and Immigration Appeals Act which came into force in early 1993 and the means were given by the opening in December 1993 of a new detention centre in Oxfordshire which doubled the available places for the Immigration Service. This was seen to be an 'operation waiting to happen', and a clear case of unjustified unaccountable immigration control, 'a travesty of natural justice' which treated genuine visitors to this country 'as if they were in a concentration camp' (Lord Gifford quoted in the *Guardian*, 24 January 1993). Further, the discretionary interpretation of guidelines by immigration officials excluded MPs from intervening in cases of detainees who were related to their constituents. The death of a Jamaican woman, Joy Gardner, during the enactment of a deportation order on 28 July 1993 due to being gagged and suffocated by three plain-clothes police and a Home Office immigration official was an earlier indication of serious flaws in government practice, particularly when this case closely followed a Home Office decision not to review or question its deportation procedures. The prospect of 'new routinisation' of harassment of black visitors to Britain seems likely.

EUROPEAN IMMIGRATION POLICY: FORTRESS EUROPE OR MIGRATION MANAGEMENT?

Article 100c of the Treaty of Maastricht gives the European Commission new authority to develop immigration policy. How this power will be used is the subject of political struggle and debate and some of the themes of this debate are considered in this section. The existence of an international refugee crisis is without question and the escalation in numbers of refugees, asylum-seekers and illegal migrants across the globe has led to the wider process of the politicisation of migration issues and renewed pressure for control. In Britain, however, what many people failed to realise was that through the 1980s and 1990s the government 'no longer had absolute control over entry and settlement in the UK and that what power it has now will diminish within the bounds of [European] Community law' (Dummet and Nichol 1990: 258, quoted in Miles 1993).

The ending of much of the primary labour migration into western Europe in the 1970s was accompanied by the emergence of explicit discourses on immigration control within individual nation-states. This led to increasing restrictions on family reunification: the immigration trend of the 1980s. The reality of continuing migration flows such as family reunification, the recruitment of foreign labour to fill specific gaps in the labour market (e.g. teacher vacancies in Tower Hamlets), people seeking asylum and movement of nationals of other EC member states do, however, contradict the rhetoric of increasing control. Further, notions of establishing a strong 'perimeter fence', for example on the coasts of Spain, Italy and Greece, are evidence of wishful thinking rather than realistic policy, as is the refusal of some governments, for example Germany, to define themselves as 'countries of immigration'. The constraints on governments' ability to deliver strict control in line with rhetoric are sometimes 'explained' by reference to the problems of controlling specific migrant groups. This is evident in the emerging European Union policy on visas. The Treaty of European Union signed at Maastricht will forbid any member state from running its own visa policy after June 1996 when a common policy will come into operation. This will force the United Kingdom to scrap preferential arrangements which allow citizens of most Commonwealth countries the right to visit relatives in Britain. The European Commission's proposed list of countries, whose nationals will need a visa to enter, has been dubbed a 'blacklist' by officials because most of the people to whom restrictions will apply are from African or Caribbean countries. Not a single white Commonwealth country is included, with Canada and New Zealand being specifically exempt from restrictions. The government are likely therefore to 'snub' the black Commonwealth and to gain European support for cutting the ties of Empire. Tory inclinations to resist EU plans are likely to be overridden by stronger inclinations to be hostile towards black British citizens, whereas opposition to EU policy is more evident where it is perceived to lead to some relaxation of controls. In opening a Commons debate on Europe, John Major emphasised the need for an island nation to retain border controls, in order to protect the nation from terrorists, smugglers and illegal immigration, which is in conflict with EC policy to allow freedom of movement of its citizens (Hansard, 15 May 1992). The conflict over the elimination of internal frontier controls is likely to escalate, given recent proposals by Raniero Vanni d'Archirafi, the EC's Single Market commissioner, which would oblige member states to permit people who are not EU nationals to travel freely once they have satisfied an immigration officer at the EU's external frontier.

Demographic factors may also play a significant role in shaping migration policy. European fertility rates have fallen greatly since the mid-1960s and the baby boom in Britain will create a high old-age dependency ratio as overall population is likely to remain static (see Chapter 10). As Baldwin-Edwards (1992) has noted, the prospect of a future shortage of labour in Europe combined with demographic pressure from countries in the Mediterranean basin such as Algeria and Turkey may be seen as complementary trends. The impossibility of shutting the Mediterranean coastal perimeter is clear and both legal and illegal immigration will continue. As in Britain in the 1960s, immigration policy may well be implemented in conflict with the needs of the economies of Europe. The more politically acceptable migration of non-racialised groups of workers, for example from those countries not subject to visa controls, may be encouraged along with other labour market strategies such as further increasing female participation rates. Switzerland passed new regulations in 1992 favouring EC and EFTA labour, giving second priority to the United States, Canada and Eastern Europe and totally excluding the Third World (Baldwin-Edwards 1992). The shape of future policy will also crucially depend on final agreements with EFTA countries and future membership of the EC.

During the 1990s the development and enactment of joint, or harmonised, European immigration policy is taking place. The secret Schengen and Trevi agreements have provided the basis for immigration controls that have been racialised and signified in particular ways. In 1994 the EU's most hard-line interior minister Jacques Pasqua, described as France's answer to the Front National, has articulated the spirit of these secret agreements. Sending back illegal immigrants to their home country 'by the planeload and the boatload' until the world 'gets the mesage', combined with measures to develop racialised internal policing of controls are proposed. But his programme of controls, under the banner 'immigration zero', had eight of its key provisions challenged by France's constitutional council in August 1993 as it was felt that they deprived foreigners of basic rights. Also President Mitterrand distanced himself from these restrictions, saying 'we must not create foreigners when they could become French'.

A similar distance was maintained by Major's government when Churchill called for a complete halt to the 'relentless flow' of immigrants in order to preserve the British way of life, following the twenty-fifth anniversary of Enoch Powell's speech which prophesied 'rivers of blood' as a result of New Commonwealth immigration. This may indicate two trends: first, political and ideological struggle over inclusive and exclusive notions of national identity; and second, the possibility that authoritarian populism may be balanced by liberal pragmatism at the European level. This has recently been indicated in the Green Paper on European Commission policy on 'migration management' drawn up by the Social Policy Commissioner Padraig Flynn. This is the first substantial statement to be made by the EC and results in part from elucidation of sections of the Maastrict Treaty.

Increasingly restrictive policies have emerged on a confusing number of different tracks within and outside the EU which create the impression that the only goal in sight is a protectionist Fortress Europe. This is seen to be motivated by racism (Webber 1991) and in particular the reconstruction of Judao-Christian Eurocentric racism (Sivanandan 1989). This has been criticised for its simplistic homogenisation of migration flows and its conceptual ambiguities (Miles 1993). A key concern has been the increase in 'white' migrants from Eastern Europe, although many of these come under the fastest-growing category of non-EC migration which is highly skilled non-manual labour from other industrialised nations. The reality of migration patterns belies the focus on 'black' immigrants from the Third World. Also black people are not a universally excluded category and some millions of black people in the EC have full citizenship rights and are not the object of control. They can be differentiated from others, e.g. Turks in

Germany, who have been excluded from equal participation in the Single Market. The position of over nine million such Third World nationals permanently living in Europe who do not have full citizenship rights has been recognised by the EC.

The recent Green Paper proposes measures to combat discrimination and alleviate problems of poor housing and unemployment but it stops short of recommending full equality of mobility within the EC. Measures to penalise human rights violations in countries from which refugees are fleeing and the targeting of overseas aid to assist in the retention of local populations were seen as necessary in attempting to pre-empt migration. Measures to harmonise asylum policy and improve arrangements for coping with sudden influxes of crisis victims are also set out. The secretly agreed measures to improve police identification and expulsion of illegal immigrants are challenged and emphasis is placed on legislating against employers who give jobs to such migrants. Governments are urged to emphasise the economic and social benefits of immigration and greater openness about the complex reality of migration flows would facilitate that debate. The prospects of the European Community following Britain's lead and establishing racist immigration law which is broadly effective, 'balanced' by anti-discrimination measures which are not, may be what the future holds. Indeed, the EC may find itself playing a primarily restraining role on those governments that breach international conventions in their over-zealous immigration practices and harassment of immigrant communities, rather than a pro-active role in promoting policies that recognise the benefits of the effective management of migration and that free movement and fundamental human rights are central precepts of the European Union. Such a perspective is unlikely to be promoted by a Tory government; whether Labour could offer this lead is considered in the next section.

LABOUR POLICIES: CONFUSION AND UNCERTAINTY?

The last Labour government gave an amnesty to illegal immigrants, passed the Race Relations Act 1976 and established the CRE. But the party were also responsible for passing the Commonwealth Immigration Act 1968, the introduction of restrictive amendments to immigration rules and laying the basis for the 1981 Nationality Act in their Green Paper in April 1977. Labour's confusion and uncertainty over how to handle 'race' and immigration policies does not augur well for clarity of leadership on these issues in the future. These problems were evident in the retreat from moral opposition to racist immigration legislation in the 1960s and have been compounded by the strength of racism among its white working-class voters and the overwhelming support for Labour among black minority ethnic voters. In the 1979 general election 'race' and immigration issues were seen as vote-losers, statements were moderated and policies downplayed. In particular, there was no recognition of racism in immigration legislation and hence no proposals for repealing such laws. By 1983 Labour had reversed its policies, partly in recognition of the importance of the black vote in the inner cities and partly in response to the rising optimism and buoyancy of the urban left. The party emphasised total opposition once again to racist immigration controls and offered to repeal the 1971 and 1981 Acts.

This spirit was echoed in the actions of local government in the 1980s. The Labour Party were frequently and widely associated with equal opportunity policies in employment and service delivery and with explicit anti-racist policies in housing and education, using their power to promote such measures through control of land and contracts. This had facilitiated significant changes in the workforce of some local authorities and in the involvement of Afro-Caribbeans and Asians in the party machine. Peach's (1991) study of Afro-Caribbeans in Europe suggests that it was socialism rather than capitalism that gave rise to migration to Europe in that the economic sectors that drew in Caribbean workers were health and public transport in Britain and the Civil Service and the nationalised sector in France. Municipal socialism in the 1980s was continuing this trend in opening up employment opportunities in the local public sector. But the decline of the urban left in the late 1980s, after the Thatcher government won the battle over local government finance, signalled the decline of high-profile Labour Party support for anti-racism. The national leadership has often appeared as defensive, evasive or embarrassed in the face of attacks on anti-racism from the right, which were particularly fierce prior to the 1987 election. The retreat from anti-racism was evident in the omission of Labour commitment to repeal immigration and nationality legislation in the manifesto used during that period.

One key factor in Labour's defeat was felt to be the 'London factor', a reference to the perception of some explicitly anti-racist London councils as extreme and the disinclination of the leadership to respond. The inability of Labour to handle effectively defensive and exclusive notions of 'race' and nation among its own supporters remained a blind-spot during this period. The challenge to racism within the Labour Party was channeled particularly through the campaign for black sections. This was particularly influential in the mid-1980s and despite formal opposition to the establishment of black sections at the 1984 conference, the political agitation for change was significant in leading to the endorsement of fourteen black parliamentary candidates across a range of seats in 1987. A negotiated compromise was reached in 1990, acknowledgement was given to the success of this campaign in assisting in the election of four black MPs, and a measure of black self-organisation in the party and representation on the National Executive Committee were secured. However, the problems of long-established patterns of patronage and favouritism combined with a racialisation of internal Labour Party politics still present formidable barriers to the development of black minority ethnic representation. A recent study in Birmingham showed that selection procedures were dependent on mobilising networks of influence and these networks were often structured by ethnicity and racial inequality. In this case an Asian candidate was blocked from selection (Solomos and Back 1991).

Labour faced further problems in squaring their secular or Christian socialism with the demands of Muslim Labour voters in the conflict over Salman Rushdie's book *The Satanic Verses*. The problems were compounded by the rise in anti-Muslim feeling during the Gulf War in 1990. The leadership again found itself torn between condemnation of the *fatwa* and Islamic fundamentalism, support for freedom of expression and support for the Gulf War and condemnation of anti-Muslim racism and related attacks, and support for cultural pluralism and the right to protection from blasphemy. Over Hong Kong the Labour leadership had previously shown its inability to construct popular support around its 'race' and immigration policies. Its opposition to the British Nationality (Hong Kong) Act 1990 on general and unconvincing terms and its refusal to specify alternative proposals for allowing in citizens from Hong Kong were in fact a capitulation to the perceived hostility of the electorate. This showed clearly Labour's inability to argue a case for the positive economic and social benefits of immigration, given the proven contribution of Hong Kong citizens to economic enterprise, and an end to the racialisation of immigration controls, as Gaitskell had done in opposition to the Commonwealth Immigrants Bill in the early 1960s.

The publication of Labour's 'Opportunities For All' in 1992 signalled an attempt to reconstruct a coherent position on issues of citizenship, racial equality and racial attacks. This also indicated an attempt to overcome Labour's divisions and re-establish 'ethical socialism' in this policy field. Evidence of this came in Labour's debate on these issues in the House of Commons in 1992 and in the opposition to the Asylum Bill which Roy Hattersley called 'a squalid appeal to racism' in the run-up to the general election in 1992. For their pains, Labour were attacked subsequently by the tabloids for welcoming a 'flood of immigrants' and for threatening 'our jobs and way of life'. This was reinforced in the last few days of the election by Sir Nicholas Fairbairn, the Tory candidate for Perth and Kinross, who said that under a Labour government 'Britain would be swamped by immigrants of every colour and race and on any excuse of asylum or bogus marriage or just plain deception' (*Independent on Sunday*, 5 May 1992).

The denial of these statements by Major clearly rang hollow given the support for such statements among the Tory, and indeed part of Labour's, grassroots. This sentiment clearly emerged in the failed attempt of a black Conservative candidate in Cheltenham to become the first black Conservative MP, who was openly called a 'bloody nigger' by members of his local Conservative Association. There was also evidence here of coded 'new racism' in the reference to dislike of 'outsiders' (Woodbridge 1993). In the overall voting, the substantial increase in support for all three black MPs in London indicated that Labour had managed to dispel the 'London factor' and association with the imagined extremes of anti-racism.

The widely held view that Labour are keeping 'race' and immigration policy on the 'back-burner' is partly substantiated by evidence that the proclaimed success of tackling racial inequalities in Labour local authorities has been either rather shallow or in the process of reversal. Also, concerns over the black vote have been dissipated by the experience that many such voters have little viable alternative and that it appears easier to maintain their support compared to particular groups of white marginal voters. The problem of disentangling racism in the party machine seems intractable, yet the prospects of slowly increasing black minority ethnic representation seem equally certain. The impact of such representation can, however, be overestimated and therefore recurring problems of capitulation to racist immigration policy and an inability to present and sustain a coherent anti-racist position are likely to remain. The rediscovery of morality in the new 'ethical socialism' (given that it avoids the pitfalls of the Tories 'Back to Basics' campaign) which is linked to high-profile opposition to explicit and coded racism combined with a rediscovery of the economic value of black migrants in building such a vision, may provide the basis for a radical reappraisal of future policy in this field. The role of Labour in building policies around these issues in Europe is also highly significant, with examples such as MEP Glynn Ford's conduct of the parliamentary inquiry into racism in Europe. But at present confusion and uncertainty at the national level is likely to continue, restraining active promotion of positive policies.

CONCLUSION

Racist discourse and racist attacks remain a marked feature of British society. The failure of anti-racist approaches to engage adequately with the shifting and contradictory elements of these discourses and practices is also equally evident. The ambivalence in state regulation and control of racist attacks is clear in the government's opposition to strengthening the law on racial hatred and introducing new offences of racial assault and racial harassment, and in the restriction of the responsibility to prosecute publishers of racist material to the Attorney General. On the other hand, the limitations of turning to individual rights-based law in the British context are markedly apparent in the field of racial discrimination. The extreme right's electoral prospects look bleak, as the 1992 general election results show, and it is important not to overestimate the political threat they pose. But, their instigation and incitement of racial attacks are increasingly a real threat to societal security. The 'weak' management of racism and the 'strong' management of migration by government and the European Commission look set to characterise political responses in the 1990s.

CORE READING

Castles, S. and Miller, M.J. (1993) *The Age of Migration*, London: Macmillan.
Hall, S. (1992) 'The Question of Cultural Identity', in Hall, S., Held, D. and McGrew, T. (eds) *Modernity and its Futures*, Cambridge: Polity/Open University.
Layton-Henry, Z. (1992) *The Politics of Immigration*, Oxford: Basil Blackwell.
Miles, R. (1993) *Racism after 'Race Relations'*, London: Routledge.
Wrench, J. and Solomos, J. (eds) (1993) *Racism and Migration in Western Europe*, Oxford: Berg.

SUPPLEMENTARY READING

Baldwin-Edwards, M. (1992) 'The Context of 1992', *Runnymede Trust Bulletin*, 252.
Balibar, E. (1991) 'Is There a "Neo-racism"?', in Balibar, E. and Wallerstein, I. (eds), *Race, Nation and Class*, London: Verso.
Barker, M. (1981) *The New Racism*, London: Junction Books.

Bauman, Z. (1990) 'Modernity and Ambivalence', in Featherstone, M. (ed.) *Global Culture*, London: Sage.

BBC (1992) *Black and White in Colour 1969–1989*.

Board of Deputies of British Jews (1994) *A Very Light Sleeper: The Persistence and Dangers of Anti-Semitism*, London: Runnymede Trust.

Bulpitt, J. (1986) 'Continuity, Autonomy and Peripheralisation: The Anatomy of the Centre's Race Statecraft in England', in Layton-Henry, Z. and Rich, P. (eds) *Race, Government and Politics in Britain*, London: Macmillan.

CCETSW (Central Council for Education and Training in Social Work) (1991) *Rules and Requirements for the Diploma in Social Work*, Paper 30, 2nd edn, London.

Commission for Racial Equality (1985) *Immigration Control Procedures: Report of a Formal Investigation*, London.

Elias, N. (1982) *The Civilizing Process*, vol. 2, *State Formations and Civilization*, Oxford: Basil Blackwell.

Foot, P. (1965) *Race and Immigration in British Politics*, London: Penguin.

Garcia, S. (ed.) (1993) *European Identity and the Search for Legitimacy*, London: Pinter.

Gilroy, P. (1990) 'The End of Anti-racism', in Ball, W. and Solomos, J. (eds) *Race and Local Politics*, London: Macmillan.

Gordon, P. and Klug, F. (1986) *New Right, New Racism*, Nottingham: Searchlight.

Hainsworth, P. (ed.) (1992) *The Extreme Right in Europe and the USA*, London: Pinter.

Hobsbawn, E. (1980) 'Are We Now Entering a New Era of Anti-Semitism?', *New Society*, 11 December.

Kellas, J.G. (1991) *The Politics of Nationalism and Ethnicity*, London: Macmillan.

Mason, D. (1992) *Some Problems with the Concepts of Race and Racism*, Discussion Papers in Sociology No. S92/5, University of Leicester.

Medical Foundation (1992) *Victims of Torture*, London.

Miles, R. (1989) *Racism*, London: Routledge.

Peach, C. (1991) *The Caribbean in Europe: Contrasting Patterns of Migration and Settlement in Britain, France and the Netherlands*, Research Paper in Ethnic Relations No.15, CRER, University of Warwick.

Rex, J. and Tomlinson, S. (1979) *Colonial Immigrants in a British City: A Class Analysis*, London: Routledge & Kegan Paul.

Saggar, S. (1992) *Race and Politics in Britain*, Hemel Hempstead: Harvester Wheatsheaf.

Sivanandan, A. (1989) 'Racism 1992', *Race and Class* 30(3).

Skellington, R. and Morris, P. (1992) *'Race' in Britain Today*, London: Sage/Open University.

Smith, M.L. and Stirk, P.M.R. (eds) (1990) *Making the New Europe: European Unity and the Second World War*, London: Pinter.

Smith, S. (1989) *The Politics of Race and Residence: Citizenship, Segregation and White Supremacy in Britain*, Oxford: Polity.

Solomos, J. and Back, L. (1991) *The Politics of Race and Social Change in Birmingham: Historical Patterns and Contemporary Trends*, Research Paper No.1, Birkbeck College.

Waever, O., Buzan, B., Kelstrup, M. and Lemaitre, P. (1993) *Identity, Migration and the New Security Agenda in Europe*, London: Pinter.

Webber, F. (1991) 'From Ethnocentrism to Euro-racism', *Capital and Class* 32(3).

Woodbridge, S. (1993) *Race and the British Right, 1978–1992: An Introductory Research Guide*, Kingston upon Thames: Kingston University.

Conclusion

Robert Leach

Any review of government and public policy in the mid-1990s must emphasise the extent of the changes that have taken place over the last ten or fifteen years. Those changes are profound, and have major implications for the British system of government, even if those implications have as yet been only imperfectly realised. Indeed, they have involved little in the way of overt amendments to the existing constitution or even to the formal machinery of government. The main principles of the constitution, as inferred by leading authorities – the unitary state, Cabinet government, ministerial responsibility, formal parliamentary sovereignty – can still be discerned. The principal institutions – Crown, Cabinet, Parliament, the great departments of state – have been but little disturbed. Indeed critics, such as the pressure group Charter 88 and the maverick Thatcherite Ferdinand Mount (1992), complain of inertia. Their sweeping proposals for reform show little sign as yet of any place on the government agenda. Yet beneath the apparent immobilism in formal constitutional arrangements, there are massive changes in the way in which British government is conducted.

Perhaps the most significant developments have involved a fundamental questioning of the whole scope and functions of government. From the early nineteenth century onwards there has been a steady growth in the effective responsibilities of government. Only in the last fifteen years has there been a determined attempt to reverse that growth of functions, and reduce what had hitherto been regarded as the legitimate sphere of state action. The most obvious manifestation has been the privatisation programme, which has not only returned to private ownership the manufacturing and transport enterprises, but public utilities such as water, with important implications for health and social needs. In local government over a million houses have been transferred from the public sector to the private sector through the right-to-buy policy. These changes of ownership have been accompanied by the deliberate encouragement of private sector provision in health care, housing, public transport, education and training, institutional care, and a whole range of ancillary and professional services. Private sector competition and the introduction of internal markets in health and education have also impelled remaining public sector organisations to behave as much like the private sector as possible. Beyond that, state responsibility for the overall management of the economy, and particularly for unemployment, has been denied, and state welfare responsibilities have been questioned and partially eroded.

Yet there is a central paradox to this neo-liberal anti-statism. This significant reining back of the frontiers of the state have not resulted in any significant reduction in government activity, as measured by the volume of legislation or in terms of public spending. Indeed the governments of Margaret Thatcher and John Major have been relentlessly interventionist. No previous government, Conservative or Labour, has intervened so regularly and extensively in local government. The Civil Service has experienced its biggest upheaval since the Northcote–Trevelyan reforms in the nineteenth century. Industrial relations, the National Health Service, housing, education and training have all suffered a more extensive programme of enforced change over the last fifteen years than over the preceding thirty. Radical interventionism rather than *laissez-faire* has been the order of the day (Gamble 1988).

One explanation of the paradox is that intervention is needed initially to restore the conditions of market choice. Once this has been done, governments will be permitted to govern less. Yet the pace of legislative change shows no signs of slackening some fifteen years after the election of Thatcher's first administration. The New Right state gives no more indication of 'withering away' than the Marxist state.

Part of the answer is that governments find it difficult to divest themselves of responsibilities even when they want to. Despite all the government's disclaimers of responsibility for economic management, they are still widely blamed for unemployment and indicators of poor economic performance. Privatisation has not effectively removed telecommunications, water, gas and electricity from the realm of public policy. The pricing policies and performance of these privatised companies are seen as legitimate areas of public concern with implications for government action. Indeed, the establishment of public regulatory bodies and the retention of government reserve powers involve a clear acknowledgement by government of continued responsibility. Similarly the introduction of competition and internal markets into the public sector necessitate government intervention. While the state continues to provide the bulk of funding, and services are provided to users on the basis of need rather than ability to pay, these can never be genuinely free markets, but managed markets, with government effectively responsible for providing the framework for competition.

But of course the ideology that has driven recent governments, and still drives the present government, is complex and never purely neo-liberal. Thatcherism and the New Right drew not only on classical liberalism but also on a Tory tradition which emphasised authority and order rather than liberty, and obligations of obedience and duty. The implication was that while the state should withdraw from some areas, it had a positive responsibility to intervene in others. Thus Conservative governments have imposed a National Curriculum in education, and attempted to instil moral and religious values through the enforcement of the daily act of worship, and predominantly Christian religious education in schools. More ambitiously still, John Major appeared to be accepting government responsibility for personal morality through his variously interpreted 'Back to Basics' programme. The Wilson and Callaghan governments were widely accused of attempting to intervene in areas (e.g. incomes policy) where they had little effective power, resulting in failure, disillusion and a crisis of ungovernability. Some Conservative ministers have shown a readiness to assume responsibility for social and moral behaviour and attitudes, where lack of effective means make eventual failure even more probable.

Thus an apparently anti-statist philosophy has not resulted in a significant narrowing of the scope of public policy, although it has involved a significant restructuring of the way in which policy is delivered. Yet this too has its para-doxical elements. For example, critics castigate the government for increasing centralisation, while the government themselves have claimed that they have increased delegation and the decentralisation of decision-making. There is an element of truth in both views. Reforms in education and health care have certainly involved some transfer of power downwards to schools, hospitals and practices. The introduction of executive agencies into the Civil Service require extensive managerial delegation. Thus some important aspects of policy may be made at lower levels. Yet at the same time the government have removed or weakened subordinate levels of government with an independent political base (see Chapter 4), and increased their own control in the crucial area of resources. While the proliferation of quangos and agencies indicate a fragmentation of administration, control of patronage involves a centralisation of effective political power. Indeed, one marked contrast between the present period and the heyday of the political consensus in the 1950s and 1960s is an apparent departure from the then prevailing convention of bipartisanship in appointments to non-elected governmental bodies. In consequence, the United Kingdom increasingly resembles a one-party state as far as real participation in the public policy process is concerned.

The changes in government are real enough. Different people hold the levers of power from those fifteen years ago. The old mandarin class in the Civil Service has ceded some power to the new executive managers. Professional heads of department in local government find their empires carved up, with managers of direct service organisations and direct labour organisations or institutional bosses now calling the shots. Consultants in the health service have had to accommodate the claims of the new breed of financial managers. This has involved some delegation and decentralisation, sometimes to appointed laypersons, sometimes to professionals, sometimes to managers, and sometimes to an extent at least to final consumers. The government indeed have claimed to empower consumers, both through competition and choice provided through market mechanisms, and through the performance standards laid down in the Citizen's Charter. Yet decentralisation through market mechanisms to consumers and service users is not the same as decentralisation through the ballot box, or the active participation of citizens in the political process. Thus elected local councils have ceded power to appointed quangos, voluntary organisations, and business interests, and the local democratic process has been effectively bypassed.

Moreover, while the number of elected local authorities has been further reduced, there are no signs at present of any compensating devolution of power to elected national or regional assemblies.

The changes that have taken place or are still proceeding are pregnant with implications for the British constitution, even though there has been no manifest constitutional change. Executive agencies have effectively narrowed ministerial responsibility, and that in turn has called into question parliamentary account-ability. The 'new magistracy' of appointees sits uneasily with the notion of representative government.

How stable is the evolving new system of government likely to prove? Many of the changes are very recent, and some of the most important are still in the process of implementation, so that it is difficult to assess their likely permanence. The most obvious challenge to the new system could come from the ballot box. Four successive election victories have given Conservative government an impression of permanence. Yet the apparent stability of the Conservative vote through four general elections masks considerable fluctuations in party support, as evidenced in local elections, European elections, parliamentary by-elections and opinion polls. Moreover Tory dominance has been exaggerated by the peculiarities of the British electoral system and the divisions of the opposition. Thus government by another party or parties is probable sooner or later. How much difference that would make to the system of government is another matter. Already it seems probable that much of the Thatcherite revolution will remain undisturbed, including the bulk of the privatisation programme, executive agen-cies, and decentralised management in education and health care. The interesting question is how far a Labour or Labour/Liberal Democrat government would be prepared to surrender the levers of power they inherit. Would patronage simply be exercised in the Labour interest, or would patronage be reduced? Would business interests continue to enjoy their entrenched involvement in so many areas of public policy, notably including education and training, or would there be a revival of ostensibly tripartite decision-making involving union interests?

A government of any colour would still face some of the significant and growing problems in health and social policy posed by demographic trends. The costs of providing adequate pensions and health care will continue to escalate, with uncomfortable implications for government spending and taxation, which will sharpen the debate over the balance between state and private provision, and intensify the divisions between the generations and between different classes of pensioners. These trends reflect similar problems over most of the Western world.

UK governments will also have to face up to problems of resource depletion and environmental pollution which are global in scale. Some Green issues may be capable of absorption within mainstream politics without too much difficulty, but it is likely that some very uncomfortable choices will have to be made, involving cut-backs in present living standards. This too could have knock-on effects on state welfare provision, the expansion of which has been previously financed substantially out of economic growth.

Indeed, external constraints are likely to have an increasing impact, whatever the party complexion of the government at Westminster. Concentration on the domestic UK sphere inevitably exaggerates the impression of autonomy in UK public policy. Many of the trends discussed already, including privatisation and marketisation, are essentially global. Problems in implementation may initiate a reaction, towards more government planning and/or a return to a more corporatist style of policy-making. Yet this too is likely to reflect trends elsewhere.

More specifically, the European Union is likely to have an increased impact on British government and public policy. The impact of the Union on certain areas of policy such as agriculture, energy and the environment is already clear enough, and it is likely to grow on fiscal policy, education and social policy. Yet it might have an impact also on the whole British system of government – towards regional devolution for example, or towards a change in the UK electoral system.

Beyond that there are more fundamental threats to the existing system of UK government and public policy. The United Kingdom is a multi-national state based on a voluntary union of the constituent national elements. The continued participation of Northern Ireland in that union is increasingly doubtful and problematic, while growing support for Scottish and Welsh nationalism suggest a distinct possibility of the break-up of the United Kingdom. How far Scottish and Welsh separatist feelings could be assuaged by a significant devolution of power to national assemblies is a moot point, but a transfer in power at Westminster seems certain to lead to some major changes in the government of Scotland and Wales with potentially far-reaching implications, including an explicitly federal system. Alternatively, growing nationalist support could lead to an attempt to take power from below.

There are other darker threats. Older commentators like Jennings (1966) and Punnett (1987) used to draw attention to the homogeneity, deference and consensus that they thought characterised the British system of government. There is some scope for debate as to whether these features were real or imagined, or if real, how they had been created or manufactured. Few commentators would, however, make similar claims for the present system of government and politics. Familiar divisions between 'haves' and 'have-nots' have intensified over the last fifteen years, and the fragmentation of British society has been increased by gender, race, religious and national differences. Less homogeneity may not inevitably involve a fundamental collapse of consensus. Much depends on how successfully minorities are brought within a pluralist society and political system, and this depends more on the attitudes and behaviour of the majority than the minorities themselves. Alternatively, prejudice and discrimination may intensify divisions and feelings of separateness.

More serious even than ethnic or religious tensions may be the growing gulf between those in full-time permanent work, and those who are jobless or only on the fringe of the mainstream economy; between those who own their homes, and those who are homeless, or dependent on various forms of sub-standard or temporary accommodation; between those who have a stake in the economy and society and those who have not. Talk of an underclass may be exaggerated, but a growing section of the population seems alienated from orthodox mainstream party politics. But if they are alienated they are not necessarily cowed and passive, and may be far from deferential. In these circumstances, rioting becomes the normal form of political expression. There is a significant break-down in law and order in parts of Britain's major cities, which would have been unthinkable thirty years before.

These trends too are far from unique to the United Kingdom. They can be found elsewhere, for example in Italy, the former Eastern Germany and Russia, indicating again that developments in the United Kingdom to some extent reflect global developments. Yet at one time the government and politics of the United Kingdom seemed to represent an island of stability and tranquillity in a world of violent upheaval. Now there is no guarantee of continued stability. British government and public policy could be moving closer to the world norm.

REFERENCES AND ADDITIONAL READING

Gamble, A. (1988) *The Free Economy and the Strong State*, London: Macmillan.
Jennings, I. (1966) *The Law and the Constitution*, 5th edn, Cambridge: University Press.
Mount, F. (1992) *The British Constitution Now*, London: Heinemann.
Punnett, R.M. (1987) *British Government and Politics*, 5th edn, Aldershot: Gower.

Index